JAN 13 '72	DATE DUE		
JAN 25 '72			
FEB 15 '72			
JUL 13 '73			

GAYLORD 234   PRINTED IN U.S.A.

A Centennial Volume
Edited by Peter Quennell

MARCEL PROUST

1871–1922

SIMON AND SCHUSTER
New York

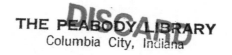

Published in the United States by Simon and Schuster
Rockefeller Center, 630 Fifth Avenue
New York, New York 10020

First U.S. printing
SBN 671-21013-0

Library of Congress Catalog Card Number: 70-153473

Designed by John Wallis

Picture research by Ann Mitchell

Manufactured in Great Britain

Contents

Foreword

MARCEL Proust was born at Auteuil just over a hundred years ago; and, to commemorate the occasion, eleven writers, English, French and American, have written the essays assembled here on various aspects of his life and work. Each has pursued an individual line; and the reader will note that the opinions they express are sometimes complementary, and sometimes contradictory. This, the editor believes, is as it should be. Proust was a man of protean genius; and to every student of his work he exhibits a slightly different aspect of his character.

Passages quoted at length are taken from the English translation by C K Scott Moncrieff, except in the case of *Le Temps retrouvé*, where Mr Andreas Mayor's more recent version has been used. For permission to reprint them we are indebted to the generosity of Messrs Chatto & Windus, London, and Random House, Inc., New York; we would also like to thank Chatto & Windus for permitting us to quote from *The Letters of Marcel Proust*, translated and edited by Mina Curtis. The extracts from *Sylvia* by Emmanuel Berl on p. 92 and from *Premier Cahier de Jean Cocteau* on pp. 188–90 are quoted by permission of Editions Gallimard. We would particularly like to thank Madame Mante Proust for allowing us to quote from Proust's notebooks and to reproduce many original photographs.

Peter Quennell

Introduction

Peter Quennell

ARCEL PROUST died in Paris, at 44 Rue Hamelin, on 18 November 1922, before he could complete the gigantic literary monument that he had been patiently planning and raising since the summer of the year 1909. Huge packets of type and manuscript, the pages festooned with half-illegible addenda and blackened with savage deletions which had swallowed up entire paragraphs, heaped the ugly little bamboo table that stood beside his death-bed, and overflowed from the shelves of the table along the near-by chimney-piece. Three of the seven sections of *A la Recherche du temps perdu* still awaited publication; and, although *La Prisonnière* had been typed and corrected, none of them was yet in proof. Among the papers that the novelist left behind him were many feverishly scribbled notes, showing changes he intended to make and new episodes that, given the opportunity, he would have worked into his narrative.

Proust had originally become a novelist during the last years of the nineteenth century, when he had written a lengthy novel entitled *Jean Santeuil* – a trial-run for its great successor – which he abandoned about 1900. Several important themes, afterwards fully developed in *A la Recherche*, were foreshadowed in this prentice essay. But, despite some splendid passages, *Jean Santeuil* is a strangely shapeless book, which lacks both a sense of direction and an adult sense of style. It was an almost miraculous revelation that, early in January 1909, had launched the author on his life-work. Having dipped a fragment of toast into a cup of hot tea – for the purposes of his story, it is a cup of *tilleul*, while the toast becomes a shell-shaped cake – he noticed that its lingering sweetish savour summoned up the vanished world of his youth with extraordinary clarity and vividness. Thus he had suddenly grasped the mystic relationship between the present and the past:

. . . Once I had recognized the taste of the crumb of madeleine soaked in her decoction of lime-flowers which my aunt used to give me . . . immediately the old grey house . . . rose up like the scenery of a theatre . . . and with the house the town, from morning to night and in all weathers, the Square where I was sent before luncheon, the streets along which I used to run errands, the country roads we took when it was fine. And just as the Japanese amuse themselves by filling a porcelain bowl with water and steeping in it little crumbs of paper which . . . the moment they become wet, stretch themselves and bend, take on colour and distinctive shape, become flowers or houses or people . . . so in that moment all the flowers in our garden and in M. Swann's park, and the water-lilies on the Vivonne and the good folk of the village and their little dwellings and the parish church and the whole of Combray and of its surroundings, taking their proper shapes and growing solid, sprang into being, town and gardens alike, from my cup of tea.[1]

Not until the beginning of July, however, did he finally attempt to give the vision substance; and about that time, for some sixty hours at a stretch, the lamp in his bedroom, which was also his living-room and workroom, had never once been turned off. He had begun the momentous journey into the past that would absorb all his energy and all his genius. His aim was two-fold; he hoped not only to produce a work of art but to perform a solemn act of expiation. Proust was a man who had wasted time. Now he set out to show that the time we lose – the experiences that have vanished apparently beyond recall – may yet be recovered through the power of art, and that memory, if rightly invoked, can restore the past in all its freshness. For he had bitter regrets. During the first thirty-eight years of his life Proust had been a spoiled child; and he knew that, while they still lived, he had disappointed both his parents. He would never settle down to any regular calling; and, little by little, he had allowed himself to become a chronic invalid. His parents were quiet middle-class people. As often as Proust was prepared to leave his sick-room, he spent his time flitting distractedly around the worlds of art and fashion.

The elder son of Dr Adrien Proust, a well-known medical specialist, whose invention of the *cordon sanitaire*, prompted by the cholera epidemic of the year 1866, had earned him international acclaim, and of his wife, the former Jeanne Weil, the daughter of a prosperous stockbroker, a sensitive and cultured Jewess, Marcel Proust was born at Auteuil on 10 July 1871. From his father he had inherited the spirit of scientific curiosity; from his mother, whom he always adored, a romantic, introspective strain, which, combined with the effects of ill-health, made him painfully nervous and excitable. One childish tragedy he describes both in *Jean Santeuil* and in *A la Recherche du temps perdu*. His mother had denied him the good-night kiss that meant he could go to bed happy. It was an incident he could never forget and, perhaps, could never quite forgive; and it left Proust with the settled conviction that those we love, to whom we have entrusted our hearts and peace of mind, will ultimately betray our trust; that deception, jealousy and heart-break must form the emotional background of every adult love-affair. This tragedy seems to have occurred when he had already reached the age of seven. When he was nine, another decisive event helped to mould the future artist's destiny. He suffered his earliest attack of nervous asthma – an affliction that remained with him until he died.

INTRODUCTION

In real life, his mother refused him her kiss one summer at suburban Auteuil; in *A la Recherche* he transfers the episode to a very different setting. Adrien Proust had been born at Illiers, not very far from the cathedral city of Chartres and some hundred kilometres south-west of Paris, where his father had owned a grocer's shop; and, year after year, the family returned to Illiers, to stay with their country relations, the Amiots, in the Rue du Saint-Esprit, nowadays renamed Rue du Docteur Proust. Here Aunt Élisabeth, prototype of the novelist's Tante Léonie, obstinately kept her bed, served by the devoted Ernestine Gallou, who gave the novelist numerous hints for Françoise. Proust loved the small provincial house, and the sweet-smelling atmosphere, which combined so many delicious rustic scents, of his aunt Élisabeth's secluded rooms. In his book, he would enlarge the tiny scrap of garden that lay behind the Amiots' house, adding the much larger Auteuil garden. He also altered and greatly improved the church that, slipping 'its belfry into every corner of the sky', looks out over the roofs of Illiers.

To visit the town is a strangely moving experience. We feel that we stand upon familiar ground. Yet is Illiers, after all, quite the place that we remember? Since our last view – in the pages of a masterpiece – it appears to have undergone a subtle change; so that it recalls one of the sacred places of childhood, which, if we are unwise enough to revisit them in later life, seem to have grown smaller, meaner, more prosaic. There are still *madeleines* to be bought at the baker's shop – 'those short, plump little cakes . . . which look as if they had been moulded in the fluted scallop of a pilgrim's shell'. But nowadays they are often rather stale, put aside, no doubt, for Proustian tourists; and I was obliged to scatter the remains of the cakes I purchased across the surface of the River Loir – which Proust in his novel calls the Vivonne – the placid stream that divides Combray-Illiers from the extremely uninteresting garden named the Pré-Catalan, once the pleasure-ground of Proust's uncle. It is in the Pré-Catalan, enlarged and embellished as Charles Swann's stately and spacious park, that the Narrator first catches sight of Madame Swann, Monsieur de Charlus and Gilberte, Swann's seductive daughter.

Similarly, 'the old grey house', occupied by Tante Léonie, which today bears an impressive memorial plaque, has become even greyer and more uninviting. The church of Saint-Hilaire, on the other hand – at least, the ancient tower of the church – answers all our expectations. The interior of the building was extensively redecorated some time in the nineteenth century. It contains no Gothic windows, no precious medieval arras; no sepulchral slabs, emerging

from the pavement, threaten to trip up a visitor. Proust's celebrated porch –
'black, and full of holes ... worn out of shape ... just as if the gentle grazing
touch of the cloaks of peasant-women going into the church ... had managed
by age-long repetition to ... impress itself upon the stone' – is probably based
on his memories of the much more important church at Saint Loup-de-Naud.
Yet the tower of Saint-Hilaire is still unchanged, with 'its little iron cock veer-
ing ... in all directions'; and so are its inhabitants. 'From the tower windows',
we read, it 'let fall at regular intervals flights of jackdaws', which wheeled away
as though their old home above the square had become 'of a sudden uninhabit-
able'; then, their agitation no less suddenly subsiding, drifted back again
into their former places. Proust, who seldom designed a portrait without com-
bining the most revelatory traits of several different human characters,
employed exactly the same technique when he depicted a landscape or a
building.

Here as elsewhere, it is not a question of what Illiers has lost as of what the
imaginative artist has added. In the introductory volumes of *A la Recherche du
temps perdu*, besides drawing a vivid picture of the background of his own
childhood, he has evoked the essential spirit of Youth. Nothing else he wrote
is quite so poetic; and, in this particular field of writing, his great book has no
exact equivalent. One of Proust's masters was the wayward Gérard de Nerval;
but *Sylvie*, set beside *Du Côté de chez Swann*, is merely an enchanting fairy-tale;
while another memorable evocation of Youth, Eugène Fromentin's novel
Dominique, despite the marvellous passages that Fromentin devotes to flowers
and trees and the flocks of migratory birds that swept high over his family house
near La Rochelle, lacks any solid human characters.

Du Côté de chez Swann is the fountain-head from which the whole flood of
the author's adult achievement, narrowing and deepening as it goes, and becoming suffused with many tragic stains – before it disappears, it is darker than
Lethe or Acheron – ultimately takes its source. Only in his first volumes, and
among the personages they introduce, do we encounter lasting goodness; and
there alone are we allowed to breathe the atmosphere of genuine happiness.
True, the Narrator is a somewhat uneasy child, tormented by ill-health and an
unbalanced affection for his devotedly conscientious mother. But within himself, despite all his griefs and discomforts, he has still an unceasing fund of joy;
to the world around him he brings that exquisite freshness of vision which,
according to Coleridge, distinguishes both the gifted child and the poetic genius.
It is 'the character and privilege of genius', Coleridge declares, to 'carry on the

feelings of childhood into the powers of manhood; to combine a child's sense of wonder and novelty' with our humdrum adult view; and this Proust does again and again in the pages of his first volume. His aunt's garden had become the Earthly Paradise from which he had been banished when he entered adolescence, but whither he returned, by a prodigious feat of imaginative recreation, as a sick and ageing man.

During the process, not only did he enlarge the garden, substituting a place of lawns and flower-beds for a meagre backyard; he gave every detail a symbolic value:

At length my mother would say to me: 'Now, don't stay here all day; you can go up to your room if you are too hot outside, but get a little fresh air first . . .'

And I would go and sit down beside the pump and its trough, ornamented here and there, like a gothic font, with a salamander, which modelled upon a background of crumbling stone the quick relief of its slender, allegorical body; on a bench without a back, in the shade of a lilac tree, in that little corner of the garden . . . from whose neglected soil rose, on two steps, an outcrop from the house itself and apparently a separate building, my aunt's back-kitchen. One could see its red-tiled floor gleaming like porphyry. It seemed not so much the cave of Françoise as a little temple of Venus. It would be overflowing with the offerings of the milkman, the fruiterer, the greengrocer, come sometimes from distant villages to dedicate here the first-fruits of their fields. And its roof was always surmounted by the cooing of a dove.[2]

Among the men and women who populate the garden at Combray, the Narrator's maternal grandmother, Madame Amédée, who shares her daughter's solicitude for the little boy's health, is certainly the most endearing. She is passionately devoted to an open-air life, loves to expose herself to wind and rain, worships Nature and everything that is simple and natural, abominates the artificial symmetry that Tante Léonie's new gardener tries to impose upon his flowers, and, when she passes the rose-trees, will surreptitiously remove a stake or two, 'so as to make the roses look a little more natural, as a mother might run her hand through her boy's hair, after the barber had smoothed it down, to make it stick out properly round his head'.

The excuse that Madame Amédée finds for ruffling the rose-trees is a visit to the garden-gate. Its bell has just sounded, heralding, presumably, the approach of Charles Swann, the rich neighbour, son of an old friend, who, with his wife and daughter – a girl of about the Narrator's age – occupies a near-by country house. He arrives alone; Marcel's relations do not receive the mysterious Madame Swann, who is said once to have been a loose woman and is now reported to be living in sin with their frequent guest, a certain Monsieur de Charlus. It is an indication of the goodness of Marcel's mother that she is determined to speak to Swann, if not of his wife, at least of the daughter whom he dearly loves; though her husband brushes aside the suggestion: *'Mais non! tu as des idées absurdes. Ce serait ridicule.'*

Charles Swann the family likes for himself, and because his father had been 'a heart of gold'; but they prefer to ignore the circumstances surrounding his questionable domestic life, just as they remain happily ignorant of his connections with the Great World, his friendship with the Prince of Wales and the most distinguished members of *'le gratin'*. The Narrator, on the other hand, is fascinated by Swann because their neighbour, he learns, often entertains at his house in Paris the famous novelist Bergotte; and he is also fascinated by the idea of Gilberte Swann, when he hears from her father that Bergotte sometimes takes the little girl to visit historic towns and ancient buildings:

I felt so keenly how pleasant and yet how impossible it would be for me to become her friend that I was filled at once with longing and despair. And usually, from this time forth when I thought of her, I would see her standing before the porch of a cathedral, explaining to me what each of the statues meant and, with a smile which was my highest commendation, presenting me, as her friend, to Bergotte. And invariably the charm of all the fancies which the thought of cathedrals used to inspire in me, the charm of the hills and valleys of the Ile-de-France, and of the plains of Normandy, would radiate brightness and beauty over the picture I had formed in my mind of Mlle Swann; nothing more remained but to know and to love her.[3]

At this point, two important themes emerge that are destined to dominate the whole succeeding narrative. Through Swann we catch a first glimpse of the Faubourg Saint-Germain, and of the Guermantes, the splendid ducal line, whose ancestors are commemorated in the modest church at Combray; through the romantic and nostalgic emotions that Gilberte arouses, Marcel conducts his earliest researches into the origin of human love, which is usually aroused, he very soon discovers, not by the real qualities of the beloved being herself, but by the series of private dreams and fantasies that we elect to weave around her person. Marcel desires Gilberte, not so much because she is slender and russet-haired and has an exquisitely sly expression, as because he associates her with Bergotte, and with the monuments of the legendary past that she has seen in Bergotte's company.

That love is subjective, and almost always irrational – since the idea we form of the creature we love has seldom any solid basis – such is the recurrent message

At Home

Marcel Proust
(right) and his
younger brother,
Robert, born
May 1873.

right: Marcel Proust
with his mother and
brother, about 1896.
far right: Proust in
youth between Robert
de Flers (left) and
Lucien Daudet.

right: Adèle Weil, the
novelist's grandmother,
portrayed with special
tenderness in his
descriptions of
Combray.
far right: Marie de
Bernardaky, Proust's
early playmate, who
contributed to his
portrait of Gilberte
Swann.

above: Proust's father in the piazza San Marco, Venice.
above left: Marie Nordlinger, who helped to introduce Proust to his intercessory spirit, John Ruskin.

His parents' drawing-room, which Proust preserved as a family shrine in the rue Hamelin.

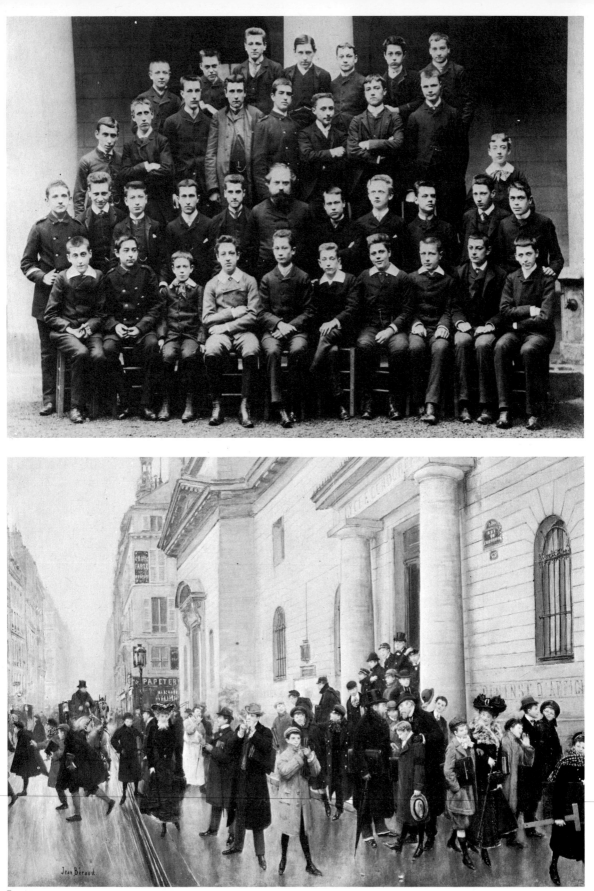

above: The tennis-party; Proust, in the role of troubadour, kneels at
the feet of Jeanne Pouquet.

top left: Proust and his contemporaries of the Lycée Condorcet, 1886-7.
left: Sortie du Lycée Condorcet during Proust's boyhood; picture
by Jean Béraud.

above left : Proust about 1896, when he published his first book *Les Plaisirs et les Jours.*
above right : Proust by Jacques-Emile Blanche; his heavy black beard, writes Jacques Porel, gave
him the look of an El Greco portrait.
top : Alfred Agostinelli, Proust's secretary and 'captive', destined, like Albertine, to die in
tragic circumstances, with Odilon Albaret at the wheel, 1907.
opposite : Proust as a young man by Jacques-Emile Blanche; at a time when he still frequented
the Faubourg Saint-Germain.

17

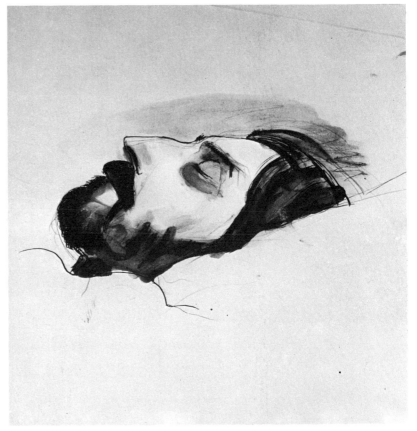

above : Photograph of Proust, taken in
May 1921, on the occasion of his last
visit to the Jeu de Paume, where he
admired Vermeer's *View of Delft*.

above : Proust on his death-bed; November 18th, 1922; sketch by
Dunoyer de Segonzac.
top : Proust's bedroom in the rue Hamelin; proofs and manuscripts
are piled on the bedside table and overflow along the chimneypiece.

of *Un Amour de Swann*, the story of Swann's unhappy pursuit of the woman who afterwards became his wife, which Proust suddenly begins to unfold towards the conclusion of his opening volume. Here is an anticipatory version, a study in miniature, of the Narrator's own existence. He loves Gilberte; and, later, far more deeply, Albertine, the girl he encounters among her enchanting companions, the frieze of 'young girls in flower', at the seaside town named Balbec. On both occasions, it is an image he loves – the image he has himself created – and the discrepancy between the girl and her image causes him incessant anguish. He enjoys but he never possesses Albertine; that is to say, although he imprisons her, he can never oblige her to give up her secret, or tell him exactly who or what she is. Albertine meets a tragic end; but, even after her death, his jealous suspicions continue to roam around her fading memory. As La Rochefoucauld had observed: '*La jalousie nait toujours avec l'amour, mais elle ne meurt pas toujours avec lui.*'

All these sufferings still lie far ahead during the period of his youth from which Proust drew his raw material for the two volumes of *Du Côté de chez Swann*. But before he embarked on his conquest of the Great World (the subject with which Marcel Schneider deals elsewhere in the present book) and possibly even before he left school, he had discovered that his passions and emotions had a strongly homosexual bias. He remained a homosexual so long as he lived; and it is a fact that we cannot afford to ignore when we are considering his creative genius. It has been said that, whenever Proust depicted a girl, he was thinking of a boy, and that his feminine personages are designed to form a screen behind which he hid his real interests. This is clearly untrue. Yet we must concede that there is some degree of ambiguity about the character of Albertine, and that his account of their strange relationship would be far less puzzling had she been a young man. The Narrator is said to have shut his mistress away in his family apartment under the guardianship of his devoted servant Françoise – a move that might well have proved difficult had she been a young girl, who had hitherto lived a fairly conventional life and had solid middle-class relations.

André Gide, moreover, records in his *Journals* two successive conversations with Proust during the early summer of 1921. 'Far from denying that he was a homosexual', Proust claimed 'never to have loved women save spiritually and never to have known love except with men . . . He says he blames himself for that "indecision" which made him, in order to fill out the heterosexual part of his book, transpose "*à l'ombre des jeunes filles*" all the attractive, affectionate, and charming elements contained in his homosexual recollections, so that for *Sodome* he is left nothing but the grotesque and the abject.'[4] But, although *La Prisonnière*, portrayed in later volumes, may perhaps have been a male captive – and Proust, we know, during the final stages of his life, had a number of nameless masculine inmates, whom his friends sometimes glimpsed at a distance wandering through his darkened rooms – he never ceased to love women, and to pay them passionately romantic homage. As a sensualist, he always desired men; as an imaginative artist, what chiefly concerned him was not the sex of the person one loved, or the manner in which one 'made love', but the psychology of Love itself.

Thus he had courted and flattered both the charming actress, Louisa de Mornand, who was afterwards deeply hurt when she suspected that he had used her features in his devastating portrait of Odette de Crécy, and, among his aristocratic acquaintances, the comtesse Adhéaume de Chevigné, whose voice, mannerisms and bird-like profile Proust attached to his wonderful Oriane de Guermantes. He was also momentarily attracted by Mademoiselle Jeanne Pouquet, his friend Gaston de Caillavet's future wife, and is thought at one time to have loved an unknown girl he met at Cabourg, the Norman seaside resort he transformed into Balbec, where the 'little band' of *jeunes filles en fleurs* had first troubled his imagination. Like many homosexuals, apart from admiring women, he was deeply interested in their way of life, the whole decorative *mundus muliebris* that had once excited Charles Baudelaire. Following the poet's lead, Proust believed that Fashion was an important and delightful manifestation of the spirit of a period; and, on another page, the reader will find an essay that describes the scrupulous care with which he dressed his heroines, and how lengthily and elaborately he distinguishes between their varying types of elegance. The duchesse and the princesse de Guermantes adopt completely different modes; and, when Marcel becomes the protector of Albertine, he immediately takes her wardrobe in hand, and decides that she must wear the creations of the great Spanish dressmaker Fortuny, who, with the help of brocades and painted velvets, seemed to have brought back the vanished world of Veronese and Carpaccio.

Had Proust's temperament not been homosexual, would he have depicted women quite so feelingly and lovingly? Three factors determined his life as an artist – his homosexuality, his Jewish blood and the physical condition that left him a lifelong invalid. Each separated him, to some extent, from the world he was describing. On the moral, social and physical planes, he was always an outsider; and the sense of his own separateness, as a paederast who loved women, a Jewish *arriviste* never quite accepted by many of the patrician circles he frequented, and a sick man whose sickness obliged him to live a peculiarly unnatural life, at once intensified his gift of observation and quickened his creative powers. What he lacked in real familiarity – the familiarity that may breed contempt and boredom – he made up in deep poetic sympathy. No aristocrat could have depicted the Faubourg Saint-Germain with so much literary style and spirit; no experienced lover of women have produced his astonishing portraits of Oriane de Guermantes and Odette Swann.

Being an outsider, he was constantly informing himself. Unlike a writer who believes that he is observing his subject 'from the inside', he could never satisfy his thirst for knowledge. He asked unending questions; and some of his acquaintances, much as they valued his talents, found this procedure oddly tiresome. One of his last victims was Harold Nicolson, at that time a youthful member of the British Foreign Service, who used to relate how Proust had buttonholed him, demanding to be enlightened about the social behaviour of the English upper classes. Together, he suggested, they should enact a little scene, in which Nicolson impersonated the Duchess of Devonshire, while he himself undertook the role, first of a fellow grandee, then of a titled Jewish guest, a Lady Sassoon or a Lady Rothschild. While greeting him and shaking his hand, Nicolson was to illustrate the exact nuances of voice and attitude that the Duchess would have employed on each occasion. Nicolson was obliged to admit that she would have extended the same greeting with more or less the same gesture – a statement that enraged the inquisitive novelist. Such a reply, he felt, could not be serious. '*Vous vous moquez de moi!*' he protested indignantly. Would his young friend please begin again?

Proust's view of the aristocracy (as Marcel Schneider points out) had a romantic and phantasmagoric, rather than a realistic colouring. It was part of the visionary picture of France that he had been building up since childhood, and that he derived from his attachment to French cathedrals, 'the hills and valleys of the Ile-de-France, and the plains of Normandy'. Though, at first sight, a loosely constructed book, *A la Recherche du temps perdu*, despite its vast length and the immense variety of divagations for which the author finds room, possesses an astonishingly comprehensive pattern. Nothing is superfluous; not a detail is wasted; for every incident is linked up, either with something that has gone before or with something that has yet to come. All the varying aspects of the story – personal, social, historical and topographical – are meticulously interwoven; just as past and present, memories and observations, merge into the same design.[5]

Even before he embarked on his great work, Proust seems to have had a remarkably definite idea of what, as a novelist, he meant to say. The only question was how to discover a form that would both allow him the requisite degree of freedom and provide a literary framework that might hold the book together. He had made three attempts. *Les Plaisirs et les Jours*, a sheaf of occasional pieces, with a flattering preface by Anatole France, pretty illustrations by Madeleine Lemaire and lively musical embellishments by his friend Reynaldo Hahn, appeared on 13 June 1896. Some of the stories contain a preliminary sketch of a subject that he was afterwards to develop in *A la Recherche du temps perdu*; but this slender volume had an expensively precious air that exasperated many readers. His contemporaries felt that Marcel was wasting his talents; and the world at large dismissed him as a snobbish young dilettante who hung around the fashionable salons. In *Jean Santeuil*, though it was a far more serious effort, he eventually lost faith; while for the collection of essays, often brilliant pieces of work, that appeared long after his death under the somewhat misleading title *Contre Sainte-Beuve*, he himself could never find a publisher.

He needed a guide; and, during the last five or six years of the nineteenth century, or perhaps a little earlier, Proust encountered the books of John Ruskin. He was now tiring of his struggles with *Jean Santeuil* – 'je travaille (he confessed) *depuis très longtemps à un ouvrage de très longue haleine, mais sans rien achever*'; and, towards the end of 1899, he began translating Ruskin's *Bible of Amiens*. It was a happy decision. Not only did Ruskin's love of the French cathedrals send him to Amiens and Cha tres, to Autun and to Bourges, 'the cathedral of hawthorn'; but in Ruskin's approach to art and idiosyncratic prose style he discovered a way of thinking and feeling that deeply stirred his own genius. Although he was never to imitate Ruskin, the old prophet's soaring descriptive flights – as when he pictures the symbolic statues of Amiens, the fantastically sculptured porches of Bourges, wreathed with a myriad spiny, flowering branches, or the explosive effect made by the pinnacles of St Mark's as they leap up against the azure sky – had a lasting influence upon Proust's use of language. Ruskin and Proust had a similar devotion to Nature, the same attachment to its smallest beauties; and, reading Ruskin's casual description of the cherry tree outside his window, which suggested 'twenty coral necklaces with their strings broken, falling into a shower', or his sketch of a wild snapdragon, its 'upper two petals thrown up like the sharpest little fox's ears', we immediately think of Marcel Proust, for whom even a stick of asparagus might become the subject of poetic reverie.

In character and upbringing, there was also a strong resemblance between these two extremely different artists. Each was the child of a devoted, demanding mother; each had had a sickly childhood; each suffered from nympholeptic attractions towards a series of very young girls, and from a curiously unbalanced sexual temperament. But it was in his role of artist and visionary prophet of art that, to Proust, the older man seemed most impressive. Ruskin (he wrote) had given his life, or the better part of his life, to an unswerving cult of Beauty. But – a significant reservation – 'this Beauty, to which he elected to consecrate his life, was not conceived of as a means of embellishing and sweetening existence, but as a reality infinitely more important than life itself, to which, indeed, he would have been ready to sacrifice his own. From this idea ... Ruskin's whole aesthetic system springs.' Ruskin would become the prophetic guide who, though he may not have strengthened Proust's desire to write – he had been endlessly scribbling ever since he grew up – gave him the direction and sense of dedication he had always needed. In May 1900, accompanied by his mother, who read Ruskin's *Stones of Venice* aloud as they travelled, Proust visited Venice for the first and last time. The evening of his arrival he spent with Marie Nordlinger, Reynaldo Hahn's delightful English cousin, herself a Ruskinian enthusiast, revising his translation of *The Bible of Amiens* beneath the shadow of the great church; and, next day, he awoke to see the Evangelist's angel radiant in the spring sunshine. The seraph 'bore me', he said, 'on his flashing wings a promise of beauty and joy greater than he ever brought to Christian hearts . . .'

Nine years later, Proust experienced the final literary revelation; but, meanwhile, his health had grown worse, and his reputation as a rich and snobbish idler had become more and more embarrassing. Few of his friends continued to take him seriously. He was '*le petit Marcel*', '*le gentil Marcel*', who kept such odd and anti-social hours, but who, when he entered a party, frequently wearing a shapeless fur-lined greatcoat over his tail-coat and his white tie, was funnier, wittier, and sometimes crueller than half a dozen ordinary human beings. One trait struck every friend or acquaintance – his huge dark, greedily receptive eyes, which appeared perpetually to be imploring help or demanding information. In her valuable little book, *Robert de Montesquiou et Marcel Proust*, the duchesse de Clermont-Tonnère describes their earliest meeting: 'Astonished, I inquired who was this strange young man, leaning in so exaggerated a pose upon the back of a chair . . . on which Mme Straus was seated. "It is the little Proust", they told me.'

Particularly remarkable were the thickness of his black dishevelled hair, the long aquiline nose that gave him a peculiarly oriental aspect – he looked definitely Assyrian once he had let his beard grow – and the immense dark eyes that revealed no personal feeling but seemed, as they swept around the company, to be two reflectors ready to absorb every visual ray that might reach him from the outer world. Through his lips, often twisted by a sidelong smile, proceeded an extremely individual voice, *'un peu puérile, caressante, gentille, chargée de mille inflexions gracieuses'*. It reminded the writer of those sticky little hands which very young children sometimes pass over one's face and clothes; *'c'est tendre et poisseux; on est à la fois flatté et un peu ennuyé'*.

Proust concentrated on any spectacle that interested him with an effort he did not disguise – as if, by marshalling all his powers of observation and imagination, he hoped to force the object he gazed at to divulge its inmost secret. Thus Reynaldo Hahn describes how, while they were walking one day in the eighteen-nineties around the gardens of Réveillon, Madame Lemaire's country house, Proust paused and inquired, gently, half-apologetically, whether it would annoy Reynaldo if he stayed behind a moment; 'I want to have another look at those roses', he said. When Hahn, after a prolonged stroll, came back to the same point, he found his friend still contemplating the roses in an attitude of deep absorption, thoughtfully gnawing one end of his moustache which he had clenched between his teeth.

Many years later, in April 1912, when he was already well launched on *A la Recherche du temps perdu*, though none of its volumes had as yet been published, the market-gardeners of Rueil, a small suburban town near Paris, were astonished to see a taxi draw up from which emerged a thin, sallow, dishevelled man, wearing a fur-lined coat above a nightshirt. It was a cold, rainy evening; and there was some talk of calling the police – the passenger and his driver bore an alarming resemblance to a pair of then notorious motor-bandits. But, once the passenger had gazed long and intently at the rows of blossoming apple trees visible across a muddy field, he climbed slowly back into his seat and the taxi drove away. Proust had been documenting for his latest chapter, and had caught the exact impression he required: 'As far as the eye could reach [the trees] were in full bloom, scandalously luxurious, wearing ball dresses with their feet in the mire.' And now he could go home to bed.

INTRODUCTION

Later still, though he seldom left his room, he retained his thirst for information, and would issue urgent appeals, usually between ten and twelve at night, summoning any friend or acquaintance who could bring him the latest news of Paris. Jacques Porel, the only son of the great actress Réjane, who was one of Proust's idols, describes in his delightful book of memoirs[6] an invitation that he received from the novelist during the year 1917. The messenger was Céleste Albaret, Proust's devoted housekeeper and nurse. With her frail elongated body, her fixed smile and her small head, she reminded Porel of a Gothic saint. Monsieur Proust, she announced, '*tout en s'excusant, insiste que M. Porel vienne le voir, boulevard Hausmann, demain soir, à onze heures*'.

Porel obeyed; and, on the next night, having waited half an hour – Proust, he heard from Céleste, was in the throes of an asthmatic crisis – he was admitted to the novelist's bedroom, the famous cork-lined room so often described by biographers, where he lay prostrate, heavily muffled up, his yellow-grey face and heavy black beard giving him the look of an El Greco portrait. His dark eastern eyes had a strangely imploring gleam – '*il me fit penser à un corbeau blessé*' – and his cajoling voice was thick with veronal, or with one of the other drugs that he took to wake or sleep. But he soon rallied, and began to pour forth a flood of superbly entertaining talk which lasted far into the small hours. He spoke of their friends, of his favourite books, of Balzac, Saint-Simon, Stendhal, Meredith, Chateaubriand, Dickens, Picasso, Dostoievski – and, naturally, of Marcel Proust. But Proust was no self-centred invalid; '*je n'ai iamais connu* (Jacques Porel remarks) *quelqu'un qui, autant que lui, sût vous intéresser à vous-même ... Proust connaissait, mieux que quiconque, l'étendue de la solitude humaine, mais il savait aussi la nécessité de prétendre l'ignorer*'.

For Proust, however, human friendship, much as he professed to value it, evidently had its limitations; '*il n'a jamais, je crois, donné à l'amitié un sens plus profond que celui: les jolies manières du cœur. Et puis au-delà, le néant*'. What really engaged him, and never failed to refresh his imagination, was the work of great artists. Those were his true friends, writes Jacques Porel; he knew the great masters so well that he had ceased to be afraid of them. He discussed them just as he discussed his friends; and when, on one of his rare visits to a restaurant, the conversation revolved round Balzac's characters, Porel felt that the author of *La Comédie Humaine* might at any moment cross the street, push his way through the door and sit down at the same table. Monsieur Porel has told me that Proust's favourite story by Balzac was *La Femme Abandonnée*, that *Bleak House* was his favourite novel by Dickens, and that he preferred Dostoievski, strangely enough, to all the other Russian novelists.

Proust, in fact, was the most 'literary' of novelists; that is to say, although he was passionately concerned with life, and drew an immense quantity of precious raw material from his own immediate observations, he was deeply versed in the literary culture of France, and owed an incalculable debt to writers as different as Baudelaire and Gérard de Nerval, Balzac, Chateaubriand and Saint-Simon. His link with Saint-Simon was particularly close and fruitful. Like Proust, the malevolent 'little Duke' was at once a romantic snob who adored the social world – which for him meant the splendid system that had its centre in the Sun King – and a ferocious critic of the aristocracy. Saint-Simon's style, his habit of piling up a tremendous succession of relative clauses into a single hugely complex sentence, had a permanent effect on that of Marcel Proust, whose long sentences reflect the rococo intricacy of the ideas that lay behind them, but, as they unroll through line after line until they have almost brimmed the page, often puzzle and exhaust his readers. It was the Saint-Simonian aspect of his narrative that so much annoyed his earliest critics. Even André Gide considered his style difficult; while critics of less account decided that a writer who was prepared to spend many paragraphs describing just how his hero turned over in bed did not deserve their serious notice.

Proust was undeterred. The first two volumes of *A la Recherche* had had a rather mixed reception; but, as soon as he had launched out on his pursuit of past time, he could see, stretching straight ahead through the years, the road he knew he had to travel. One of the chief characteristics of genius is an ability, not only to surmount misfortunes, but to turn them to creative profit. In 1905 Proust had lost his mother – his father had died in 1903; and, though her loss plunged him into 'unknown regions of grief', it also enabled him to take a step forward. While Madame Proust continued to share his life, she retained her obsessive hold upon her son; and, during her lifetime, he could not begin a novel that dealt with so many themes she would certainly have found repellent.

Similarly, his asthmatic condition, which had tormented him since he reached the age of nine, became at last a useful adjunct. He entered a sanatorium; but his disease defeated the specialists – no doubt because the patient was not prepared to help himself. Unconsciously, writes Mr George Painter, he 'preferred his asthma and the way of life it necessitated to the health of ordinary human beings'[7]; for illness enforced the personal solitude that he required if he were to write his book. From the year 1909 onward, Proust adopted the

The *château du cycle*, Bois de Boulogne,
about 1900 by Béraud.

existence of a literary hermit. About this time he began to sever his connections with the fashionable world; and before long the smooth young man of fashion, painted by Jacques-Emile Blanche, developed into the haggard recluse who rarely left his bed until the night had fallen and, when he did emerge, had the air of a revenant, a ghostly apparition swaddled in scarves and shawls, wandering through the vacant perspectives of the Ritz or occasionally surveying a crowded ballroom from a sofa near the door.

Many well-known writers, including Cocteau and Colette, have described the bizarre effect he made. He was all black-and-white, with his deathly pallid face, his dark eyes, his shock of black hair and his black untidy overcoat. Jacques Porel has likened him, as he lay abed, to a wounded crow beside the path; and Francis de Croisset, I am told by his step-son-in-law, the vicomte Charles de Noailles, used to say that he resembled a '*chaud-froid de corbeaux*', so bleakly unappetizing was his habitual guise. In his last period, Proust was a night-bird; and a series of sinister stories are told about his nightly frequentations. Having at length escaped from his mother's influence, he seems to have descended deep into 'the Pit of Sodom'; and it has even been said that, like his character, the lesbian Mademoiselle Vinteuil, he deliberately profaned his parents' image. Whatever the truth may be, the idea of such a profanation undoubtedly attracted him; and he certainly gave away some of his parents' discarded furniture to a Parisian male brothel.

Yet nothing he did was done without a purpose; and both his knowledge of evil and his knowledge of good contributed to the masterpiece that he was now creating. *A la Recherche du temps perdu* (of which *Du Côté de chez Swann* came out in 1913, *A l'ombre des jeunes filles en fleurs* in 1919, *Le Côté de Guermantes* in 1920, and *Sodome et Gomorrhe* between 1921 and 1923) slowly assumed its monumental shape. Balzac had raised a considerably larger edifice; but *La Comédie Humaine* lacks the artistic unity that Proust imposed upon his novel. This he had accomplished by making his book the record of a single man's experience. Yet, strangely enough, Proust's Narrator is not a very solid personage; we believe in his feelings and sufferings rather than in the man himself; as an individual, he is drawn with far less care than any of his fellow characters.

Though Proust and his Narrator are clearly much alike, and everything that happens to the Narrator had – no doubt under a somewhat different guise – also happened to the novelist, *A la Recherche* is not an autobiographical book; for the Narrator, having set out to investigate the past, looks far beyond his own experience, and is mainly interested in what he finds there because it illustrates some general truth, and clarifies his views on Time and Art and the nature of the human passions. Nor was Proust attempting to write history. *A la Recherche* draws a miraculously vivid picture of French social life over a period of some forty years. But the novelist makes no attempt to achieve historical exactitude; and, as Marcel Schneider usefully points out, there are a number of second-rate novelists who probably give a much more accurate impression of the society that Proust describes, for example when he is portraying the Guermantes and the Faubourg Saint-Germain. The social historian is a studious collector of facts; and, notwithstanding his passionate interest in facts, which he continued to amass until the very end, Proust's aim was to distil a poetic essence from the information that filled his secret notebooks, and to portray his characters, not as they actually were, but as, he felt, they should have been – as they *might* have been, had they acquired sufficient strength to realize all their hidden possibilities.

Thus *A la Recherche* is a work of fiction, built upon poetic principles. In *Contre Sainte-Beuve* we find a tribute to Chateaubriand, written while Proust was still comparatively young, that may serve to illuminate his own method. Again and again, he writes, amid Chateaubriand's descriptions of events and his solemn musings about human destiny, we hear a note that belongs to him alone; *'ce qui est son cri à lui . . . on sent bien ce que c'est qu'un poète'*. He may be discussing, perhaps, the Great Condé; *'on sent sous sa phrase une autre réalité'* – far superior to the prosaic kind of reality that gives events, even ideas, their historical importance. Proust, too, has this distinguishing note, which constantly recurs throughout his narrative. He is a novelist who believes that life can only be understood, or really enjoyed in moments of poetic exaltation, and that those moments can sometimes be caught and preserved through the regenerative powers of memory.

As he wrote, he left nothing unchanged; no single face, landscape or incident that he drew up from his memories of the past was sufficiently vivid, sufficiently characteristic, to provide the material his story needed, until it had been passed through his creative imagination, and there combined with a host of other memories to give it the necessary strength and point. All his personages had a composite origin. Oriane de Guermantes, we know, was derived from the comtesse Greffulhe and the comtesse de Chevigné, both luminaries of the Faubourg Saint-Germain, but also from Madame Straus, the elegant Jewish *salonnière*, a witty and sharp-tongued woman, who contributed the famous Guermantes turn of phrase. Similarly, Charles Swann seems to have originated partly in Charles Haas (the only Jewish member of the Jockey Club) partly in the

more learned Charles Ephrussi (once the employer and patron of the young
Symbolist poet Jules Laforgue) and, at the same time, perhaps in Proust himself. Similarly, when he was creating the baron de Charlus, he grafted on to the
romantic and fastidious Robert de Montesquiou some of the squalid and sinister
attributes of a certain baron Doasan, like Proust, an experienced frequenter of
the homosexual underworld.

Proust, however, while producing a composite portrait, did not follow the
example of those eighteenth-century art-dealers who were accustomed to
assemble a pile of fragments, which they patched together, with one or two
modern additions, to form a perfect 'antique' statue. Before he completed his
reconstruction, he had planted a fiery seed of individual life; and none of the
men and women from whom he borrowed a face, a hand or gesture can have
been more *alive* than Charlus, Swann, Odette, Madame Verdurin, Cottard and
Brichot, Bloch, Legrandin, Françoise or the duc de Guermantes. Proust had a
marvellous eye for the traits, quirks, oddities and vices that constitute a human
character. In Parisian salons, we are told, he was an extraordinarily accomplished mimic; his imitation of Madame Lemaire bidding her guests farewell
and paying them effusive compliments, then, as she slowly ascended the stairs,
giving the little dog that trotted behind her real opinion on the company, was a
particularly brilliant piece of comic acting. Proust and the Comic Spirit is a
subject that deserves a separate essay. *A la Recherche du temps perdu* may be considered, in some respects at least, a tragic book; but, almost to the end, it is
constantly illuminated by entrancing gleams of humour. Sometimes the humour
is broad and ribald. The elderly Monsieur Nissim Bernard, for instance, a
homosexual visitor to Balbec, the uncle of the Narrator's friend Bloch, had
fallen in love with a young man employed at a local farm, whose ruddy face suggests a ripe tomato. Unluckily, there is a second tomato, the favourite's heterosexual twin-brother; and, when the short-sighted Monsieur Nissim Bernard
happens to pay court to the wrong tomato, he invariably receives a black eye.

More delicate is Proust's treatment of the rich middle-class hostess Madame
Verdurin. She is surrounded by 'the faithful', a group of especially privileged
intimates, among her chief supporters being the ignorant and garrulous Dr
Cottard whose idiotic pleasantries enchant his friends. One of his jokes had so
delighted the hostess that, during her paroxysms of amusement, she had actually put out her jaw. Henceforward she adopts a wise precaution. Amid the
fine eighteenth-century furniture she and her husband have collected, she keeps
a long-legged Swedish chair:

From this lofty perch she would take her spirited part in the conversation of the 'faithful', and would revel in all their fun; but, since the accident to her jaw, she had abandoned the effort involved in real hilarity, and substituted a kind of symbolical dumb-show which signified, without endangering or even fatiguing her in any way, that she was 'laughing until she cried'. At the least witticism . . . she would utter a shrill cry, shut tight her little bird-like eyes . . . and quickly, as though she had only just time to avoid some indecent sight or to parry a mortal blow, burying her face in her hands . . . she would appear to be struggling to suppress, to eradicate a laugh which, were she to give way to it, must inevitably leave her inanimate. So, stupified with the gaiety of the 'faithful', drunken with comradeship, scandal and asseveration, Mme Verdurin, perched on her high seat like a cage-bird whose biscuit has been steeped in mulled wine, would sit aloft and sob with fellow-feeling.

The Comic Spirit naturally declines as Proust moves towards his closing volumes. From Combray he travels through Balbec on into the Faubourg Saint-Germain, where he observes the marvellous Guermantes at home, but discovers that the Great World, interesting and attractive though it may often appear from an artist's point of view, is after all '*le royaume du néant*', a place of frustrated hopes and lost illusions. In one of the novelist's greatest tragic passages, he describes how Swann, having been condemned to death by a specialist, visits the duchesse de Guermantes, thinking that his old friend, whose sympathy he counts on, should be the first to hear the news. Oriane, however, is setting out for a party; and the duc de Guermantes, who detests feminine unpunctuality, is sharply nagging in the background. Flustered and over-wrought, she refuses to accept the suggestion that Swann must very soon die, scatters a few evasive consolatory remarks, hastily enters the waiting carriage and is driven away beside her husband.

In *Sodome et Gomorrhe*, *La Prisonnière* and *Albertine disparue*, while friendship is dismissed as a fraud, love is also found wanting, whether it be the love of the Narrator for Albertine, or the love of Charlus for his selfish protégé Morel. Proust's lovers always embrace a cloud; but, once the cloud itself has evaporated, passion lingers on as jealousy. The title of Balzac's novel, *Les Illusions perdues*, may very well have haunted Proust; and to the idea that we can seldom arrive at the objective truth about our fellow human beings he gives a new and disconcerting twist. Whereas in the ordinary novel, remarks Mr Leo Bersani, the characters admit to mistakes that are subsequently put right, 'Marcel's incomplete or distorting impressions of other people' reveal 'the universal unreliability' of any judgements we may venture to form about the world beyond our own immediate ken.[8] The whole world is a baffling maze of illusions. Only the artist can provide a golden clue that may ultimately lead us through the labyrinth.

In his last volume, *Le Temps retrouvé*, which he did not live to publish, Proust depicts the downfall of his last illusions, but pays a splendid tribute to the healing powers of Art. I cannot quite agree with Pamela Hansford Johnson that *Le Temps retrouvé* is a cheerful book. Although the conclusion is soberly optimistic – Art has prevailed against the ravages of Time; the Narrator has himself achieved salvation – during its course he deliberately and brutally demolishes every idol he has so far raised. In his earlier volumes, one of his most appealing personages is the Narrator's aristocratic friend, Robert de Saint-Loup, an impulsive enthusiast, who to his inherited nobility joins a deeper nobility of heart and mind. Saint-Loup has married Gilberte Swann; but, when the Narrator visits their house at Tansonville, he finds that his old friend has become a practising paederast and callously neglects his wife for the sake of Charlie Morel, once the baron de Charlus's homosexual protégé.

Proust's description of the effect of his homosexual proclivities on Robert de Saint-Loup – contrasted with their effect on Charlus, now a drivelling and decrepit invalid, faithfully tended by his sinister henchman Jupien – is a marvellous essay in imaginative analysis:

He came several times to Tansonville while I was there, and I found him very different from the man I had known. His life had not coarsened him or slowed him down . . . on the contrary . . . it had given him, in a degree in which he had never had it before . . . the grace and ease of a cavalry officer. Gradually, just as M. de Charlus had grown heavier, Robert . . . had . . . become slimmer and taken to moving more rapidly, a contrary effect of an identical vice. This swiftness of movement had, moreover, various psychological causes; the fear of being seen, the wish to conceal that fear, the feverishness which is generated by self-dissatisfaction and boredom. He was in the habit of visiting certain low haunts into which . . . he would hurl himself in such a way as to present the smallest possible target to the unfriendly glances of possible passers-by, like a soldier going into an attack.[9]

Previously, the Narrator has learned from Gilberte herself that the little red-haired girl he had once adored was neither innocent nor unapproachable, and that the gesture he remembered her making behind the boundary of her father's park, which he had thought was a movement of cold contempt, had been really a shameless invitation to join her in her wicked games. So much for innocence. Meanwhile the whole social system of the Faubourg Saint-Germain has collapsed into a vulgar farce; Madame Verdurin is the present princesse de Guermantes – the prince has been unmasked by the narrator as yet another secret invert; the duc de Guermantes is the besotted lover of the aged Odette Swann; the duchesse de Guermantes, a coarsened elderly woman, who has long since lost her elegance, throttled by jewels, her 'salmon-pink body almost concealed by its fins of black lace'. Yet, at the same gathering where the narrator beholds this apocalyptic scene, he enjoys his second moment of illumination, which confirms his belief that the Past can still be recovered, and that, amid the nightmare of lost illusions and changed identities, Art, and Art alone, can save him.

For the purposes of his novel, the incident is said to have taken place just after the end of the First World War. By 1918, however, the production of *A la Recherche du temps perdu* was already under way. During those last years he worked against time, and the outer world grew more and more unreal. But in 1921, about 24 May, instead of following his customary procedure and going to sleep as soon as day broke, he rose early and, despite an alarming attack of vertigo, managed to travel across Paris to the Jeu de Paume, where he visited an exhibition of Dutch pictures that included Vermeer's *View of Delft*. It was 'the most beautiful picture in the world' he decided; and, having seen it, and gazed with his usual passionate intensity on a 'little patch of yellow wall' – the detail that had so delighted Bergotte – he lunched at his old haunt, the dining-room of the Ritz, and slowly struggled home to bed.

From this adventure he derived his magnificent description of the death of Bergotte – one of the three great creative intelligences, Bergotte the novelist, Elstir the painter and Vinteuil the composer, evolved by Proust from his personal recollections of a variety of modern artists. In *A la Recherche du temps perdu*, except for his mother and grandmother, they are the only characters who escape reproach – intercessory spirits in whom the author came to believe, as Balzac had believed in Bianchon, the famous physician of the *Comédie Humaine* to whose professional skill he appealed upon his death-bed. On his own death-bed, Proust remarked that, having himself reached the same condition, he would like to enlarge his account of his imaginary novelist's final hours; and, when he had dictated the passage to Céleste, he said that the result was 'very good'. Then, 'I must stop', he added, 'I can't do any more'. Some manuscripts were scattered across the bedclothes; and, during his agony, Céleste noted that his hands were plucking feverishly at the tumbled pages. Proust died late in the afternoon of 18 November 1922, at the age of fifty-one. The journey he did not live to finish had lasted nearly thirteen years.

1

The Making of a Novel
Philip Kolb

WHEN MARCEL PROUST was a student in his philosophy year at the lycée Condorcet, he wrote a composition that his professor, Monsieur Darlu, criticized severely. Across the top of the first page, Monsieur Darlu wrote the comment: 'extremely vague and superficial', pointing out with a touch of irony that the selected topic was 'very complex'. The seventeen-year-old boy had ventured to demonstrate how a scientist draws conclusions enabling him to derive a law from factual knowledge. The grade that young Proust received, out of a possible 20 points, was . . . 4. The professor did, however, make one encouraging remark. He conceded that there was 'some progress in composition'.[1] The boy deserved encouragement. He would continue to make progress in composition until he eventually became a novelist who, today, is widely recognized to be the greatest whom France has produced in at least one hundred years.

The qualities of his style, the depth of his psychological penetration, the heights of his poetic genius, and the charm of his humour, were indeed appreciated quite early by some of his critics. Despite that recognition, paradoxically enough, the general reading public, even today, seems to retain an image of Proust that is in some respects blurred and distorted. For many people, perhaps a majority, the name of Proust brings to mind a pathetic, Chaplinesque figure, something like the stock character, or caricature, of a Frenchman in English light comedy of a few generations ago, or perhaps a type that Ionesco might conjure up. Proust is still seen as the legendary figure fabricated about 1919, when he first came into the public eye, that same straw man of whom the same tales and anecdotes – half truth and half fiction – are purveyed about the recluse in his cork-lined room, with his effete, ingratiating manner and his excessive tipping of the doorman at the Ritz. Need it be pointed out that the person so portrayed fails to measure up to the sort of man capable of producing so monumental a masterpiece as *A la Recherche du temps perdu*?

What is perhaps a cause for greater concern is the fact that his novel is frequently misrepresented. Even professional people sometimes write about it without having read it with sufficient comprehension. They speak, for instance, of Proust's 'cycle' or 'series' of novels, or of the author's indifference to morality or religion. And the potential reader, curious about Proust, may end up reading disquisitions on him and his life, or on his work, instead of reading his *novel* to understand and enjoy it. Admittedly this is not easy. Proust has nothing in common with authors of popular fiction or adventure stories. He cannot be expected to appeal to the same public as Simenon or even Sartre. His style inevitably perplexes most of those who first encounter it; those serpentine sentences are bound to exasperate or discourage the average reader, unless and until one has become inured to Proust's sentence structure. And that takes time and patience. Even then, the uncompromising length of his novel is a challenge to the most intrepid reader. And there are other problems. When we consider the myriad of obstacles that the ailing Proust had to overcome, first, to get his material in order, to write it and get it into print, and then to persuade critics and public to read a novel so completely unconventional, we marvel that he did succeed, against countless odds, in winning for it such a multitude of readers in every civilized country in the world.

All of this represents an almost incredible achievement. And it has not taken long. Although Proust was born a century ago, and died half a century ago, his novel in its entirety was not published until 1927, and then only in a text replete with errors. The corrected text, which we owe to Messers Clarac and Ferré, has been available less than twenty years, and a complete corrected English translation remains yet to be done. Meanwhile a flood of new Proustiana is upon us, honouring the author on his first centennial. Some of the new publications will no doubt shed light on the author or his novel. But how much of it will misinform or obfuscate the reading public?

Proust was an author devoted to the search for Truth. Assuredly then, he deserves better than to be made the perennial victim of misinformation and misunderstanding about his aims and his accomplishments. While he did not claim to give us ultimate truth, he did seek it; and he presents what he found in his novel. So we can at least strive to discover the truth about him and his work. We shall examine certain prevalent ideas about his novel – bearing a singular similarity with notions entertained by some of Denis Diderot's critics concerning the works of that renowned encyclopedist – and then we shall go behind the scenes, so to speak, to find out whether those ideas are corroborated by evidence of Proust's practices in the actual composition of his work. It is possible to make such an excursion by means of a huge collection of Proust's manuscripts, notebooks and other materials which the Bibliothèque Nationale has acquired from Proust's family.[2]

My examination of these materials has convinced me that Proust's notebooks hold the key to many problems concerning his work. The solution of these problems depends on our capability in deciphering Proust's handwriting – at times almost illegible – and on our being sufficiently conversant with Proust's universe to penetrate the full significance of that mass of documents. As we shall see, the notebooks reveal some of the hidden intent of his novel, and some of the secrets of his methods and practices in planning and writing it. We shall then see how different he was from the kind of novelist many of his critics have supposed him to be.

In this connection, we pause to consider a curious parallel between Proust and Diderot. It is worthy of note that Diderot was one of the few French writers of the eighteenth century with whom Proust has any real affinities. Diderot seems to foreshadow Proust in observing the contradictions and inconsistencies of human conduct. He dared to depart from literary traditions in character depiction by showing in fictional form how complex man's nature really is. Proust would carry that idea a step farther, systematizing and stylizing the presentation of his characters in an invention that he chose to call his 'prepared' character (*'le personnage "préparé"'*). In Diderot these tendencies seem already to be suggested in the whimsical paradox of such a title as *Est-il bon? est-il méchant?* – where Diderot refrains from drawing conclusions. Here we have the innovation of an author who makes no claim to omniscience. We find another example of what Proust would try to demonstrate in this title: *Sur l'inconséquence du jugement public de nos actions particulières.*

An even more marked parallel can be seen, however, in the similarity of attitudes expressed by Diderot's and Proust's respective critics. Diderot has frequently been reproached for the alleged weaknesses of improvisation, disorder, and the inconsistency with which he delineates character. But recently, Professor Pommier's research on *Le Rêve de d'Alembert* has shown that Diderot actually exercised considerable care in the revision of that particular work. Professor Etiemble, in an article full of spice and vinegar, has examined the structure and meaning of the *Pensées philosophiques*, and takes to task such old-line critics as Daniel Mornet for their strictures concerning Diderot's composition, his alleged improvisation and the incoherence of his characters. Still more recently, Professor Roger Kempf has made some pertinent observations along the same lines in his book entitled *Diderot et le roman.*

Oddly enough, these very same criticisms of improvisation, disorder and lack of consistency in character depiction, have been formulated against Proust. They were put into circulation when *Swann* was first published in November 1913, and have been repeated periodically from that day almost down to this. A few brief quotations will show the tenor of these charges. When that first volume of Proust's novel came out, most of the critics judged it from a narrowly traditional point of view, applying to it the standards of the so-called classical French novel. Paul Souday, literary critic of *Le Temps*, one of the big-wigs of the critical world, thought that *Du Côté de chez Swann* resembled an English novel, and remarked superciliously, 'We French and Latins prefer a more synthetic process'.[3] Another influential critic, Henri Ghéon, in a long review article in the *Nouvelle Revue Française*, gave the novel some ambiguous words of praise interlarded with back-handed censure. He was the first, I believe, to accuse Proust of making no choice or selection of material, of simply spreading out before the reader in a confused, haphazard way what he has dredged up from the depths of consciousness. The same critic charged Proust with a lack of logic in character depiction, of seeking the diverse and contradictory aspects of a character instead of tracing the line of his development.[4] Ironically enough, some writers (André Maurois for example) have recently credited Ghéon with being one of Proust's discoverers! We shall return to this question later. Here, then, are the very same criticisms that had been levelled against Diderot. They were to be repeated by other critics as the successive volumes of *A la Recherche du temps perdu* issued forth. When *A l'Ombre des jeunes filles en fleurs* came out, in 1919, Proust won the Goncourt prize and suddenly found himself famous. But no sooner had the prize been awarded than a hue and cry was raised. A critic named Gasquet called Proust the 'crudest of improvisers'[5]; it seems probable that he had scarcely had time to glance at the novel. The literary critic of an important newspaper, *Le Journal des Débats*, whose name was Jean de Pierrefeu, greeted the award with surprise and indignation. Caustically, he said that Proust was known for some clever and malicious parodies, and a compact volume having the bizarre title *Du Côté de chez Swann* and neither a beginning nor an end. Acidly, the critic went on: 'To that first volume he has added a second one which prolongs the first, and he is preparing two more on the same theme. There is nothing to prove that he will stop going on his merry way; in my opinion, only fatigue or death can stop him in the task he has undertaken of searching for his lost time.'[6] This last pun simply echoes one of Ghéon's insidious jibes. These are mere samples of the critical incomprehension that plagued Proust throughout his career.

We return then to the question: how can we ascertain the facts as to Proust's aims and achievements? We have one piece of evidence of capital importance concerning the structure of his novel. In a letter addressed to Madame Emile Straus in August 1909, Proust states: 'I have just begun – and finished – a whole long book.'[7] Curiously enough, this important statement has been misinterpreted by one of Proust's most distinguished biographers. Nevertheless, it is clear from this and corroborative testimony that Proust – in the spring of 1909 – had written a first draft of the introductory and concluding chapters of his novel. The intervening portions he was to write subsequently. By proceeding in this manner, he was able to lay a solid foundation for the structural elements of his novel before going on to fill in its central narrative parts, where he develops his characters and illustrates his themes. In the opening chapter, set in the quaint provincial town of Combray, he presents the principal themes that will recur intermittently to form a unifying network throughout the novel. He also names some of the principal characters and the places that form a setting for the novel. In the last chapter of *Le Temps retrouvé*, he will explain the significance of the themes set forth at the beginning, and give a final summing-up, revealing the goal towards which the narrator's seemingly aimless peregrination has been leading, and the lessons he has learned about life and art. That is how the narrator discovers his vocation: he will regain past time – time passed aimlessly – through Art.

On the question of whether or not Proust improvised his novel, a decisive answer can best be found in the notebooks he used in its preparation. They bear testimony to the great amount of painstaking work which went into the planning and execution of the final version. The archives in the Bibliothèque Nationale include eighty-two large notebooks and four small ones, as well as a quantity of manuscript materials, typescripts and proof sheets. But that collection is not complete. Altogether Proust must have used at least one hundred and thirty notebooks, during the composition of his novel, in addition to the other materials. Nor does this estimate take into account the manuscript of his early novel about Jean Santeuil, covering well over one thousand pages in print, where the young author tried his hand at so many of the same themes, characters and episodes that later were to reappear, in revised and perfected form, in the novel of his mature years.

A general survey of the notebooks discloses three types of entries. First, there are the passages we can recognize as belonging to Proust's novel in various stages of its composition. Then, there are the many notations he scribbled down to remind himself about some aspect of the novel's form or content which he wanted to bear in mind later in writing some particular section. And, finally, there are certain texts extraneous to the novel, such as literary criticism or pastiches.

We can give only a passing glance to the actual texts of the novel. But they show clearly how mistaken the critics were to insinuate that Proust had simply set out to write the random thoughts that came into his head. Certain passages he rewrote many times, revising and correcting indefatigably. These texts belong for the most part to the early years of the novel's composition, before he had acquired the stylistic mastery that marks practically everything he wrote during the last decade of his life.

Evidence against the charge of improvisation is even more overwhelming when we consider the many notations concerning his plans for the structure of the novel, the balance and symmetry of its parts, and the details of its composition. At times he would jot down the outline for an entire section. In one such notation, he reminds himself of the contrast he wishes to obtain between the Narrator's first and second visits to the seaside resort called Balbec. The note is labelled 'Capitalissime', that is to say, *of the utmost importance*, and begins:

Second trip to Balbec. First I show that I had come the first time to seek the unknown, now I come looking for what is known to me. I had come there seeking an eternal mist, etc. I come looking for memories of dining behind the blue windows with the sun's rays on the shutter (perhaps I should place here what I say about returning to Balbec in the part already written). I had come to look for a Persian church. I was coming to seek what Elstir had told me of the church and the seas he had painted and which I'll find in spite of myself (that will explain without my saying so, the descriptions of Turneresque seas). I had come for an unknown society. I was coming now above all because I knew everybody.

The reference to 'Turneresque seas' alludes to Proust's descriptions of the sea, evocative as Turner's paintings as interpreted by Ruskin. Clearly these descriptions are intended to illustrate Elstir's vision of nature and his impressionistic conception of the art of painting. Another such note gives the arrangement of scenes in the third volume, *Le Côté de Guermantes*. Still another is headed: 'The articulation of this chapter can be . . .' and is followed by a listing of the events in the final chapter. These samples show what attention Proust devoted to problems of structure and organization, and how he calculated his effects, working out in advance the slightest details in the distribution and counterbalancing of scenes and sections.

Another category of notations deals with the characters in the novel. Here we see to what a great extent Proust relies on his memory of persons he had known, their actions, speech and even gestures in actual conversations and incidents. It is evident that he bore specific models in mind for each character, and almost every one is a composite creation. Proust has himself stated, towards the end of *Le Temps retrouvé*,[8] speaking of the novelist in general terms: ' . . . there isn't a gesture of his characters, a quirk, an accent, which has not been inspired by memory; there is not a name of an imaginary character beneath which he cannot see sixty names of persons seen, of whom one has posed for a grimace, another for the monocle, this one for a fit of anger, that one for the impatient thrust of an arm, etc.'

In one notebook, I find a curious sidelight on Proust's manner of composing or compounding his characters. It concerns the character named Bloch, a school friend of the Narrator who is so precocious that he considers the supreme merit of poetry to consist in having absolutely no meaning. He is also precocious in other ways, since he is the first to introduce the Narrator to a house of ill fame. But he does lend the Narrator a book by Bergotte, who will become the Narrator's favourite living author. Unfortunately, Bloch makes a bad impression on the Narrator's family, who find him objectionable not because of any prejudice but because he is ill-mannered and irresponsible. Bloch confirms this impression by his rude and tactless behaviour. He had begun by annoying the Narrator's father, who, seeing him come in with wet clothes, had asked him with keen interest: 'Why, M. Bloch, is there a change in the weather; has it been raining? I can't understand it; the barometer has been "set fair".' This drew from Bloch nothing more instructive than: 'Sir, I am absolutely incapable of telling you whether it has been raining. I live so resolutely apart from physical contingencies that my senses no longer trouble to inform me of them.'

Finally, Bloch had upset the whole household when he arrived an hour and a half late for luncheon, covered with mud from head to foot, making not the least apology, merely saying: 'I never allow myself to be influenced in the slightest degree either by atmospheric disturbances or by the arbitrary divisions of what is known as Time. I would willingly reintroduce to society the Chinese opium pipe or the Malayan kriss, but I am wholly and entirely without instruction in those infinitely more pernicious (besides being quite bleakly bourgeois) implements, the umbrella and the watch.'[9]

Bloch is the chap who, in Madame de Villeparisis' drawing-room, knocks over a vase containing flowers and spills all the water on the carpet. Simultaneously, another guest, admiring the hostess as she paints flowers, happens to say to her: 'Really, you have the fingers of a fairy'[10]. Bloch takes this remark to be an ironic reference to his clumsiness; and, to cover up his shame, instead of apologizing he affects an insolent bravado and retorts: 'It's not of the slightest importance; I'm not wet.'[11]

Here is the notation concerning Bloch in one of Proust's notebooks: 'Combine in his speech the conversation of Max Lazard, Bernstein, Gregh and Lanson . . .' We see here the process of amalgamation at work. The first name, Max Lazard, was that of a well-known, erudite economist who had married into the Ellisson family, whom Proust had known from childhood. The second model is one of the foremost playwrights of Proust's time, and one of his friends, Henri Bernstein. The third one, Fernand Gregh, was a poet of considerable reputation with whom Proust had been friendly since his early twenties, and a future academician. Gregh is the only one of the four who has previously been recognized as a model of the character Bloch. Assuredly the most surprising of the four names is that of Lanson. This name appears nowhere in Proust's correspondence, and I knew nothing of Proust having met anyone of that name. Checking the Paris directories of the period, I found only one listing of the name Lanson, that of Gustave Lanson, the Sorbonne professor, author of the celebrated history of French literature. I still was dubious that the eminent Lanson could have been a model for the vulgar Bloch. As far as I know, he was not even Jewish. But I did observe that his name is linked with that of Gregh, in the notebook entry, and followed by the parenthetical remark: ('these last two 3rd December'). On re-reading Gregh's memoirs, I found an explanation for the linking of the two names. For Gregh tells how he had become friendly with Lanson – it was indeed the Sorbonne professor! – who had a cottage in the Fontainebleau region, near-by, where Gregh and his family used to spend their vacations. Gregh even calls attention to Lanson's conversation, which, of course, reflected his vast erudition.[12] It seems safe to assume, therefore, that Proust had met Lanson through Gregh, and that he was similarly struck with the quality of his conversation, studded with literary quotations. In Bloch's speech, we have then an amalgamation of elements taken from these four models, and probably others as well.

Curiously enough, although Bloch represents a non-assimilated Jewish milieu, only two of the four original models named in our source had Jewish origins. Yet it is largely on the basis of Proust's portrayal of Bloch and his family that the author has been accused of antisemitism. To my mind there is little justification for the charge. He had close ties with the Jewish people, and I find no evidence that he ever attempted to hide or deny these relationships. If Bloch is a buffoon and a boor, he is so because Proust saw him that way, just as he

Paris

'Every
morning I
would hasten
to the Moriss
Column to see
what new
plays and
words it
announced.'
Photograph
of 1898.

III

right: Polaire in the Bois, with dog and motor-car.

right: Bicycling and walking dress, at the beginning of the new century.

opposite: Taking the air in the Bois de Boulogne.

overleaf: The Moulin Rouge about 1896.

above : Late nineteenth-century Paris;
the place Saint-Augustin.

right : Fashions in the Bois, on the eve
of World War I.

above : The place de la Bastille, 1909; by Luigi Loir.
top : The Universal Exhibition, 1900; the Palace of Electricity
and the Palace of Waters.

saw Swann, also Jewish, as a man of tact and distinction. He considered it the duty of a novelist to be impartial, showing the nature of man and society as he views them.

In actual practice he assembled the elements of each character in much the fashion he states in the passage quoted earlier from his final volume. He appears then to be justified in claiming, as he does in his famous dedicatory epistle addressed to Jacques de Lacretelle: ' . . . there are no keys for the characters of this book, or else there are eight or ten for a single one . . .'[13] Not only does this statement apply to characters, their physique, habits, facial expressions, their gestures, attitudes, voice and pronunciation, but also to Vinteuil's music, and even to descriptions of churches, all inspired by specific models that Proust had observed, that he remembered and artfully moulded together in his immortal creations. Proust's notebooks show us that he collected the elements for his characters much in the manner of the entomologist gathering species. He even affixes to his notes concerning certain characters, as a sort of label, the names of the persons he is thinking of as he plans certain passages.

Even the metaphors associated with certain characters are carefully selected for use as leitmotif. Thus he specifies, in one of his notes:

Extremely important. For what I think I possess in Albertine there must be some of the most beautiful images of Balbec, for example the blue mountains of the sea (which I can perhaps indicate as reappearing when I hear music in the morning so that Albertine reminding me of the music reminds me of the blue mountains but this is not necessary (since the music isn't perhaps until later). In any case solid metaphors and the same ones well linked.

This note shows us how he prepares passages in *A l'Ombre des jeunes filles en fleurs* and *La Prisonnière*, where he achieves such superb poetic effects associating Albertine with the sea.

Obviously, Proust had nothing in common with the writer who simply improvises as he writes. Like Balzac, he made numerous marginal additions to his manuscript and proof sheets. Céleste Albaret used to paste additional pages into his notebooks at the sides or bottom of the sheets, making elongated accordion-like pages that extend in some instances as much as six feet in length. But such insertions, at least in Proust's case, are not necessarily after-thoughts. They may well be passages that Proust had planned or actually written earlier; he may simply have hesitated to choose the place where their insertion would be the most effective. In some instances he wrote alternative passages, as in the

The avenue de l'Opéra during the last
years of the nineteenth century.

case of Saniette's death. Proust did not live long enough to make the necessary corrections.

Such interpolations inevitably add to the over-all length of Proust's text; they pose the question: is Proust's novel too long? This is a fair question, and it deserves a fair answer. What justification is there for a novel three or four thousand pages long? Admittedly, this is a matter of proportion. It depends on the aims of the author, and the measure of his achievement.

The plot he selected was basically simple: the Narrator's quest of a vocation. Only the significant episodes in that quest are included; but they are told in full or, we might say, in depth: the scene of his mother's goodnight kiss, marking his parents' failure to cure the child's neurotic tendencies; his early ambitions to become a writer, marked by a consultation with Monsieur de Norpois, who instils doubt in the child concerning his own literary talents; his initiation by la Berma to dramatic art; his introduction by Bloch to the work of Bergotte, and by Gilberte Swann, to the writer himself, who teaches him some lessons about literature, and to Elstir, who teaches him about art; experience of love, through Gilberte and Albertine; experience of society, through Madame de Villeparisis and the duchesse de Guermantes; experience of friendship, through Saint-Loup; knowledge of sexual aberrations, through Mademoiselle Vinteuil and the baron de Charlus. His life at Balbec – where he meets the Guermantes clan and Albertine – he owes to Gilberte's father, Charles Swann. These experiences lead him to conclude that happiness is attainable neither through friendship nor love. His doubts about the reality of art are dispelled by hearing Vinteuil's posthumous work, and, encouraged by Vinteuil's example, he finally decides on the pursuit of a nobler happiness through artistic creativity in the writing of his novel.

Time is the novel's great theme, as its title indicates. As Proust explained when his first volume appeared, he wanted to isolate 'that invisible substance of Time'; such an experiment required duration. Events of purely social significance, such as a marriage towards the end of the novel between persons who, in the first volume, had belonged to different social milieux (Gilberte Swann and Robert de Saint-Loup), would indicate the passage of time, taking on, as he put it, 'the beauty of patina on leaden surfaces at Versailles that Time has shrouded in an emerald scabbard'. Then, 'as a village which, while the train winds along its way, appears to us first on the right, then on the left, the diverse aspects of the same character will seem, in the eyes of others, like successive and different people, giving us the sensation that Time has elapsed'. Certain characters, as we shall see, turn out to be different from what they had appeared to be earlier, as in life.[14] Here again are the characters he had 'prepared' in the first volume so that they would do later exactly the opposite of what we should have expected.[15] A novelist can hardly hope to achieve such objectives unless his novel has considerable amplitude.

Despite this need for liberal dimensions, the notebooks show us that an impressive amount of material was sacrificed. Such passages include entire episodes (concerning Odette Swann, for instance, or the baronne Putbus) as well as notations for dialogue or description. Then there are some striking cases of condensation. I find an earlier text, for example, of a comic episode telling of Proust's little brother Robert's separation from a pet goat. In the revised version Proust has substituted the Narrator for his brother, and eliminated the other members of the family, even the goat. Only his mother remains; it is she who discovers the Narrator bidding a tearful farewell, not to a goat but to his beloved hawthorn bushes. The original version covers seven full pages of the printed text; they have been reduced to one paragraph of just twenty-five lines.[16]

The amount of material he sacrificed in this manner must have been considerable. Contrary to the general impression of Proust, as we have seen, he has on occasion condensed his text rigorously, or eliminated material entirely. In a letter to Robert Dreyfus, he expresses indignation because one of his critics had accused him of noting everything; he protests: 'No, I don't note anything. He is the one who makes notes. Not a single time does one of my characters close a window, wash his hands, put on his overcoat, make an introduction. If there is anything new in this book, it's that, and it's not intentional. I'm just too lazy to write things that bore me.'[17] We should perhaps not take this statement too literally. Proust simply means that he includes details only when they are relevant and significant; he feels that nothing in his novel is really superfluous. And every element is interlocked with the rest.

On the question of his novel's length and its complexity, I find one inscription in the notebooks that is illuminating. Proust is outlining an unexpected twist in the relationship between Charlie Morel, the baron de Charlus and others; and he adds this explanation: ' . . . things are more complicated than people believe, complexity as well as the symmetry that organizes it, being an element of beauty'. Here, I believe, is one of the tenets of Proust's artistic credo, one of the secrets of his art. Not only does he strive for certain effects through the architectural organization and symmetry of his novel's parts; he considers that the complex adjustment of that inner structure adds an element of truth, and, as a consequence, contributes to the beauty of the whole. Whether or not we agree, we can see that this complexity is intentional; it is studied; and it has an aesthetic *raison d'être*. Proust's aim was to imitate the sort of complexity we encounter in life itself. The effect obtained is something akin to that achieved by Mozart in the finale of the *Jupiter* symphony, where he combines five themes in counterpoint.

That complexity is at once apparent in Proust's characters. For, as he had explained, he presents them at first according to their reputation in society, or the Narrator's first impressions of them, so that they seem to have certain traits and to belong to a certain type; but on better acquaintance, they are revealed to be quite different from what those first impressions seemed to imply. A good example is the composer Vinteuil, who appears at first to be a sad, timid, insignificant piano-teacher; after his death, his music will reveal his true inner nature, which, on the contrary, is joyful and audacious, filled with the inner conviction of a man possessed of great creative powers. So Proust has purposely misled us; imitating real life, he wishes to show how false our first impressions may be. But this is an artful, stylized imitation of life, that Proust varies to suit individual cases in the novel. When the critic Ghéon complained that Proust's characters were illogical, he had simply failed to comprehend an original technique of character presentation. He had failed also to note that Proust was making use, in an original way, of observations about erratic quirks in human nature which Diderot had made before him in a less systematic manner. These successive revelations concerning Proust's characters have an additional function in his novel. For each new perspective contributes to our impression of the passage of time. This, as we have indicated, is one of the novel's major themes. Here then is that kind of complexity which Proust uses to enhance his artistic effects.

An illustration of another sort of complexity in the development of character can be seen summarily in the portrait of the princesse de Parme. The Narrator, when presented to her at a dinner in the salon of the duchesse de Guermantes, is struck by her friendly, almost humble manner; he explains it in this humorous, litany-like recital of the Princess's education:

> Her friendliness sprang from two causes. The first and more general was the education which this daughter of Kings had received. Her mother (not merely allied by blood to all the royal families of Europe but furthermore – in contrast to the Ducal House of Parma – richer than any reigning Princess) had instilled into her from her earliest

childhood the arrogantly humble precepts of an evangelical snobbery; and today every line of the daughter's face, the curve of her shoulders, the movement of her arms seemed to repeat the lesson: 'Remember that if God has caused you to be born on the steps of a throne you ought not to make that a reason for looking down upon those to whom Divine Providence has willed (wherefore praised be His name) that you should be superior by birth and fortune. On the contrary, you must suffer the little ones. Your ancestors were Princes of Trèves and Juliers from the year 647; God has decreed in His bounty that you should hold practically all the shares in the Suez Canal and three times as many Royal Dutch as Edmond de Rothschild; your pedigree in a direct line has been established by genealogists from the year 63 of the Christian Era; you have as sisters-in-law two Empresses. Therefore never seem, in your speech, to be recalling these great privileges, not that they are precarious (for nothing can alter antiquity of race, while the world will always need petrol), but because it is useless to point out that you are better born than other people or that your investments are all gilt-edged, since everybody knows these facts already. Be helpful to the needy. Furnish to all those whom the bounty of Heaven has done you the favour of placing beneath you as much as you can give them without forfeiture of your rank, that is to say, help in the form of money, even your personal service by their sick-beds, but never (bear well in mind) invite them to your parties, which would do them no possible good and, by weakening your own position, would diminish the efficacy of your benevolent activities.[18]

WE HAVE seen something of Proust's aims, his practices and his achievements. His philosophy professor, back in 1888, had been wise to encourage him for his progress in composition. Young Proust learned his lesson of avoiding any tendency to be vague or superficial. We have seen how he bases his slightest observation on the memory of living models. He never would overcome his penchant for complex subjects; that is because he could see more than most of us. But he would know how to make complexity serve his artistic purposes. Nor would he lose interest in the subject selected for that school composition: the problem of deriving the laws of nature from observable facts. Indeed he would spend most of his life probing, with a scientist's curiosity and tenacity, the psychological laws that determine human conduct.[19] But he would do much more. For he would transform the manifold observations stored up in his phenomenal memory, through his powers of imagination, his poetic fantasy, his humour, and the magic of a style which is perhaps his greatest attribute, to create one of the enduring works of fiction. Many who enter the labyrinth of his novel may get lost and give up. There are no short cuts. But few of those who persevere all the way fail to find the journey richly rewarding.

2

The Faubourg Saint-Germain

Marcel Schneider

WHEN MARCEL PROUST set forth on his journey in pursuit of vanished time, it was eternity he discovered rather than his own past – eternity so far as we can apprehend it, with the wretched means at our disposal, during those moments of vision which strike us like flashes of lightning and leave us irradiated and for ever changed. Such transfiguring moments we owe to the recollections that spring up, unsought, in the depths of the involuntary memory. Thus Proust was to exalt the gift that, thanks to the taste of a madeleine steeped in a cup of limeflower tea, or the sensation of treading the irregular pavement of a courtyard, had enabled him to arrest the passage of time and gain a miraculous insight into the hidden world that lies beyond. Wordsworth had already composed his *Ode on the Intimations of Immortality from Recollections of Early Childhood*; and the work of Proust reflects the same disquietude, the same anxiety to transcend the ordinary limitations of our spirits and our senses.

The author of *A la Recherche* certainly did not intend to become the portraitist and chronicler of modern society between 1890 and 1910 that many of his readers, following certain biographers and critics, even now believe he was. The man who wrote in one of his private notebooks, 'I have a clear view of life up to the horizon; but it is only what lies beyond the horizon that I am interested in depicting,'[1] could not be expected to produce a realistic, accurately detailed picture of the social scene beneath his eyes. Like Balzac, Proust was a visionary artist. The world that he imposed on his readers was the world he carried in himself – that of a sick, over-sensitive child, at once sadly spoiled and wonderfully gifted, who breaks his toys as soon as they are no longer useful, or have ceased to please his fancy.

His personages – endowed with such an extraordinary strength of life that we say, 'she is a Madame Verdurin: she is a Françoise' whenever we meet a middle-class blue-stocking, hag-ridden by her snobbish ambitions, or a devoted and despotic servant – have a verisimilitude and an air of universality that have made them household names. But, above all else, they are *Proustian* personages and bear the seal of their creator's complex and mysterious genius. Proust's duchesses are as different from real existence as may well have been Balzac's from those who actually flourished during the reigns of Louis XVIII and Charles X. They are more characteristic, more seductive, more truly conceived – with a truth derived from art, which is not the simple truth of nature They are not portraits; still less are they caricatures; but original products, evolved from the dreams, desires and aspirations of the novelist who created them.

MARCEL SCHNEIDER

Despite all the 'keys' we have been offered by critics, and the evidence of some of Proust's contemporaries who have announced that they recognized themselves – or whom others have professed to recognize – in the pages of *A la Recherche du temps perdu*, it was the novelist who provided his characters with the central nucleus of their being, with the innermost secret of their personality. What he asked from the living man or woman was merely some detail of the clothes they wore, some remark in a certain set of circumstances, some habit or some personal defect – anything that might help to form the envelope, but could never have conferred the spark of life, or taken the place of the creator's imagination, had his imaginative energies proved insufficient. When we are discussing Proust, writes François Mauriac in his *Journal*, we should speak, not of observation but of absorption. 'During the course of his apparently frivolous youth, he absorbed everything that came his way. He assimilated the world that he was afterwards to rediscover in his own mind through one of the greatest poetic miracles in the history of our literature.'

The relationship of Proust with aristocratic society affords a particularly vivid illustration of the method that Proust employed while he was reconstituting the actual world. On the one hand, he borrowed the material that his involuntary memory furnished him; on the other, he allowed his creative impulse to work along independent lines, regardless either of objective accuracy or of ordinary social scruples. Novelists who are today decried, such as Paul Bourget and, especially, Abel Hermant, have painted far more lifelike pictures of the fashionable world at the beginning of the twentieth century; but it is to Proust we refer as our touch-stone, because, after all, he was a man of genius. That genius, however, makes his testimony doubly suspect. Smaller artists have less commanding voices; but it is to them the careful historian refers when he seeks an approximate rendering of the real facts.

The historian of literature need not concern himself with sociological exactitude, but must stick as closely as he can to the artistic truth of the writer he is studying; which means, in most cases, that he must enter into the nightmares, the fantasies and the obsessions of the man whose work he values. With Proust, we observe the most astonishing change of position that any novelist has yet displayed. At the end of his book, the same aristocratic world, whose favour he had once courted, and where he had eagerly sought the right of entry, is painted in the darkest and most brutal colours. Did he repent of having intrigued for the social privileges that had so long dazzled him? Was he determined to mortify himself by demolishing a society that had once struck him as

An *evening party*, by Jean Béraud.

the only milieu in which a man of his quality could live at ease? Having over-praised the fashionable world, he subsequently reversed the process. His savage denunciation was the revenge he exacted for his earlier complacencies towards the Great.

IT WAS about his fortieth year that Proust, under the two-fold influence of sickness and the book he knew he had to write, gave up the fashionable world that, earlier, he had loved so dearly. Only a dozen years remained, to settle accounts with his fellow human beings and achieve *A la Recherche du temps perdu*. The novelist who wrote, in *Le Temps retrouvé*, that, 'the world being the kingdom of nothingness, between the merits of different *femmes du monde* there are insignificant graduations', was no longer the lively young man, with a magnificent Charvet tie spread across his breast and a white orchid in his buttonhole, painted by Jacques-Emile Blanche, but the recluse who, obeying Pascal's advice, now seldom left his own room.

'The kingdom of nothingness' – his phrase evokes Pascal; Proust did not believe that a novelist, particularly a poetic novelist, could eschew the functions of a moralist. Thus he judges; he condemns; he fulminates. With the zeal of a religious neophyte, he burns what he had formerly adored. For it is certainly true that he once adored society – and, more than all else, that section of aristocratic society, its most elegant and refined aspect, which is customarily styled '*le gratin*'. But, towards the close of his existence, he had definitely turned against the great world, against those who were merely distinguished by their rank, their position or the fortune they had inherited; though he continued to dispatch effusive letters to Anna de Noailles and Robert de Montesquiou, both aristocratic friends of exceptional distinction.

Meanwhile, sick and feverish, knowing that he had not very long to live, he blasted the society that had formed the focus of so many dreams. He retouched his picture and wilfully darkened its colours. The duchesse de Guermantes ceases to be a unicorn, a phoenix, an ideal shape that had stepped down from the imagery of a stained-glass window, to reveal herself as frivolous, spiteful, deplorably uncultivated and, worst of all, '*à côté*', or what in Spain is called '*cursi*'. 'The duchesse de Guermantes,' he one day informed the duc de Guiche, of whom he had made some use when he was depicting Saint-Loup, 'resembles a tough barnyard fowl whom I formerly took to be a bird of paradise – By transforming her into a puissant vulture, I have at least prevented the public assuming that she was just a commonplace old magpie.'

Similarly, he revenges himself against Saint-Loup, who had played so cour-ageous a part during the First World War and done his duty in the front line, by attributing to him amorous tastes that we should never have guessed from his liaison with *Rachel-quand-du-Seigneur*. As for the baron de Charlus, the most generous and gifted character in the earlier volumes of his book, he savagely blasts him and shows Charlus falling into the lowest sexual excesses. Does he not portray the baron being flagellated by male prostitutes in the brothel kept by his old friend, the waistcoat-maker Jupien? Aristocratic society has lost even the code of good manners that had once distinguished it. The guests assembled by Charlus at the house of Madame Verdurin, to launch his protégé, the vio-linist Morel, do not so much as greet their hostess; while she herself makes a base attack on the baron, so that he is only saved from an ignominious retreat by the unexpected appearance of the Queen of Naples, who offers him her regal arm.

Nor does the purse-proud bourgeoisie escape the novelist's furious indigna-tion. As she grows older, Madame Verdurin, always an insupportable woman, becomes more petty, more pretentious and more perfidious. Proust rounds off the essential absurdity of her character by exhibiting her, in *Le Temps retrouvé*, after the end of the War, at a time when 'good society' no longer exists, as the new princesse de Guermantes. On Monsieur Verdurin's death, she has married the duc de Duras – an intermediate step towards the Guermantes union. Every-thing falls to pieces, everything loses its quality, in the last two volumes of *A la Recherche du temps perdu*, love as well as friendship, heroism as well as personal devotion. The thesis of the book is that nothing retains its reality except the magisterial work of art. Proust labours the point, encompasses his most flattering portraits with hideous shadows. It is a ruthless judicial inquiry to which he subjects the social world; and the world hesitates to recognize itself in these violently distorted pages, where, one after another, every per-sonage in the story is convicted of meanness, vice and degradation. What remain intact are Vinteuil's *Sonata* and the canvases that Elstir painted.

In a novelist who had woven so many dreams around the associations of the name Guermantes and around the poetic legend of the ancient French nobility, this volte face may seem at first surprising. But for Proust the nobility was a myth; and he continued to venerate the myth, even as he designed the most condemnatory picture of the great world to be found in twentieth-century writing. The fact is that the nobility has disappeared – that caste, '*la race mystérieuse aux yeux perçants, au bec d'oiseau, la race rose, dorée, inapprochable*', which had inspired his youthful visions. Had he not been an assiduous reader of Balzac, Proust might still have reached the same conclusion as the author of the *Cabinet des Antiques*.

My dear children [says, at the end of this story, the duchesse de Maufrigneuse to Victurnien d'Esgrignon and his aunt] there is no longer a nobility: there is nothing but an aristocracy. Napoleon's *Code Civil* has destroyed their parchment deeds as the invention of the canon had already destroyed the feudal system. You will be much more noble than you are now once you have acquired some money. Marry whom you like, Victurnien; you will enoble your wife. That is the most solid of the privileges which the French nobility preserves today.

Balzac could not have predicted that, after 1848, this nobility would be condemned to idleness, and that its most talented representatives, instead of becoming marshals and ambassadors, would be racing enthusiasts and clubmen, obliged to devote their leisure to horses and the pursuit of *petites femmes*. In 1915 Proust reproached the nobility, now simply an aristocratic caste, with frivolity, callousness, a complete lack of regard for anything that did not concern the antiquity of their own lines and the value of their alliances, and with the contempt they showed for science, literature and the arts. It was a world, he alleged, '*distrait, oublieux, futile*', whose comprehension did not extend even to such poetry as possesses 'a colouring of history, beauty, picturesque attraction, the comic spirit and frivolous elegance' – the kind of poetry that comte Robert de Montesquiou was so apt at distilling from the circumstances of his social milieu, but in which Montesquiou had wasted his life and earned the ironic comments of *le gratin*.

Like Montesquiou, Charlus is a 'Professor of Beauty', who cultivates the frivolous with so much systematic application that Proust attributes to him the belief that 'birth allied to beauty and other sources of prestige, is the only thing that lasts' – and that 'the War, like the Dreyfus Affair, is a vulgar and fugitive phenomenon'. Charlus practises the same social detachment as Proust; but he does not do so for the same reasons. Because they are both poets – the baron a mere dilettante, Proust a great imaginative artist – each of them stands back from reality, and judges it according to principles that no other member of their entourage is qualified to understand.

Yet, although misunderstood by his own milieu, Proust does not pretend that the people are the repository of all the moral virtues, as do our contemporary 'progressive' writers; nor does he look on the capitalist bourgeoisie as the last word in modern civilization. He emphasizes the spitefulness of the servant Françoise, the rapacity of the waistcoat-maker Jupien, the absurdity and stupidity of the Verdurins, the Cottards and Brichots. But it is for the aristocracy that he reserves his sternest sentence. Did he wish to rival La Bruyère, whom he admired – one remembers the severity of La Bruyère's judgements upon the Court and upon the Great – and Pascal, whom he sought to follow? At the time Proust renounced the 'beau monde', he also constituted himself its pitiless judge. He raised his tone and, now a Father of the Church – a church in which the work of art has replaced the body of Christ – proceeds to thunder against 'the Kingdom of nothingness'.

YET how much trouble it had once cost him to achieve the conquest of the social world! Since he was an adolescent, it had been apparently the main objective of his life. His contemporaries were wrong there. They believed that 'le gentil Marcel' would see his dearest wishes gratified if he were blessed with an invitation from comte Robert de Montesquiou or from Montesquiou's cousin, the romantic, the Wagnerian comtesse Greffulhe. They could not have been expected to guess that his real objective was the Book, but that the book that dominated his existence had to find its path through the World.

Proust's mother, who did not receive guests, never went out at night and disliked all worldly agitation, devoted herself solely to her duties as a wife and to bringing up her two sons. Professor Proust, on his side, had no social relationships, apart from those with his colleagues at the *Faculté de Médecine* and with the members of the *Académie des Sciences morales et politiques*, to which he wished to be elected. The result was that their elder son, who since his childhood had dreamed about the names of the nobility,[2] had, unaided, to secure the right of entrance, and then establish his position, in this completely unknown universe. The Narrator of *A la Recherche du temps perdu* had a good deal more luck; his grandmother had once known Madame de Villeparisis, and his parents were friends of Charles Swann, though they did not suspect that Swann had close relations with the great world. A different stroke of good fortune fell to Marcel Proust's share. At the Lycée Condorcet he had two friends, both of whose mothers kept salons, Gaston de Caillavet, son of the Madame de Caillavet who, in 1893, became the Egeria of Anatole France – we remember that France was to produce a preface for Proust's first collection of writings, *Les Plaisirs et les Jours* – and Jacques Bizet, whose parents had been the composer of *Carmen* and Geneviève Halévy, daughter of the composer of *La Juive*.

In her widowhood, Madame Bizet, a beauty with the eyes of a tzigane and 'a primitive, oriental, melancholy grace', had married a rich barrister named Emile Straus, illegitimate offspring of one of the barons Rothschild; and she entertained at her house both artists and men and women of fashion. Madame Straus's witticisms were widely quoted; and Proust was afterwards to make good use of them by putting them into the mouth of the duchesse de Guermantes. Before he left school, at an age when most boys are chiefly devoted to sport, Marcel Proust was laying an effusive siege to both these ladies, who, although they did not belong either to *le gratin* or to high financial circles – the young Forain called them 'the Jewesses of Art' – had the knack of assembling important guests.

During his military service at Orléans in 1889 and 1890, Proust also made the acquaintance of Robert de Billy, a future ambassador, who gave a more definite shape to his reveries about the inaccessible Faubourg Saint-Germain. Proust had beautiful manners, but lacked that air of elegance, that désinvolture, which is only to be acquired in aristocratic company. His desperate amiability was construed by many observers – more by men perhaps than by women, who have never been averse from homage – as merely a sign of a pushing desire to make himself conspicuous, and to gain the position that a Rastignac or a Lucien de Rubempré occupies in Balzac's novels. Against him were the facts that he came of a 'perfectly honourable' but unassuming middle-class family, and that his mother was a Jewess; which, at the time of the Dreyfus Affair and the spell of virulent antisemitism that accompanied it, was a very serious drawback. To his credit were his intelligence and sense of fun; the gift of amusing lazy people, who perpetually demand to be entertained, is the surest and quickest means of succeeding in the social world. 'His imitations were the delight of the salons,' we learn from his biographer, André Maurois.

It was in 1891, after the completion of his military service, that his real conquest of the world began. Madame Straus's salon, which was situated at the intersection of the Avenue de Messine and the Boulevard Haussmann, in the Parc Monceau, a quarter that had recently become fashionable, served him as his starting-point. The studio of Madeleine Lemaire proved even more useful. She and Madame Straus were the ladies who had invented '*Tout-Paris*'. Until about 1880 there had been 'good society' and the life of the Boulevard, High Finance and various groups of artists; and these milieux rarely intermingled. Geneviève Straus and Madeleine Lemaire, however, had the idea of mixing all the different worlds – or, rather, of picking from each world everything that was most intelligent and most 'amusing', and of confronting disparate elements without striking an inharmonious note. It was a question, essentially, of appearing modern, '*à la page*'.

Madeleine Lemaire, who lived in Rue de Monceau, occupied a little house, fronted by a little garden and prolonged, behind the house, by a courtyard, where stood the artist's little studio. There she painted her famous roses, which fashionable society disputed the privilege of acquiring at extremely high prices. The enthusiasm then expressed for the artist who, according to Alexandre Dumas *fils*, had created 'more roses than anyone else since God', is nowadays difficult to understand. Her flowers seem to have been cut out of tin; and even their colours are unpleasant. But in 1890 Madeleine Lemaire was a person to be reckoned with; she decorated the menus of the Rothschilds, illustrated the poems of Montesquiou – and embellished Proust's first book.

She received at tea-time nearly every day, each Wednesday of the spring season gave musical and literary afternoons and, once a year, held a fancy-dress ball, for which all fashionable men and elegant women felt it their duty to obtain a card. 'At her house', writes Philippe Jullian in his biography of Montesquiou, 'one met *tout le monde*, even more than at Madame Straus's salon, but also princes of Orléans, grand-dukes, Sarah Bernhardt and Pierre Loti, together with anyone rich enough to pay an extravagant price for a fan, and anyone thought to show promise. Madeleine Lemaire had a genuine flair for talent.' She had detected the artistic gifts of Reynaldo Hahn and Proust alike; and it was with her that Proust met the princesse Mathilde, at whose house in the Rue de Berri he afterwards became a guest, the comtesse Greffulhe and Madame de Chevigné, whom he was presently to use as models, and, on 23 March 1893, Robert de Montesquiou himself.

This was an important date in the novelist's worldly career; for Montesquiou at that time was an arbiter of elegance, the Petronius of *fin de siècle* society. To please him was to see the portals of the Faubourg Saint-Germain opening before one. Montesquiou's moral reputation might well cause head-shaking among the more prudish old ladies; his birth – the Montesquiou-Fezensac are descended from the Merovingian kings of France – his air of authority, his insolence, his cult of Beauty had made him uncontested ruler of the smart and worldly life. To Proust's first letter he replied by sending him his own photograph, inscribed with the line: *Je suis le souverain des choses transitoires*. Proust now felt that he had already won the battle. In fact, that battle had only just begun; for Montesquiou, who was at once reticent, greedy of admiration and suspicious, proved much more difficult to conquer than Geneviève Straus and Madeleine Lemaire. The

People and Places

At the restaurant; cover-design by Toulouse-Lautrec, 1895.

left : Friday at the salon;
by Jules Grün.

left : Maxim's and its patrons;
a caricature by Sem.

left : A gambling-club;
picture by Jean Béraud.

opposite : An evening party
in the 1880's.

Sarah Bernhardt in
her drawing-room.

left : Nijinsky in 1909;
a year before he was first
admired by Proust.

The acrobat, painted between 1883 and 1885 by James Jacques Joseph Tissot: probably the Cirque Molier, known as *Le Cirque Amateur*, where aristocrats performed circus feats.

below: The Master of Ceremonies by Béraud.

La Loge by Jean-Louis Forain, painter, draughtsman and anti-Dreyfusard caricaturist.

above: A meet in the forest, about 1905.

La promenade au Bois
by Giovanni Boldini.

ensuing relationship was a blend of flirtations and squabbles, of advances and abrupt retreats. An amalgam of Plato and King Ludwig II, Montesquiou wished to initiate his disciples into the cult of Beauty and, at the same time, rule over their minds and hearts. But he was always on his guard against their ingratitude and their selfish private motives.

When Proust wrote, 'I shall ask you to be kind enough to show me some of those women friends in whose company you are most often described: the comtesse Greffulhe, the princesse de Léon ...', Montesquiou pulled a wry face. He wished to be loved and admired for himself, not as a mere intermediary between the fascinating *gratin* and '*le petit Proust*'. He had no idea of the book that the '*gentil Marcel*' had now begun to plan; still less did he foresee the deplorable role that he himself would play in it. On him Proust was to model the character of Charlus, attributing to him sensual and masochistic traits that Montesquiou did not possess. Proust had hoped to capture Montesquiou's esteem by introducing to him Léon Delafosse, a young and exquisitely handsome pianist, who, when he wrote *A la Recherche du temps perdu*, was to become the violinist Morel and take an unpleasantly ambiguous advantage of the baron's good graces. Montesquiou encouraged Delafosse's career, and seemed to delight in his companionship; but Proust gained nothing from having brought them together; and, once Delafosse had deserted Montesquiou, the latter bore Proust a lasting grudge because he could offer no assistance.

The comtesse Greffulhe, born Elisabeth de Caraman-Chimay, possessed a mysterious beauty that resided above all in her dark and enigmatic eyes. Sure of her own perfection, she could write with complete simplicity to her cousin Montesquiou: 'I have never been really understood save by you and by the sun.' She was accustomed to stay at Sandringham as the guest of the Prince and Princess of Wales and, at her house in the Rue d'Astorg, received grand-dukes, archdukes, ambassadors and famous artists. Although her intelligence and culture were strictly limited, she knew how to hold and charm distinguished men. On Montesquiou's advice, she gave fêtes and artistic receptions that caused a considerable worldly stir. Montesquiou procured an invitation for Proust to one of these fêtes; and, through the enchanting comtesse Greffulhe, the future novelist glimpsed the delicate and romantic outline of his princesse de Guermantes-Bavière. 'She was wearing', he notes, 'a coiffure of Polynesian grace and mauve orchids that descended to the nape of her neck, like the "*chapeaux de fleurs*", of which we read in M. Renan's pages.'

He was never on terms of close friendship with comtesse Greffulhe; but he was better acquainted with the comtesse Adhéaume de Chevigné, born a Sade; and he conferred her aspect and her way of life, her hoarse voice and her arched nose, which suggested the beak of some marvellous bird, on his portrait of the duchesse de Guermantes. According to François Mauriac, however, if she had recalled Oriane in her youth, she retained few traces of Proust's heroine once she had put her youth behind her; and Mauriac, when he was presented to Madame de Chevigné, saw only 'a dry, cynical old woman; whereas the comtesse Greffulhe, whom I knew when she was very aged at the Rue d'Astorg, did not say a word or make a gesture that was not pure Guermantes (and sometimes Guermantes of the most stupid kind)'.

The comtesse de Chevigné took little interest in writing, and was particularly uninterested in the works of '*le petit Proust*', which she pronounced intolerably tedious. Marie-Laure de Noailles, the grand-daughter of Madame de Chevigné, relates, in her *Journal d'un Peintre*, how one day her grandmother made use of her services to pack away into a basket the letters she had received from Proust: '"These", she said, "are the cacklings of that bore Marcel". Despite the protests of Reynaldo Hahn, never would she consent to read them . . . Proust's eyes I recognize in Suzy Mante-Proust (his niece), as they were painted by Jacques-Emile Blanche. Proust's look was stranger than Blanche could paint.' But then, the vicomtesse de Noailles saw Proust only towards the end of his life; and Blanche had portrayed him while he was still a young man: 'I saw Marcel,' she writes, 'once and once only, at my first ball in the house of the Etienne de Beaumonts. It was midnight. Perhaps he had just got up. Powdered, pale, puffy like Oscar Wilde after his prison-years, he collapsed on a sofa to the left of the door and fixed his gaze upon the room.'

Proust was scarcely more successful with a great lady and celebrated patron of art who then dictated fashionable taste, the princesse Edmond de Polignac, a member of the American Singer family. She has been thus described in Igor Stravinsky's *Chroniques*: 'An excellent musician, who had an enormous fund of general knowledge, and was undoubtedly a gifted painter, she protected and encouraged art and artists. I shall always remember with gratitude the evening parties at which I executed in her house a number of my new works – for instance, besides the *Noces* and *l'Histoire du Soldat*, my *Concerts* and my *Sonata*, which is dedicated to her, *Oedipus Rex*, etc.' Stravinsky omits *Renard*, which she had commissioned and which belonged to her, just as she had acquired the *Socrate* of Erik Satie and *Le Rétable de maître Pierre* of Manuel de Falla.

Even in childhood, Winnareta Singer had displayed unusual gifts; and, when

she became the princesse Edmond de Polignac, she received painters and musicians at her salon in the Avenue Henri-Martin, in her county house at Villerville
and in her palace on the Grand Canal. She played duets with Fauré, painted in a
style somewhere between Manet and Berthe Morisot, loved receiving and holding a salon, and commissioning the works of artists. Not only did she allow
Stravinsky to give at her house private parties that were a kind of dress rehearsal
of his latest compositions; but she subsidized Diaghilev when he was anxious
to put on *Mavra* and *Renard* at the Paris Opéra.

As a mark of their friendship, which had never been very warm, but which
he himself had found flattering, Proust wished to dedicate *A l'Ombre des jeunes
filles en fleurs*, the book that, in 1918, would obtain the Prix Goncourt, to
the memory of her husband, prince Edmond de Polignac, who had died in
1901.

The five volumes of Swann [he wrote to the princesse] contain not a single woman
who bears the remotest resemblance to you. Nor does any of the characters, even in the
slightest degree, recall the Prince ... I should very much like to give you pleasure.
My letter of the other day – the kind of letter one writes when one is undecided what
one really thinks, with all the vagueness of truth – was hardly calculated to please you.
Perhaps the dedication may do so, and clear up a misunderstanding that has lasted
twenty years.

Yet the misunderstanding was never to be cleared up. Madame de Polignac,
fearing that a malicious interpretation might be put on Proust's tribute to the
late prince, and being no more appreciative than Madame de Chevigné of the
author's literary genius, declined to grant him the permission he sought; and
A l'Ombre des jeunes filles en fleurs appeared without a dedication.

Proust was happier in his friendship with the three Roumanian ladies who,
at that period, were dazzling Paris – Anna de Noailles, Princess Bibesco and
Princess Soutzo, today Madame Paul Morand. The long correspondence of the
poetess and the novelist reveal the variety of affectionate and thoughtful bonds
that linked the brilliant talker and her friend who always loved to listen. Princess
Bibesco has published her recollections in *Au bal avec Marcel Proust*. Finally,
reading Paul Morand's *Journal d'un attaché d'ambassade, 1916-1917*, one gets a
clear impression of the relationship, so full of charm and gentle gaiety, that
existed between Proust and Princess Soutzo. Proust's name and that of his
future wife recur on every fifth or sixth page. For example, under the date
26 April 1917:

Proust imitates his guardian-housekeeper: 'Celeste tells me that one can see the out-line of M. Morand's face in the tone of his voice.' Then he describes the 'terrible drama of his life'. He had assured Madame de Chevigné that he never went out in the evenings. Hélène Soutzo, unaware of this pious fraud, innocently remarked before the comtesse that the lift-boy at the Ritz led Marcel Proust directly to her room without troubling to announce him; 'which indicates', said the distraught Marcel, 'that I am nowadays on more familiar terms with the princesse than with the comtesse'. It pro-voked a dramatic crisis and, after three days' gestation, a long letter from Proust to Madame de Chevigné, beginning with the words: 'When what one has loved seems stupid . . .'

Elsewhere Morand notes: 'Proust really lives in the past. His works are *The House of the Dead*, the *De Profundis* of the middle classes.'

Before he attended balls with Marthe Bibesco, Proust, about 1897, had be-come closely associated with her cousins Emmanuel and Antoine, and would say of the latter that he was 'the most intelligent Roumanian prince the French have'. It was the Bibescos who brightened his imagination by describing the minor details of their social life, the strokes of wit that had amused them and the events that they had found arresting. Like Reynaldo Hahn, Lucien Daudet, Bertrand de Fénelon, prince Radziwill (Loche) and the Castellanes, they used to visit Proust after a dinner party or a play, that they might tell him, while it was still fresh, the gossip that would be circulating next day.

Proust was under no illusions as to the interest that many of his friends took in his own literary efforts. Witness this letter to Antoine Bibesco, dated 18 April 1914, where Proust reports a telephone conversation he had had, on the subject of *Swann*, with the marquis d'Albuféra, a descendant of Marshal Suchet: 'But, my dear Louis, have you read my book? . . .' 'Read your book? You've written a book?' 'Of course, Louis; I've even sent you a copy' 'Well, *mon petit Marcel*, if you sent it me, I must certainly have read it. The only trouble is that I wasn't quite sure that I had ever had it.'

Less frivolous were his relations with the young duc de Guiche, the future duc de Gramont, who would collaborate in founding an Institute of Optics, both theoretical and applied, and who was more concerned with problems of optics and hydrostatics than with the gossip of the great world. Later, asked to recall his memories of Proust, he replied that he had known him as 'an obscure little young man who occupied the end of the table at Madame Straus's dinner parties'. The phrase had a great success, and was afterwards used to suggest that Proust had been despised and rebuffed by a society that, in fact, had given

Robert de Montesquiou, 1897;
portrait by Giovanni Boldini.

him an affectionate welcome, and entertained and warmly praised him – not, it is true, as a novelist, the literary celebrities of the day being France, Loti, Hervieu, Hermant and Barrès, but as a conversationalist and diverting companion. Given *le gentil Marcel*'s age, was he likely to have been seated at the centre of Madame Straus's table, the place reserved for bishops and royal highnesses – or, failing them, for Academicians?

Once he had himself become a celebrity after his book had been awarded the Prix Goncourt, he never played the great man; and this is how he answered the young comte de Gaigneron, who, in 1919, expressed his admiration for his work :

> Your 'my dear M. Proust' immediately made me feel that I was vice-president, in some department or other, of the local *comité bonapartiste*, and that the signature would prove to be
>
> 'Your affectionate Napoleon.'
>
> But I need not tell you that receiving a letter from Prince Victor would be as indifferent to me as receiving a word from you is precious. The brother himself of the said Victor, who is more intelligent than the Pretender, and whom I knew when I was still almost a child at the Princesse Mathilde's house, has left me a recollection of that icy bearing to which the proud timidity of Princes so very soon descends (on the amiability of Highnesses who are not timid, see *A l'ombre des jeunes filles en fleurs*, my grandmother's meeting at Balbec with the Princesse du Luxembourg, and the Princesse de Parme in the next volume).[3]

Here Proust identifies himself with the Narrator of *A la Recherche*, speaks of 'my grandmother', and, to explain the behaviour of royal highnesses, does not hesitate to mention such-and-such an episode in his book, when addressing an unknown correspondent. At all events, his desire to please a new generation of readers is clearly evident; he wishes to be for them what Montesquiou had been for him. On this subject, Morand in his *Journal* makes the following note, dated 16 December 1916: 'It is unbelievable that Proust (except, luckily, in his books) should have been influenced by Robert de Montesquiou, the lion of his youth. Montesquiou managed to turn himself into a character in a bad novel, while Proust has created an admirable work.'

THERE is no denying, of course, the important fact that, if Marcel Proust had not frequented ducal and aristocratic houses, he would have failed to depict the Guermantes with so much truth. But the truth involved was that of great literature, and had little to do with the reality of social existence in France during the period of the eighteen-nineties. When we read the recollections of Elisabeth de Gramont, of the comtesse de Pange, born a Broglie, of Boni de Castellane and of Robert de Montesquiou, to cite only those names which are best known to the general public, one is aware of the vast gulf that separates the illustrious families of his age from Proust's representation of the Guermantes.

To invent the Guermantes, he did not merely add up a succession of details borrowed from the Gramonts, the Noailles, the Polignacs or the La Rochefoucaulds. He had recourse to the material provided by his memory and his poetic imagination, selecting from among the data furnished by the contemporary social scene only such features as would strengthen and vivify the substance of his personal visions. Realists seek to propagate the deceptive idea that an artist imitates and reproduces what he has previously observed; whereas he himself is always his richest source of information. Proust had imagined his Guermantes; he did not sketch them from the life; nor did he draw them from the innumerable notes that he must have made in the various noble houses to which he had obtained an entry.

The Guermantes, 'an almost royal house, more ancient than the house of Capet', did not exist save in the mind of a writer for whom the nobility, now a vanished race, still remained the object of his privileged imaginings. Proust did not abandon reality for the world of the imagination; he did not make use of the historical event to evolve a literary fiction. He took the opposite course, moving away from the imaginary towards a reality that belonged to him alone; with the result that *A la Recherche* offers us a Proustian vision of the world, a universe that bears his special stamp. All he asked of those who surrounded him was to lend support to his dreams and his intuitive convictions.

Proust, in love since childhood with a legendary golden race, who occupied Renaissance palaces, where they patronized artists and shared the life of men of genius, lived long enough to become an exile among the men and women of the present day. The like of his fabulous creations could scarcely have continued to exist in France under the Third Republic; neither the state of morals nor the restrictions of modern society would have permitted their survival. The Guermantes have no real affinity except with the sixteenth-century Guises, the Montmorencys and the Lorraines, and bear little resemblance to the Gramonts or the Noailles as they existed about 1900. They are conceivable, moreover, only at a time when there was still a French Court; and there was no court during the age in which Proust situated his *A la Recherche du temps perdu*. Hence the ambiguity that always surrounds the Guermantes, who think and behave as if they lived under Henri III, but must take sides on the Dreyfus Affair and the separation of the Church and State, issues that shock their hereditary pride, and that, in point of fact, they find it difficult even to understand.

Proust created a legend without the least regard for history. Here is an example. The baron de Charlus, dining with the Verdurins, is placed upon his hostess's left hand, her right being reserved for the marquis de Cambremer. If a Guise or a Lorraine had supped with a bourgeois, would he have been relegated to second place? It is inconceivable. Whether the action of the story is supposed to unfold in the sixteenth century or in the twentieth, the most modest people have an accurate idea of the laws of social precedence. But the Verdurins are not modest people. Far from it; they are *nouveaux riches*, who think they know everything but who really know nothing. In order to ridicule the Verdurins and their pretensions, Proust introduces this wildly improbable episode, and puts Charlus in a situation that would never have confronted a Lorraine or Guise – he is obliged to explain the ancient origins of his line, and that what counts is not a man's title so much as the name he has inherited.

Poor Verdurin had assumed that the marquis de Cambremer must be more important in society than the baron de Charlus, forgetting that the baron was a Guermantes. This mistake prepares the way for a scene of high comedy:

'Pardon me,' M. de Charlus replied with an arrogant air to the astonished Verdurin, 'I am also duc de Brabant, damoiseau de Montargis, prince d'Oléron, de Carency, de Viareggio and des Dunes. However, it is not of the slightest importance. Please do not distress yourself,' he concluded, resuming his subtle smile which spread itself over these final words: 'I could see at a glance that you were not accustomed to society.'[4]

Many similar scenes could also be quoted, that seem to show the Guermantes as at once contemporaries of Philip II or Elizabeth I and bizarre survivors of the past, living on under the presidencies of Sadi Carnot or Monsieur Fallières.

Proust's condemnation of the aristocracy does not arise from his disillusionment with an aristocracy whose value he had once exaggerated, but from the fact that, the nobility having been for him a myth, a poetic image, a fragment of a vanished period which only his vivifying memory could restore to life, the great world, as it is existed in his own day, must necessarily arouse his mirth and scorn. Both the novelist's broken-down health and his peculiar type of sensibility – the sensibility of a tyrannous, destructive child – had kindled in his mind a perverse attraction towards the universal void. Everything, he felt, should perish with him; everything should collapse into chaos and abjection. The splendour of the legendary nobility had grown dim; his visions of the Italian Renaissance and of the Court of Versailles had gradually disintegrated; and the horror of the actual world and of corrupt humanity had taken their place in his imagination.

Then his Jewish blood began to stir; he saw himself as both Isaiah and Pascal. Father of the Church and a prophet of the Ancient Law, he cast his stone and uttered solemn curses. Nothing contented him now except the idea of eternity; and, to justify his personal existence, he fell back upon the work of art. Like Baudelaire, he thought that only through creative effort could he hope to find salvation: 'The artist should listen to his instinct, which assures him that art is everything that is most real in life, the sternest school of human conduct, and the only true Last Judgment.' The work he creates, where plan has merged into execution, becomes the artist's Hell and Heaven. Judgement will not overtake us on Doomsday; we face it in our daily lives, thanks to the unceasing conflict waged between the combined forces of our idleness and our frivolity and the redeeming strength of our creative impulse. The work of art is a victory that we have won against ourselves.

Thus Proust causes Bergotte to die at the very moment when, once again, now for the last time, he is contemplating Vermeer's *View of Delft*:

In a celestial balance there appeared to him, upon one of its scales, his own life, while the other contained the little patch of wall so beautifully painted in yellow.[5]

Vermeer and Bergotte – and, by implication, Proust himself – here exchange their secret message. They know that they are equally great in stature – with an authentic greatness, far superior to that of the golden race of dukes and princes. They are the true stars of the human firmament. To shift from one artist towards another, is it not merely to move across the heavens, and leave one celestial body behind us that we may set foot upon a fellow star?

3

Bergotte
Elizabeth Bowen

THE NAME BERGOTTE made me jump like the sound of a revolver fired at me point-blank, but instinctively, for appearance's sake, I bowed; there, straight in front of me, as by one of those conjurors whom we see standing whole and unharmed, in their frock coats, in the smoke of a pistol shot out of which a pigeon has just fluttered, my salute was returned by a young common little thick-set peering person, with a red nose curled like a snail-shell and a black tuft on his chin. I was cruelly disappointed, for what had just vanished in the dust of the explosion was not only the feeble old man, of whom no vestige now remained; there was also the beauty of an immense work which I had contrived to enshrine in the frail and hallowed organism that I had constructed, but for which no room was to be found in the squat figure, packed tight with blood-vessels, bones, muscles, sinews, of the little man with the snub nose and black beard who stood before me . . . The nose and beard were . . . the more aggravating in that, while forcing me to reconstruct entirely the personage of Bergotte, they seemed further to imply, to produce, to secrete incessantly a certain quality of mind, alert and self-satisfied, which was not in the picture, for such a mind had no connection whatever with the sort of intelligence that was diffused throughout those books . . . which were permeated by a gentle and godlike wisdom.[1]

Confrontation by Bergotte in actuality was a dual shock. Apart from what he was like, that he should be *there* unnerved the Narrator; to whom not a hint had been dropped that the novelist was, or was to be, in the room, anywhere in the mêlée of sixteen guests at Madame Swann's overpowering luncheon party. ('Just a few people', she had informed the youth, enamoured contemporary of her daughter's, were to be coming.) That Bergotte, intimate with the Swanns, was known to frequent their voluptuous Paris drawing-room, with its white fur rugs, perpetual bowls of violets and many lamps (lit even in daylight) had for his worshipper, from the start, doubled the glamour of this exotic family, with its ambiguous past. By them, his Bergotte-obsession had been benevolently taken into account; today, they had staged for him a supreme surprise. The illustrious man, briefed to meet the occasion, was at the ready, the juvenile totally unprepared – that he rallied from this therefore shattering meeting was to his credit. In addition, this was his first sortie into what for all he was then to know was the *beau monde*. Due to Madame Swann's passion for entertaining in what she conceived as being the English manner, her luncheon party was dotted with strange rites, possible pitfalls – a mystery envelope slipped to one on arrival, a carnation recumbent on one side of one's plate; on the other 'a smaller plate heaped with some blackish substance which I did not then know to be caviare. I was ignorant of what was to be done with it but firmly determined not to let it enter my mouth.' Thanks to the *placement*, one sat within earshot of Bergotte.

Adolescent disillusionments are many, inevitable, classic subjects for comedy. But today was a major occasion, like it or not. Of the confrontations in which *A la Recherche du temps perdu* abounds, all are dramatic, most are, when later looked back upon, to be seen as historic. All are fateful, most occur without warning. The Bergotte-Narrator confrontation was to differ from others, in this peculiarity: it led on to what became almost nothing. It marked an end, rather than a beginning. Itself a climax, if only in view of the height of the expectations it flattened, it remained the one, only climax in a relationship otherwise anticlimatic, patchy, uninspirational – a relationship haunted by what it should have been, of which the most to be said was that, throughout the years, it succeeded in never quite petering out. Nothing much came of any subsequent meeting.

Bergotte the man's obnoxious, trite, meaty physical personality had at least impacted: time and familiarity were to neutralize even that. He dematerialized, leaving only a name. Disconnected from him as a being, the books remained.

B**UT** a magnified Bergotte exists on another plane. There, he is one of a triumvirate, the three artists dominant in *A la Recherche du temps perdu*. He, Elstir, Vinteuil – Writer, Painter, Composer – are ever-present in the resounding novel, few of whose major passages are uninfluenced by at least one of them. Together, they confirm the Narrator's statement: 'The only truth of life is in art.' Shown, also, to have acted on the characters' destinies, they are thereby precipitants of the plot: akin, in their way, to The Three Fates. Never, one may remark, is Bergotte granted quite the stature of Elstir, or of the dead Vinteuil. Those two retain an ascendancy. Their achievements expand, his reaches a limit. In *his* art, is the limit inherent? As an art, is writing subsidiary? Bergotte once totally had commanded the boy at Combray, who had yet to behold painting and hear music.

First-comer, the novelist ploughed into virgin soil.

B**ERGOTTE**, then only known to a few readers, who composed a sort of eclectic secret society, had been recommended by the flamboyant Bloch, an *avant-garde* comrade of the Narrator's. Bloch's subsequent banishment from the Combray household, on account of one of his more ghastly remarks, did not, happily, bring about a ban on the author he had sponsored – unhindered, the boy out there in the garden read on and on:

For the first few days, like a tune which will be running in one's head and maddening one soon enough, but of which one has not for the moment 'got hold', the things I was to love so passionately in Bergotte's style had not yet caught my eye. I could not, it was true, lay down the novel of his which I was reading, but I fancied that I was interested in the story alone . . . Then I observed the rare, almost archaic phrases which he liked to employ at certain points, where a hidden flow of harmony, a prelude contained and concealed in the work itself, would animate and elevate his style; and it was at such points as these, too, that he would begin to speak of 'the vain dream of life' of the 'inexhaustible torrent of fair forms', of the 'sterile splendid tortures of understanding and loving', of the 'moving effigies which ennoble for all time the charming and venerable fronts of our cathedrals'; that he would then express a whole system of philosophy, new to me, by the use of marvellous imagery, to the inspiration of which I would naturally have ascribed that sound of harping which began to chime and echo in my ears . . .[2]

The experience deepened, was cumulative: 'One of these passages of Bergotte's, the third or fourth which I had detached from the rest, filled me with a joy to which the meagre joy I had tasted in the first passion bore no comparison, a joy which I felt myself to have experienced in some innermost chamber of my soul.'[3]

Simultaneously, there were to be brought about two things one might have thought incompatible: identification with Bergotte, establishment of him as a father-figure. 'It was suddenly revealed to me that my own humble existence and the Realms of Truth were less widely separated than I had supposed, that at certain points they were actually in contact; and in my new-found confidence and joy I wept upon his printed page, as in the arms of a long-lost father.' Wish to exploit this ideal filial relation, to exchange views on all subjects under the sun, to confer, to be reciprocally in contact, to play, even, when need be, a consolatory role, became, during this first phase, in its Combray innocence, predominant: the father-affair proceeded apace – counteractive, in its respectable melancholy, to the former succession of psychic orgasms. 'From his books', the Narrator remembers, 'I had formed an impression of Bergotte as a frail and disappointed old man who had lost his children and never found any consolation . . . .'[4] Hence, that 'Sweet Singer with the silvery hair', to be exploded by a metaphorical pistol-shot in a Paris drawing-room.

This springtime of the romance with Bergotte has an appropriate, vernal, rural-lyrical setting: old small-town Combray, the grandparents' dignified house with its walled back-garden, the encircling countryside with its pliant contours, shallow and yet mysterious, opening-and-closing distances, changing lights. Past Combray slides, bridged, the Vivonne river. Spring warms on into early summer. Hawthorn foams into flower. A season for family walks – '*Which way shall we go?*' – *al fresco* coffee-drinking in the cool of the evenings, outdoor reading – on one occasion interrupted, dynamically, by Swann, country neighbour, paying one of his calls. 'What are you reading?' the man says to the boy. 'May I look? Why, it's Bergotte! Who has been telling you about him?. . . He is a charming creature . . . I know him quite well; if you would like him to write a few words on the title-page of your book, I could ask him for you.'[5]

I noticed in the manner in which Swann spoke to me of Bergotte something which, to do him justice, was not peculiar to himself but was shared by all Bergotte's admirers at that time . . . Like Swann, they would say of Bergotte: 'He has a charming mind, so individual; he has a way of his own of saying things, which is a little far-fetched, but so pleasant. You never need look for his name on a title-page, you can tell his work at once.' But none of them went too far as to say 'He is a great writer, he has great talent.' They did not even credit him with talent at all. They did not speak because they were not aware of it. We are very slow in recognizing in the peculiar physiognomy of a new writer the type which is labelled 'great talent' in our museum of general ideas.[6]

As a rule, Swann does not talk about people he knows – he cannot be bothered. In any event, their names would mean little to Combray (to which, these days, he is a summer *revenant*.) His consenting to talk about Bergotte to the boy in the garden is a concession *to* boyhood, to manifest hero-worship – and at that casual, vaguely effortful, random, full of thrown-away lines of which he does not compute the vital importance or foresee the effects. Why, yes, Bergotte – it transpires – dines with the Swanns every week (in Paris, that is). Nor is that all. 'He is', Swann adds, 'my daughter's greatest friend. They go about together, and look at old towns and cathedrals and castles.'[7] From that picture, inside a single sentence, desire springs. Gilberte is perceived to be the predestined love-object.

She yet has to be set eyes upon. Will she ever be? Doubt as to even that creates the requisite agonizing romantic circumstance. The Swanns being, just now, in residence at near-by Tansonville, the country house inherited from his father, the girl-child must be somewhere within the white paling bounding the park. Effectually, she might be on another planet. Tansonville is, absolutely, forbidden territory. Swann having married his mistress, a former courtesan, Combray society ostracizes the marriage. Among ladies who implacably do not visit is the Narrator's mother. Swann is still made welcome when he comes calling, for the sake of old days, and as his father's son. Madame Swann, Combray rumour has it, meanwhile is disporting herself at Tansonville with a further lover (this turns out to be the improbable Charlus). Locally, she and her daughter have been never so much as glimpsed.

LEGEND heightens the sense, or idea, that life is a novel – idea which continuous Bergotte-sessions also could have fostered in a young reader held back, so far, from life. One is subject to inevitabilities and compulsions, a sort of aesthetic pre-determination (he came to believe). In return, existence takes on shape and coherence; also, the comprehensibility of a story. Gilberte Swann, cause of her parents' marriage, had been given birth to (as the Narrator saw it) solely to play one part: hers with himself. She was someone Bergotte-begotten. She owed her first embodiment, faceless, indistinct, already tormenting, to envisagement of her beside the Silvery Singer, backed by 'the charming and venerable' façade of a cathedral. Attendant nymph. Round the nymph-image accumulated erotic fancies. A passion, one might say, by association, whetted by readiness for more.

The coming face-to-face was, as it eventuated, a Bergotte masterpiece; equally, a full-scale Proustian confrontation. The afternoon shimmers with heat and colour. The Narrator, his grandfather and his father, out walking, are at less pains than usual to give Tansonville a wide berth, the Tansonville ladies being – it is understood – sightseeing at Rheims today, while Swann is in Paris. Even, one pauses by the white paling, to look through the thinning lilacs, purple and white, into the ostensibly empty park: expanses of lawn, tall trees, artificial lake. No, not a footstep to be heard anywhere, and a bird's note is sounding unduly loud, as though raised in protest against the solitude. But then the Narrator notices a straw basket lying forgotten on the grass by the side of a line whose float is bobbing in the water. (The float dips while one watches: a fish has bitten). Betraying nothing, he hurries after his elders. Ahead of him, they have turned up a mounting field-path, flanked by the hawthorn hedge which is a further boundary of the Swann domain.

I found the whole path throbbing with the fragrance of hawthorn blossom. The hedge resembled a series of chapels, whose walls were no longer visible under the mountains of flowers that were heaped on their altars; while, underneath, the sun cast a square of light upon the ground, as though it had shone in upon them through a window . . . The flowers, themselves adorned, held out each its little bunch of glittering stamens. [The flowers] here spread out into pools of fleshy white, like strawberry-beds in spring.[8]

But far more festal, farther along the hedge comes one great pink hawthorn, clotted with blossom which has 'precisely the colour of some edible and delicious thing'. And of the thousand buds now swelling and opening, each disclosed, as it burst, 'as at the bottom of a cup of pink marble, its blood-red stain . . .'[9] Wreathed by this glory, there is a gap in the hedge. The Narrator again looks into the park. The foreground is not empty: he is transfixed.

A little girl, with fair, reddish hair, who appeared to be returning from a walk, and held a trowel in her hand, was looking at us, raising towards us a face powdered with pinkish freckles. Her black eyes gleamed, and as I did not at that time know, and indeed have never since learned, how to reduce to its objective elements any strong impression, since I had not, as they say, enough 'power of observation' to isolate the sense of their colour, for a long time afterwards, whenever I thought of her, the memory of those bright eyes would at once present itself to me as a vivid azure, since her complexion was fair; so much so that, perhaps if her eyes had not been quite so black – which was what struck one most forcibly on first meeting her – I would not have been, as I was, especially enamoured of their imagined blue.

I gazed at her . . .[10]

In return –

She cast a glance forward and sideways, so as to take stock of my grandfather and father, and doubtless the impression she formed of them was that we all were absurd people, for she turned away with an indifferent and contemptuous air . . . [A moment later, however] while they, continuing to walk on without noticing her, had overtaken and passed me, she allowed her eyes to wander, over the space that lay between us, in my direction, without any particular expression, without appearing to have seen me, but with an intensity, a half-hidden smile which I was unable to interpret . . .

'Gilberte, come along; what are you doing?' called out in a piercing tone of authority a lady in white . . .[11]

'BERGOTTE? – A flute-player', is Monsieur de Norpois' considered verdict. The elderly diplomat, ex-ambassador, is honouring the Narrator's family; he adorns their table. (Home life, in the capacious Paris apartment, had resumed its course, a number of months ago, on return from the yearly visit to Combray.) Never has Monsieur de Norpois dined here before – the *cuisine* is, he is

The room with three lamps,
by Edouard Vuillard.

to discover, excellent. His contact is with the Narrator's father, his ally on an anonymous commission. That his presence, for his hosts an event, is on his part an amiable condescension he feels, but does not allow to appear – has he not suffered himself, already, even before dinner, to be not only shown but asked to pronounce on a literary effort of their son's? He did not think highly of it, and felt bound to say so.

Wish not to exploit or tire Monsieur de Norpois causes the party to be confined to four: guest, host, hostess and the adolescent in question. All four being seated, Monsieur de Norpois blandly trollies the conversation round to the Swanns – topic agreeable to the Narrator only. *En route*, there is a minute of royal name-dropping. 'Now it is certain', he says, 'that the comte de Paris has always most graciously recognized the devotion of Swann, who is, for that matter, a man of character, in spite of all.' And, Madame Swann? 'She', the old boy declares, 'is altogether charming.'[12] The Swanns have made it. Monsieur de Norpois dined there the other night.

'Was there a writer of the name of Bergotte at this dinner, sir?' I asked timidly . . .

'Yes, Bergotte was there', replied M. de Norpois, inclining his head courteously towards me . . . 'Do you know him?' he went on, fastening on me that clear gaze, the penetration of which had won the praise of Bismarck.

'My son does not know him, but he admires his work immensely,' my mother explained.

'Good heavens!' exclaimed M. de Norpois. [13]

No, he cannot share the lady's son's point of view. Demolition of Bergotte begins. Flute-player; a quite agreeable one, but there is mannerism, there is affectation. And when all is said, there is nothing so very great. Nowhere did one find in his ennervated writing anything that could be called construction. Little action – but above all no range. 'His books', points out M. de Norpois, 'fail at the foundation, or rather they have no foundation at all. At a time like this, when the ever-increasing complexity of life leaves one scarcely a moment for reading, when the map of Europe has undergone radical alterations, and is on the eve, probably, of undergoing others more drastic still, when so many new and threatening problems arise on every side, you will allow me to suggest that one is entitled to ask that a writer should be something else than a fine intellect which makes us forget, amid otiose and byzantine discussions of the merits of pure form, that we may be overwhelmed at any moment by a double tide of barbarians, those from without and those from within our borders. I am aware that this is a blasphemy against the sacrosanct school of what these gentle-men term Art for Art's sake, but at this period of history there are tasks more urgent than the manipulation of words in a harmonious manner.'[14]

And, aha – yes: *that* reminds Monsieur de Norpois of that luckless 'poem in prose' by the son of the house. One ought to have smelled a rat: the Bergotte influence! 'You will not, of course, be surprised,' he informs the youth, 'when I say that there were in it none of his good qualities . . . But there is the same fault . . .'[15]

Given a few fireworks, let off prettily enough by an author, and up goes the shout of genius. Works of genius are not so common as all that! Bergotte cannot place to his credit – does not carry in his baggage, if I may use the expression – a single novel that is at all lofty . . . But that does not exclude the fact that, with him, the work is infinitely superior to the author . . . It would be impossible to imagine an individual more pretentious, more pompous, less fitted for human society.[16]

Bergotte, it emerges, had blotted his copy-book in Vienna.

I was Ambassador there; he was presented to me by the Princess Metternich, came and wrote his name, and expected to be asked to the Embassy. Now, being in a foreign country as the Representative of France, to which he has after all done some honour by his writings, to a certain extent . . . I was prepared to set aside the unfavourable opinion that I hold of his private life. But he was not travelling alone, and he actually let it be understood that he was not to be invited without his companion. I trust that I am no more of a prude than most men . . . nevertheless, I must admit that there are depths of degradation to which I should hesitate to descend . . . The Princess returned to the charge, but without success.[17]

The writer's brazen and cynical behaviour was, we learn, rendered the more repulsive by contrast with the moral tone of his books. The Bergotte 'moraliz-ing' had, in fact, bored Monsieur de Norpois as much as anything else – it begins to appear. 'Torturing scruples!' he grumbles, 'Morbid remorse.' His *liaison* with Madame de Villeparisis, of long standing, has been chequered by nothing of that kind.

WHAT sort of a novelist was Bergotte? He wrote *romans psychologiques* – but so did many: France cradled those. What made his work distinctive, singled it out? What characterized the Bergotte novels, basically – that is, allowing for changes in mood or manner, variations in density, gains or losses in vigour as time went on? Traceable continuity tends to underlie a creative career – a sensa-tional break *may* be made with it, but one hears of no such break being made by Bergotte. Something, therefore, like a family trait or family tendency (accentuating, probably, with the years) would have strung his successive books together: what had they in common, one with another? A particular manner of seeing, and making seen? Sensuous imagery – cause, in the first place, of the Narrator's *engouement*? A palpable temperament, with its vocabulary – thanks to which, at the outset, he was commended for an 'originality', a 'charmingness' to which Monsieur de Norpois's antipathy was itself a tribute?

That cannot have been all – the internal Bergotte could be unaccommodating and was formidable. Needing to carry the strain of revulsions, tensions, his style was of tougher fabric than first appeared. The Narrator's boyish reactions to it were not uninterruptedly rhapsodical; here, then there, he found himself brought up short – if unexpectedly stimulated – by 'harshness': discordant interpolations, provincialisms, phrases deliberately strident and anti-melodic. The Sweet Singer revealed a quite other side. (Why this was not a warning, one might wonder.) The recalcitrance was genuine; the melancholy elsewhere suffusing the lovely prose was, though not a fake, in the nature of a by-product, which had undergone a refining process – call it a sublimation, sometimes over-aesthetic, of the morose, solitary, cancer-like melancholy of the man Bergotte.

Manifestly he was a master of his craft. *Le roman psychologique* suited him – gaunt in concept though it might be in principle, it invited stylishness, and lent itself to a *désabusé* romanticism: his. Since the break-away from sentimental precedent, new, free, so far unexploited areas were offering themselves to the artist pen. At the same time, this was not a revolution; a degree of orthodoxy was still required – which can have been no hardship to Bergotte. Plot, of a kind, or at least a promising 'situation', was still *de rigueur* – of his novels' plots we are given little idea: they must have contained suspense, on whatever plane, for a Bergotte novel was difficult to put down (hence, no doubt, his ultimate surge into popularity). One would not be surprised if his plots were trite: what matter? – he did not depend on them. (The manner of telling, of *showing*, was the thing.) And the same may have applied to his characterization. His approach to character chiefly was analytical. Were his people, any of them, outstanding, magnetic, memorably disturbing? One has the impression that they were not. Not *they* were affective; what was affective was the magic of the climate in which they floated, the concentratedness of the vision pin-pointing them. As for their psychology? – they were Bergotte's creatures.

He was a visual writer. Imagery rendered his cadenced prose, above all, sensuous and concrete. The art in his novels acted upon the reader as does a

67

spectacle on an onlooker. There can have been nothing about the setting of a scene he did not know: everything came to have a magnified semblance of actuality. And actuality learned to imitate Bergotte – as when, for instance, that afternoon at Tansonville, one came to a stop at a gap in a hawthorn hedge.

How good a novelist was Bergotte? Ultimately, the judgement is left open.

WHICH of the novelists Proust knew, in Paris, as compatriots and contemporaries, was most nearly the origin of Bergotte? (A French novelist, it has to be, who was senior to Proust, though not necessarily by a great number of years. Was not Bergotte's unexpected youthfulness (of a gross kind) not the least of the shocks?) Once – that is, when I first read *A la Recherche du temps perdu*, in the nineteen-twenties – *I* would have said, Bourget. Now, re-reading the work with particular concentration on Bergotte, I find Bourget recedes. His novels, as I recollect them, were indeed 'psychological' – more drastically so, probably, than were Bergotte's – but unenhanced by the harp-soundings (or 'flute-playing') which so beatifically acted on the Narrator. He concentrated on being a fashionable iconoclast. Barrès, against whose insidious *Culte du Moi* trilogy, which was gaining ground, Bourget's *Le Disciple* aimed an ethical (and best-selling) blow, could seem the likelier of the two to have upheaved young Proust, as did Bergotte the young Narrator. Barrès was an at once clear-cut and limpid stylist: an *élitist*, both in method and aim. But Proust and Barrès, in Paris, were little in contact; there existed between them nothing equivalent, even, to the *manqué* but still-persistent relationship there was between the Narrator and Bergotte. Of the gulf opened up by the Dreyfus case, they were on opposite sides . . .

Exploratory work done on Proust and his personal world, in the last years, more and more brings forward Anatole France as a, in fact as *the*, Bergotte candidate. France it was, it now is strongly suggested, who was the Master, the awakener of and predominant influence on creative awareness – or, awareness of what it could be to be creative – in the young Proust. What France wrote inspired the early writing, and was its model. Substantially there was a France-Bergotte alikeness: snout nose, detestable little beard, thick-set physical bounciness, and, worst, lack of venerability were, in one first fell moment, to devastate Proust. The tottering idol, rather too much at home in the drawing-room in which he was first encountered, was lover *en titre* of the hostess, a distinguished *salonnière*. Of Bergotte's love life, apart from the nameless lady he arrived in Vienna with, we hear nothing till its humiliating last phases. He was said by many to be unkind to his wife; so was Anatole France. France was consistently friendly to Proust; spoke highly of him as an emerging writer, would have been glad to see more of him, wrote him a preface, and went out of his way to do him other good turns. This good-will, Proust reciprocated, if temperately.

Ruskin, on the strength of stylistic influence, keying-up effect on the Proust aesthetic and engenderment of the passion for cathedrals, has been named as at least a constituent of Bergotte. As anywhere present in Bergotte, I cannot see him. One must stop somewhere. Bergotte is a composite character: accepted? Like the otherwise very different Saint-Loup, he has group-origin. Or call it multiple origin. There are as many young-noblemen candidates for Saint-Loup as there are literary candidates for Bergotte. Both integrate, miraculously, as individuals; but Saint-Loup, besides being conspicuously attractive, to a degree which Bergotte conspicuously is not, is the more completely perceived, the more 'realized' of the two, for this reason: in Saint-Loup there is nothing of Proust; in Bergotte there is much. Bergotte is a stand-in, scape-goat, whipping-boy for his creator. Hence Proust's recurring, uneasy unjustness to him. Those Bergotte purple patches (worse, it is true, in English) the 'torrents of fair forms', and so on, could be burlesques of Proust's own at their early worst – how he once *had* written could continue to haunt him. For a long time, had he not laboured under the charge of 'preciousness?' – *he* knew what it was to be patronized as 'charming' . . . Just as he transferred his homosexuality to Charlus, Proust shifted on to Bergotte his literary guilt, with its nexus of ignominies, self-searchings and anxieties. Charges brought against Bergotte of being (socially) 'ambitious – utterly selfish', the Narrator makes no attempt to rebut. But, it is pointed out,

those vices did not at all prove . . . that his literature was a lie and all his sensitiveness mere play-acting . . . There may be a vice arising from supersensitiveness just as much as from the lack of it. Perhaps it is only in really vicious lives that the moral problem can arise in all its disquieting strength. And of this problem the artist finds a solution not in terms of his own personal life but of what for him is the true life, a general, a literary solution. As the great Doctors of the Church began often, without losing their virtue, by acquainting themselves with the sins of all mankind, so great artists often, while being thoroughly wicked, make use of their vices in order to arrive at a conception of the moral law which is binding upon us all.[18]

The notion of purgation, of self-redemption, of bought-back virtue being possible for the artist by means of art recurs throughout *A la Recherche du temps perdu*, from volume to volume. with ever-accumulating force. It interlocks, for instance, with the notion of immortality, in the passage following Bergotte's death:

Permanently dead? Who shall say? . . . All we can say is that everything is arranged in this life as though we entered it carrying the burden of obligations contracted in a former life . . . All these obligations which have not their sanction in our present life seem to belong to a different world, founded upon kindness, scrupulosity, self-sacrifice, a world entirely different from this, which we leave in order to be born into this one, before perhaps returning to the other to live once more under the sway of those unknown laws which we have obeyed because we bore their precepts in our hearts, knowing not whose hand had traced them there – those laws to which every profound work of the intellect brings us nearer and which are invisible only – and still! – to fools. So that the idea that Bergotte was not wholly and permanently dead is by no means improbable.[19]

(*'Our birth is but a sleep and a forgetting?'* It could be that amongst the torments of the artist is this – that in his case the oblivion is not complete?)

GILBERTE, as compared to the later Albertine, comes, finally, more or less unscathed out of her involvement with the Narrator. Highly romanticizable, Gilberte was not born to be a romantic's prey. The sadistic love-tactics that were to be employed with Albertine fall flat when tried out on an immune schoolgirl – Swann's cherished only child. Gilberte, tolerantly referred to by Monsieur de Norpois, that famous evening, as 'a young person of about fourteen or fifteen', would not have been much above that age when she and the Narrator began their games in the Champs Elysées; nor (so far as one can make out) can he have been much more. She gave no signs of being sexually precocious: the wrestling-match, erotic for the Narrator, was for Mademoiselle Swann, apparently, simply an agreeable rough-and-tumble. As her family saw it, this was a boy-and-girl affair – the unseriousness of it in their eyes probably diminished it in hers. She tended to be more off-hand, capricious or sullen with the Narrator when her parents were there. Only many years afterwards, when it had ceased to matter, was he to learn that still waters had run deep – Gilberte (in a womanhood made unhappy by marriage to the unfaithful Saint-Loup) gives the Narrator her version of their encounter at Tansonville. On seeing him, she instantly had desired him. (Hence the equivocal smile on the childish face, and the sliding glance.)

It was because of Bergotte that he had fallen in love with her, he tells her. That, one may take it, she knew. They had talked, talked, talked about Bergotte –

at the beginning. Bored or piqued by a little too much Bergotte, did Gilberte then set about to displace him? She did so; that she should was, after all, in the course of nature. Beside the physical girl, the ethereal Singer had not a chance – that was, as an obsession. The unattainability of Gilberte – not lessened, indeed made more to be felt by knowing her, together with not knowing if, and if so by what means, he could know her better – caused her to drain off from the Narrator any faculty for any kind of desire other than his for her. The paradox of romantic love – that what one possesses, one can no longer desire – was at work. Did he not 'possess' (through its entering into him, he into it) Bergotte's art? So now, he thought of it less. Yet it continued to play a part, to remain in association with what was happening. Gilberte, as promised, brings the Narrator a rare pamphlet of Bergotte's. This is a moment: 'As for Bergotte, that infinitely wise, almost divine old man . . . now it was for Gilberte's sake, chiefly, that I loved him. With as much pleasure as the pages he had written about Racine, I studied the wrapper, folded under great seals of white wax and tied with billows of pink ribbon, in which she had brought those pages to me.'[20] The seals, the ribbon, bespoke 'the mysterious charm of Gilberte's life'.

At the start, meetings are in the Champs Elysées – in the playground glade where they first spoke to each other – only. Suspense attends on them: sometimes for days together she fails to appear. Where is she: at home? That home, is he ever, or never, to enter? That he does do so, that not only Swann but his wife (who well might, even splendidly here in Paris, have repaid some of the snubs she had had from Combray) make him welcome, show for him such an affection that it amounts to, virtually, adopting him, leads up – as we are to know – to the luncheon party at which his main desire (as they saw it) was to be gratified.

THAT the Narrator sits in earshot of Bergotte gives Proust occasion to stress the social cynicism, the up-thrusting provincialism, yet the eventual, it could be involuntary, tunings-in of the true artist. Bergotte's conversation, as listened-in to, goes through changes of gear. One understands only too well, at first, the impression formed by Monsieur de Norpois; Bergotte had indeed a peculiar 'organ'.[21] Or, the voice is as though issuing 'from behind a mask'. It was not till later on that:

I discovered an exact correspondence with the parts of his books in which his form became so poetic and so musical. At those points, he could see in what he was saying a plastic beauty independent of whatever his sentences might mean, and as human speech reflects the human soul, though without expressing it as does literary style, Bergotte appeared almost to be talking nonsense . . .

Certain peculiarities of elocution, faint traces of which were to be found in Bergotte's conversation, were not exclusively his own; for when, later on, I came to know his brothers and sisters, I found those peculiarities much more accentuated in their speech. . . . Those young Bergottes – the future writer and his brothers and sisters – were doubtless in no way superior, far from it, to other young people, more refined, more intellectual than themselves, who found the Bergottes rather 'loud'.[22]

But, 'men who produce works of genius are not those who live in the most delicate atmosphere, but those who have had the power . . . to make use of their personality as a mirror, in such a way that their life, however unimportant it may be, is reflected by it, genius consisting in the reflective power of the writer and not in the intrinsic quality of the scene reflected.'[23]

Before the party breaks up, the Narrator has not only moved in upon, but has had – he learns – a heady success with Bergotte. 'You can't think how delighted I am,' Gilberte whispers into his ear, 'because you have made a conquest of my great friend. He's been telling Mamma that he found you extremely intelligent.' He and Bergotte leave the party together: in the carriage they talk about health – the Narrator's, defective – then, à propos, doctors.

'I'll tell you who does need a good doctor, and that is our friend Swann,' said Bergotte. And, on my asking whether he was ill, 'Well, don't you see, he's typical of a man who has married a whore, and has to swallow a hundred serpents every day, from women who refuse to meet his wife, or men who were there before him. You can see them in his mouth, writhing . . .' The malice with which Bergotte spoke thus to a stranger of the friends in whose house he had been so long received as a welcome guest was as new to me as the almost amorous tone which, in that house, he had constantly been adopting to speak to them.[24]

CRUELTY infests, as might a malevolent fever a swamp or jungle, the universe of *A la Recherche du temps perdu* – the marvel is that it does not poison it wholly: life, with its perennial innocence, survives. The characters have an astonishing resilience, a fool-hardy, desperado quality which gives them panache: almost all of them are at bay. Bergotte, for instance, knows all there dares to be known about the snake-pit of literary politics; the days of his high reputation are to be numbered (as are, indeed, those of his life on earth). Neither he nor that other whipping-boy, Charlus, can be made chargeable with the crime that is central in the vast novel: a cannibalistic romanticism. That, the Narrator,

Combray and Balbec

Illiers: an early nineteenth-century engraving.

above: The Pré-Catalan; the pleasure-ground of Uncle Amiot, which Proust transformed into the Swanns' spacious park.

top left: Saint-Jacques; the old church that dominates the town of Illiers, always overlooking its ancient roof-tops and 'slipping its belfry into every corner of the sky'.

top right: Françoise's kitchen at Illiers; 'a little temple of Venus . . .'

opposite: The Amiots' garden at Illiers; in *A la Recherche*, the garden where the Narrator's family assembled before dinner and awaited the arrival of Charles Swann.

IV 2

On the cliffs at Etretat,
a resort of Proust and
his family.

CABOURG

5 Hs DE PARIS.

GRAND·HOTEL
RESTAURANT
CAFE
DIRECTION
H·NOËL &
PATTARD.

CASINO.
THEATRE·
CONCERTS·
BALS.

LA
PLUS BELLE PLAGE

IMPRIMERIE-PAUL·DUPONT: 4. RUE DE BOULOI · PARIS.

above: Deauville at the end of the nineteenth century.
top: The Grand Hôtel at Cabourg, the Norman seaside town that Proust described as Balbec, scene of the Narrator's first meeting with Albertine.

opposite: Advertisement of Cabourg and its attractions, 1895.

Proust in 1900, on the terrace of his hotel at Venice, where, under Marie Nordlinger's guidance, he revised his translation of *The Bible of Amiens*.

At sea, aboard a friend's yacht.

alone, carries the onus of – *unless* Proust identifies with the Narrator. How far did Proust identify with the Narrator; how far objectify (and thereby disclaim) him? The destruction of Albertine, by means of a long-drawn-out demoralization, is horrible. There had been gleams of virtue, of tenderness, of aspiration to harmony in the love for Gilberte: few remained in the love meted out to Albertine. There was sporadic remorse – the 'morbid remorse' of Bergotte?; there was never pity. Albertine, after her flight and following death, had to be exorcized – and at length was.

Bergotte's writing lost attraction for the Narrator when, with time, it became easy to read:

His sentences stood out as clearly before my eyes as my own thought, the furniture in my room and the carriages in the streets. But a new writer had recently begun to publish work in which the relations between things were so different from anything that connected them for me that I could understand hardly anything of what he wrote . . . I felt, nevertheless, for the new writer the admiration which an awkward boy who never receives any marks for gymnastics feels when he watches another more nimble. And from then on I felt less admiration for Bergotte, whose limpidity began to strike me as insufficient.[25]

Ironically, a series of visits received from Bergotte, at this time, for the Narrator came several years too late. However, they, or at least the idea of them, gave comfort to his father and mother, and were felt to honour his grandmother, who here, in the family apartment, now lay dying.

Here, in another room, sat the speechless Bergotte, day after day, for hours on end – a sick man. Fame has terribly overtaken him.

The general rule is, no doubt, that only after his death does a writer become famous. But it was while he still lived, and during his slow progress towards a death that he had not yet reached, that this writer was able to watch the progress of his works towards Renown. A dead writer can at least be illustrious without any strain on himself . . . He [Bergotte] existed, still, sufficiently to suffer from the tumult . . .

The bulk of his thought had long since passed from his brain into his books. He had grown thin, as though they had been extracted from him in surgical operations. He led the vegetative life of a convalescent, of a woman after childbirth; his fine eyes remained motionless, vaguely dazed, like the eyes of a man who lies on the sea shore and in a vague day-dream sees only each little breaking wave.[26]

Now, 'the passion for Bergotte's works was unbounded'. Alone in an inclement apartment, sometimes, when chilly, with a grubby tartan rug over his knees, he was apologetic when he received company – discouraged, his visitors dwindled to almost none. Doctors contradicted each other across him. He appears miserly; actually, much of the new money has been bestowed on various derelict little girls he had hired, in the last years, to come in and sleep with him, having come to the conclusion that it is less humiliating to buy love than to fail to win it. 'What I have squandered, all the same!' he reflected sometimes. He went out only out of fear of contracting the habit of staying in – and then, only to houses in which he need not speak (he now had a speech-obstruction).

There are two instances in *A la Recherche du temps perdu* of the Narrator's stepping clear of the 'I' and entering the experience of another person. One is, when he 'becomes' Swann, for the duration of Swann's love-affair with Odette, the other, when he 'becomes' Bergotte, for the minutes before and at the moment of Bergotte's death. Bergotte had been ordered to rest. But on learning that morning, from something said by a critic, that Vermeer's *View of Delft*, lent by the gallery at the Hague, was on view in Paris, he ate a few potatoes, left the house and went to the exhibition. On the stairs up to it he had an attack of giddiness. Making his way through the rooms, he passed Dutch pictures which struck him as stiff, futile and artificial. At last he came to the Vermeer, which he had imagined he knew by heart, which he remembered as more striking, more different, than anything else he knew. And so it was. This time, thanks to the critic, he remarked for the first time some small blue figures. There, too, more precious than ever in substance, was the tiny patch of yellow wall. His giddiness increased: 'he fixed his eyes, like a child upon a yellow butterfly which it is trying to catch, upon the precious little patch of wall'.

'That is how I ought to have written,' he said. 'My last books are too dry, I ought to have gone over them with several coats of paint, made my language exquisite in itself, like this little patch of yellow wall.' Meanwhile, he was not unconscious of the gravity of his condition. In a celestial balance there appeared to him, upon one of its scales, his own life, while the other contained the little patch of wall so beautifully painted in yellow. He felt that he had rashly surrendered the former for the latter. 'All the same', he said to himself, 'I have no wish to provide the "feature" of this exhibition for the evening papers.'

He repeated to himself: 'Little patch of yellow wall, with a sloping roof, little patch of yellow wall.'

Sinking on to a divan, he felt better. . . . 'It's just an ordinary indigestion from those potatoes; they weren't cooked properly.' A fresh attack beat him down; he rolled from the divan to the floor. . . . He was dead. They buried him, but all through the night of mourning, in the lighted windows, his books arranged three by three kept watch like angels with outspread wings and seemed, for him who was no more, the symbol of his resurrection.[27]

Proust while dying thought about Bergotte's death – there was something, he made known, that he wanted to add.

Israel's Way
Sherban Sidéry

'Advice in the form of an enigma: if you cannot break the bond, at least mark it with your teeth.'

'If you look upon monsters, take care you do not become one yourself; for, should you gaze down into the abyss, the abyss may enter into you.'

NIETZSCHE: *Beyond Good and Evil*

CHER MONSIEUR, I did not reply yesterday to the question that you put to me about the Jews. My reason was a very simple one: despite the fact that I am a Catholic like my father and my brother, my mother is a Jewess. You will understand that I have a strong reason for wishing to refrain from a discussion of the kind.[1]

Such were the phrases, precise and cool and haughty, with which Marcel Proust advised comte Robert de Montesquiou both of his ancestral origins and of his attitude towards his birth. It is true that, like Michel de Montaigne, he was the offspring of a Jewish mother. Proust's mother had been born a Weil; Montaigne's came of a family of Jewish-Portuguese stock named Lopez. From this link may we not draw a conclusion? The critic Albert Thibaudet is persuaded that between these two great writers there was a genuine relationship. They display, he writes, 'the same mobility of phrase, the same lively, compelling images, the same expansive style, which closely corresponds to the continuity and plasticity of human life'; and, later, he adds that 'Bergson also shows this sense of movement' – Bergson and Proust, of course, were connected through the female line. But the most striking point of resemblance is their insatiable curiosity, which they focused upon life itself, upon the reality of life (the reverse of the world of appearances) and its many-sidedness.

There is scarcely an aspect of existence that one or other of them has not explored. Each was a man of 'universal' genius. Each was half Jewish; each was a Catholic; neither had a definite faith or possessed a Christian frame of mind. Yet neither was to die an atheist. Montaigne expired while attending the mass in his bedroom, and is said to have breathed his last at the moment of the elevation. As for Proust, he, too, according to George Painter, considered summoning a priest: 'He thought of the saintly Abbé Mugnier's efforts to save his soul,' and remembered that he was a baptized and confirmed Catholic. '"Send for the good Abbé Mugnier," he said with mingled irony and reverence, "half an hour after I die. You will see how he'll pray for me."' And he instructed Céleste to 'find the rosary that Lucie Faure brought for me from Jerusalem, and put it between my fingers when I'm dead'.

That last request was not a final volte-face, nor was it an act of piety. It was essentially a poetic gesture. In Proust's case, we cannot speak of religious half-heartedness or of death-bed conversion; still less can we assume that, at the eleventh hour, he was tempted to accept the incredible 'wager' once proposed by Pascal. We confront a totally disillusioned man, whose mind was closed against the idea of faith – shut and bolted indeed; though he was not, like

Jean-Paul Sartre, utterly hostile to religion. Is the explanation to be found in the fact that Marcel Proust had Jewish origins? Bergson, we are told, on the point of conversion, drew back owing to a sense of solidarity with his persecuted race. But then, Bergson was the product of other disciplines, that his relation Proust had never recognized.

If we are to understand Proust's godless universe, we must employ the comparative method that he himself had recommended. Here it is Racine's example we should examine. For Racine, the Christian values invariably took precedence; they determined the course of his life and his work, sometimes even more powerfully than he suspected. It was through a Christian glass that he surveyed – and misinterpreted – the dramas of the pagan world. Proust loved Racine merely because he admired his scientific insight into the nature of the passions, and his prodigious gift of representing them. The two artists appear to typify two opposing views of life, each of them governed by a different conception of fatality. Racine, being deeply impregnated with the Christian spirit, could not begin to comprehend the psychological make-up of his pagan heroes. Even his villains are Christian; great sinners in a world where the notion of sin was still unknown, they are bound to contradict their own historical reality. Without considering Athalie or Phèdre, whose problem is exclusively a Catholic one we may select a lesser personage: Burrhus. These are the words in which he addresses Agrippina, when he is bringing her the news of Brittanicus' assassination by Nero:

> *Son crime seul n'est pas ce qui me désespère,*
> *Sa jalousie a pu l'armer contre son frère,*
> *Mais, s'il vous faut, Madame, expliquer ma douleur,*
> *Néron l'a vu mourir sans changer de couleur.*

The dismay felt by Burrhus, the reader will observe, is peculiarly Christian, and implies repentance and remorse. It is not the crime itself that he condemns, so much as the *attitude* of the man who has committed the crime. Tacitus and Suetonius have a very different reaction; their anger springs from quite another source. It is virtue that the Roman historian invokes; through the lips of Burrhus, the Christian dramatist poses the problems of sin and, possibly of ultimate salvation. Proust ignores the dramatist's statement of belief. 'The Jansenist pallor', 'the Christian hair-shirt' – phrases that the Narrator attributes to Bergotte (a character partly based on Renan) – for Proust are no more than aesthetic curiosities. The interest that he allows them is dependent merely on their verbal charm. They are the reflection of abstract ideas, unconnected with the main tragedy, isolated and perfect, like the famous Racinian line, often wrongly supposed to possess a fascination that defies critical analysis:

La fille de Minos et de Pasiphaé.

To the sense of beauty – which Proust regarded as one of the means that may guide us in the lifelong pursuit of truth – he did not add the sense of sin. It was the scandal he dreaded, and not the offence; not virtue he cultivated, but nobility. His tolerance, his sympathy, his generosity were neither instinctive traits, nor did they arise from any Christian sentiment. Their use was purely to console; they were a tribute he owed to the general wretchedness of mankind. Proust's pessimism was no doubt rooted deep in his unconscious memory – the ancestral memory of a race that, age after age, has suffered unending persecutions.

It is clear that, at one period of life, Proust had been affected by Renan's influence. When he was eighteen, he received from the old man a copy of *La Vie de Jésus* with the following inscription: '*A Marcel Proust que je prie de garder affectueusement mon souvenir quand je ne serai plus de ce monde. Janvier 1889.*' An eloquent, almost a humble dedication, it reveals the magnetic quality that, despite his extreme youth, had enabled Proust to capture the attention of a man as finely intelligent as Ernest Renan. If Proust, moreover, had shown signs of Catholic leanings, he would not have been offered this gift, above all with such a dedication. And then, there was the young man's friendship for Anatole France, who not only admired Renan, but is well known to have displayed a 'smiling scepticism' about religious subjects. Proust had met France at the house of Madame Arman de Caillavet, a lady of Jewish origins, who kept a celebrated literary salon.

Proust himself would learn to smile at religion. His descriptions of the Curé of Combray, of the conduct of Tante Léonie – a bigot rather than a believer – who is chiefly interested in discovering whether Madame Goupil arrived at Mass before or after the elevation, and of Françoise's response to her employer's questions, sufficiently illustrate his point of view. The religious convictions of others he treated with indulgent lightness. Certainly he accompanied his relations to Mass – but it was in order to enjoy his private dreams. He never went to pray. (Here the Narrator and the novelist are so closely connected, and there is so little doubt that his accounts of his visits to the church are based on a direct personal experience, that we need not try to separate them.) For prayer he substituted meditation of an entirely non-religious sort. It was an ethnological and aesthetic truth that, as he watched the duchesse de Guermantes take her place and merge into the imagery of the medieval tapestry, occupied the young man's mind. The vision of reality he sought to pin down had no colouring of metaphysics.

At this stage, however, we must attempt to arrive at a more precise impression of the relationship that existed between Proust and his Narrator. We have little concrete evidence to help us; Proust seems to have done his utmost to lead his critics astray. When does the Narrator become Marcel? When does he cease to represent the novelist? The little that the author consents to tell us he put into the form of a very brief dialogue where he is addressed by an imaginary reader. 'How is it', inquires the reader, 'that, young as you were at the time (or as your hero was, if you and he are not, in fact, the same person) you already had so poor a memory?'[2] That is all the novelist will admit; but his hint is none the less indicative, and suggests a covert acceptance of the allegation. As if he feared that he might have said too much, Proust was never to repeat his half-avowal. But he authorizes us to make our own guesses; and we may conclude that, even though novelist and Narrator are not to be identified, the second is at least a projection of the first, a kind of ideal Self, as indispensable to the author as was Mephistopheles to Faust. Further than that Proust would not go for fear that he might lose his freedom.

One remembers Flaubert's famous sally: 'Madame Bovary is myself!' But, if Flaubert dared to make this remark, it was because he did not run the same risks, for his heroine was not his spokesman, and he might safely have coined a similar phrase about Bouvard or Salammbô. A similar admission, had it come from Proust, would have assumed a far more dangerous meaning. 'I am close to saying a thing that cannot be said,' 'And I to hearing a thing that cannot be heard.' Such, in Sophocles's tragedy, are the words that pass between the Messenger and Oedipus. The terrible truths that Proust designed to tell could only be allowed utterance if the speaker wore a mask; Proust's readers are permitted to divine them, though he hesitates to set them forth in words.

Around the age of fourteen, during the course of a popular game, Proust was confronted with a questionnaire, a kind of written interrogation as to the preferences of the person questioned. He was asked 'Which is your favourite virtue?' And the young Marcel replied: 'All those which are not peculiar to a single sect, the universal virtues.' An odd yet revealing reply. To begin with, we note the adolescent's tendency to generalize; a question put in the singular Proust has answered in the plural. He declines to select the smallest virtue that has not a universal application or remains the property of any one sect. But what is a sect if not a minority? And of which minority was the young man thinking? Even at this period Proust was anxious to join the ranks of other men, to become an 'integrated' character. Had he thought that he had already achieved this object, the curious reply he gave would scarcely have occurred to him. Still unaware of his own genius, he had not yet discovered that one of the conditions of genius is to stand apart from other human beings. But, dimly, though he had not yet taken cognizance of the exceptional position that he occupied, Proust *knew* that he was not like other men. By his birth, he was half affiliated to the Jewish minority; and his mother, whom he adored, had entirely Jewish origins.

Later still, though it was not his own choice, he joined another persecuted group. Meanwhile, at fourteen, may he not have already suffered from his mother's origins, and from the incomprehensible accusation that he carried in himself *the* Jewish virus? To be a Jew is to bear a burden of guilt. The *others* accuse one; they point one out; they whisper and they shrink away. The mysterious malediction, '*he is a Jew*', always hangs over one's youthful head. True, Proust lived in an age and a country where antisemitism as yet amounted to no more than social prejudice; its grimmest manifestations did not emerge until the novelist himself had died. But, during his lifetime, the threat already existed, despite the fact that, both in the middle classes and among the aristocracy, Jews and Christians intermarried; that the salons were tentatively opening their doors to Jews; and that the most exclusive Parisian clubs sometimes consented to elect a Jew – for example, Charles Haas, whom Proust used as one of his models when he was portraying Charles Swann.

This happened seldom enough, and was not allowed to go uncriticized. If a Jew hoped to stand up to Gentile opposition, whether it were latent or avowed, he must gain some form of personal prestige, grow rich, speculate, hoard money, build up a family fortune or acquire the gift of pleasing. At the best of times, he confronted many obstacles; for money excites envy, and envy always breeds hatred. The sinister Edouard Drumont, surrounded by his henchmen, was writing *La France Juive* and editing *La Libre Parole*. It was a situation that Proust could not dismiss. How, in his secret thoughts, did he regard the popular aberration that represented one side of his own family – and perhaps the dearest side – as a community of racial suspects, cut off from the world around them, a community whose virtues were peculiar to a single alien creed. When Proust's turn came to write a book, he spared his brain-child, the Narrator, his ideal self, any such humiliations. The Narrator is not a Jew. Nor is he a homosexual. He is like other men, with the added advantage of genius. For him there are no social tabus.

These twin 'blemishes' – Jewish descent and homosexuality – Proust reserves for one of his most pathetic characters, Monsieur Nissim Bernard. Experiences that were evidently those of the author are transferred to the Narrator; and, between them, they produce something more than a portrait – a judicial summing-up. During the process, the whole Bloch milieu, Uncle Nissim Bernard, Bloch's sisters and his father, and, last but not least, Bloch himself, are treated with amused ferocity and inimitable wit. One can see that the author thoroughly enjoys himself. The Narrator, on the other hand, can afford to stand aside; for he belongs to a family of practising Catholics; and his father, his mother, Aunt Léonie, and, no doubt, the rest of the clan, are all of them orthodox Christian believers. Without going so far as to indulge in antisemitism, the Narrator's grandfather abounds in pointed jokes:

... My grandfather made out that, whenever I formed a strong attachment to anyone of my friends and brought him home with me, that friend was invariably a Jew; to which he would not have objected on principle – indeed his own friend Swann was of Jewish extraction – had he not found that the Jews whom I chose as friends were not usually of the best type. And so I was hardly ever able to bring a new friend home without my grandfather's humming the 'O, God of our fathers' from *La Juive*, or else 'Israel, break thy chain' ...

Before seeing them, merely on hearing their names, about which, as often as not, there was nothing particularly Hebraic, he would divine not only the Jewish origin of such of my friends as might be of the chosen people, but even some dark secret which was hidden in their family.[3]

Here the author appears to intervene, feeling perhaps that he ought to make some comment, and explain his grandfather's eccentric ways: 'These little eccentricities on my grandfather's part (he tells us) implied no ill-will whatsoever towards my friends.' Possibly, however, they were not quite so devoid of significance as the Narrator would have had us think.

As for Bloch, whose name is clearly Jewish, he raises objections of a different order, which do not necessarily involve his connection with the sin of Israel. What offends in Bloch is the vulgarity and indiscretion that are perhaps among his individual faults. Having described with relish Bloch's entry into his parents' and grandparents' household, and the temperate welcome they accord him, the novelist feels obliged to add:

> But I was fond of Bloch; my parents wished me to be happy ... And he would still have been received at Combray but for one thing. ... Having informed me ... that no woman ever thought of anything but love ... he had gone on to assure me that he had heard it said on unimpeachable authority that my great-aunt had led a 'gay' life in her younger days, and had been notoriously 'kept'. I could not refrain from passing on so important a piece of information to my parents; the next time Bloch called he was not admitted ...[4]

One must recognize that, in this presentation of Bloch, there is a considerable degree of ambiguity; in later pages, there is nothing to show that the Narrator has felt the smallest sympathy for his Jewish school-friend. On the contrary, he seldom does him justice, but constantly depicts him as grotesque and vulgar, maintaining that the success or demi-success, that Bloch afterwards achieves in the social world, has been of the most dubious sort. Above all, we must not forget the extraordinary last portrait of Bloch that Proust drew for *Le Temps retrouvé*, where the Narrator meets him at the morning reception given by the princesse de Guermantes.

A crucial question arises: when the Narrator deals with Jews, and with the place they hold in bourgeois society, is his attitude objective? At first sight, the answer is *Yes*. As for the novelist, at first sight, *No*. It is an almost insoluble question; and if, in an attempt to solve it, one seeks to establish a Proustian parallel between this problem and that of 'the other blemish', homosexuality, one is obliged to admit that, on the subject of his Jewish characters and their failings, the writer is a great deal less eloquent. Was it because he was less involved himself, or because his feelings were less open? He speaks of anti-semitism with a certain detachment, as though he were merely commenting on social fact. At the time of the Dreyfus Affair, his attitude would be sensitive, vigilant and sympathetic, but exempt from fanaticism. He would have reacted similarly had Captain Dreyfus been a Provençal or a Breton; it was 'the inno-cent man he championed, rather than the Israelite'. With incomparable humour he analyses both the supporters of Dreyfus and his opponents, showing the futility, stupidity, the egotism, the inconsequence and the absurdity that prevail in both the warring camps.

Thus the duc de Guermantes, from conservatism, class-feeling and natural stupidity, begins as an anti-Dreyfusard, but finishes up as a Dreyfusard, simply because, at a watering place, he had met some delightful Italians who are convinced of Dreyfus's innocence. The baron de Charlus, certainly an intelligent man, believes himself to be a Dreyfusard, but talks like an idiot when he seeks to explain his point of view. Then his unconscious antisemitism rises to the surface; for Monsieur de Charlus is antisemitic without knowing it, just as, later, he will become Germanophile. His reasons are deeply hidden, the product of his complex character and of the major anomaly that deforms his private life. His pronouncements, moreover, have little value, apart, of course, from their psychological interest; they are only important thanks to the effect that they produce upon his own world. A clan as irrational and conservative as the Faubourg Saint-Germain was bound to rally around a man who, since he played a dominant social rôle, felt that he was entitled to make his voice heard, but whose authority was derived from his social position rather than from his ability to deliver a considered judgement. The novelist underlines this fact, and notes a phenomenon that becomes manifest once Dreyfus had been found not guilty:

... This was the moment when from the effects of the Dreyfus case there had arisen an antisemitic movement parallel to a more abundant movement towards the penetration of society by Israelites. The politicians had not been wrong in thinking that the discovery of the judicial error would deal a fatal blow to antisemitism. But provisionally, at least, a social antisemitism was ... enhanced and exacerbated by it.[5]

From the above passages one may, therefore, assume that what consciously interested Proust were the deductions he could draw, and the social laws that he was able to establish in his passionate pursuit of Truth. That pursuit, and the arduous discipline it imposed, had now come to govern the novelist's entire existence. It is as an observer, not as a moralist, that the Narrator records a luncheon party with the Guermantes, in company with Gilberte Swann. The Guermantes are now receiving Gilberte! But to make this possible, their dear friend Swann has had to die; at an earlier period, Madame de Guermantes had always obstinately turned down Swann's requests that she would receive his daughter. The Narrator profits from the occasion to analyse not only his host's and hostess's frivolous and unacknowledged antisemitism, but the evasiveness and snobbery – amounting almost to a denial of her parent – that characterizes Gilberte's attitude. The name of Swann, for example, is carefully avoided, lest it might chance to prove embarrassing. Though she cannot yet definitely renounce her father – who had adored her, and had seen her as his last hope that he might not be completely forgotten among those who had once been his friends – Gilberte, by a kind of manœuvre in which the Duke and Duchess join, begins to abolish his memory with a fine display of tact.

Soon she will be known as Mademoiselle de Forcheville, the name of her adoptive father, and will at length become a connection of the Guermantes, thanks to her marriage with their nephew Saint-Loup. Meanwhile, not being yet quite ready to renounce her real parent, Gilberte, when she lunches with the Guermantes, seizes the chance of making a number of preparatory moves. Some cards having just been left at the door, the Duchess remarks that she doesn't know the visitor and, turning to Gilberte, remarks that they come from a person called Lady Rufus Israel. 'Gilberte flushed crimson: "I do not know her," she said (which was all the more untrue in that Lady Israel and Swann had been reconciled two years before the latter's death and she addressed Gilberte by her Christian name), "but I know quite well, from hearing about her, who it is you mean."'

To his commentary on, or analysis of this scene, the Narrator adds a yet more striking detail:

The truth is that Gilberte had become a great snob. For instance, another girl having one day, whether in malice or from a natural want of tact, asked her what was the name of her real – not her adoptive – father, in her confusion, and as though to mitigate the crudity of what she had to say, instead of pronouncing the name as 'Souann' she said 'Svann', a change, as she soon realized, for the worse, since it made this name of English origin a German patronymic. And she had even gone on to say, abasing herself so as to rise higher: 'All sorts of stories have been told about my birth, but of course I know nothing about that.'[6]

Proust believed that our social personality is built up by the ideas of others, which naturally included the fact that one might perhaps have Jewish origins, as was clearly demonstrated by 'the others', when they refused so much as to concede that Dreyfus was a true-born Frenchman. In turn, both the duchesse de Guermantes and the baron de Charlus, each of whom pretend to support Dreyfus, maintain, without actually saying so, that he could not be considered a traitor because he was not really French. Monsieur de Charlus also delivers himself of much the same remarks – observations of an almost maniacal kind – as he has already made about the Bloch family. Yet Proust appears to be no more scandalized than a naturalist discussing the habits of a wild animal, and is content merely to record the occurrence. If, now and then, he feels obliged to underline certain oddities of behaviour, he does so in the spirit of a scientist describing the ferocity of birds or the intelligence of termites.

When the interests of Israel are concerned, the Narrator regards the problem from an entirely objective point of view; personally, he always remains detached. Was his detachment real or fictitious? This is a question one may well ask. Was it a ruse, a form of self-discipline or an ingenious literary method? The link that attached him to Israel was his mother, whose memory was evergreen. He had made Madame Proust the object of a cult; but the ambiguity of Proust's character is always an alarmingly conspicuous trait; and he could never escape from his own interior demons. We often speak of outrageous mothers; here we must reverse the order and describe Proust as an outrageous son – outrageous, surely beyond the ordinary limits.

How else could he have regarded the Jewish question with such apparent lack of feeling? Social persecution – the word 'prejudice' is far too weak – attacked the very being who had given him life and, with life, the terrible problems that resulted from his Jewish origin. It was not a conscious emotional response that drove him to produce his well-known essay on hearing how Madame van Blarenberghe had been murdered by her son; he wrote his article because the drama had touched him in the depths of his existence. The test was, so to speak, *dictated*; and, having quickly completed it, he sent his manuscript to *Le Figaro*. '*The Filial Sentiments of a Parricide*' caused an immediate sensation. Half reverie and half confession, it gives a brilliant and disturbing account of the fatal relationship between a mother and a son, which tells us much more about the writer himself than about the crime committed:

What have you done to me! What have you done to me! If we care to think of it, there is perhaps not a single truly loving mother, who, at the end of her life, often long before she comes to die, might not reproach her son thus ... For most men so painful a vision ... soon vanishes in the ordinary joy of living. But what joy, what reason for continuing to live, what human existence could resist this vision? Which is the more real – this vision or ordinary happiness? Which of them, indeed, is 'Truth'?[7]

As if to establish the truth of his theory, he invents the phrase 'profaned mothers'. Confronted with this evidence, can one safely assume that Proust took a cool, dispassionate view of his hereditary link with Israel?

Since the Jewish problem had involved a parent for whom he felt the deepest veneration, so sensitive a son could scarcely have remained indifferent. But such are the privileges of genius that, by a process of imaginative transposition which must certainly have caused him pain, the adoring son was able to cut himself free and, though it implied a kind of profanation, produce, as the laws of his art demanded, a sharply objective account, critical, analytical, satirical, of his beloved mother's race. There are moments when one is astonished by the double rôle that Proust adopts, and asks oneself if it had not been better for him to have decided he would keep his counsel. But genius will brook no opposition; and, for the man who possesses that cruel advantage, its demands are inescapable. To resist them would be beyond his strength. Paraphrasing Madame de Noailles on Rousseau, we might say of Marcel Proust that he '*grelottait de génie*', that his genius possessed him like a raging fever.

If the novelist often seems ambiguous, it was because Man, whom he had set out to investigate, is himself compact of ambiguities. All the contradictions and contrasts in human nature, all the heights and all the depths, Proust was destined to assimilate, until he had come to love his personages unornamented and undisguised. Thus Israel assumed the same footing as any of the other phenomena upon which he spent his lifework. His general statements have a strictly objective tone – for example, in the following reference to Charles Swann. His parents' old friend, he considers, must once have in turn exhibited every stage through which members of his race have passed, from the most childish snobbery and the clumsiest vulgarity to the most refined politeness; but the Swann whom the Narrator's family knew, and whom they had built up of their own imaginings, had become

a complete and living creature; so that even now I have the feeling of leaving someone I know for another quite different person when, going back in memory, I pass from the Swann I knew later and more intimately to this early Swann – this Swann in whom I can distinguish the charming mistakes of my childhood, and who, incidentally, is less like his successor than he is like the other people I knew at that time, as though one's life were a series of galleries in which all the portraits of any one period had a marked family likeness, the same (so to speak) tonality – this early Swann abounding in leisure, fragrant with the scent of the great chestnut tree, of baskets of raspberries and of a sprig of tarragon.[8]

Proust, it has already been pointed out, here borrows some of his character's traits, and lends him others of his own. When he describes Swann's habit of enlisting his friends' help, should he require an introduction or a piece of information, we know that this was a habit to which he himself was much addicted. Of Swann he writes:

It was not only the brilliant phalanx of virtuous dowagers, generals and academi-cians . . . that Swann compelled with so much cynicism to serve him as panders. All his friends were accustomed to receive, from time to time, letters which called on them for a word of recommendation or introduction, with a diplomatic adroitness which, per-sisting throughout all his successive 'affairs' and using different pretexts, revealed more glaringly than the clumsiest indiscretion, a permanent trait in his character and an in-varying quest. I used often to recall to myself when, many years later, I began to take an interest in his character because of the similarities which, in wholly different respects, it offered to my own, how, when he used to write to my grandfather . . . the latter, recognizing his friend's handwriting on the envelope, would exclaim: 'Here is Swann asking for something; on guard!'[9]

Clearly, the novelist has embarked on an indirect piece of self-criticism. Swann, nevertheless, with all his human errors, was undoubtedly Proust's favourite hero; and, later, when Swann, a dying man, drags himself, for the last time, to an evening party at the prince de Guermantes's, only to receive a private harangue from his host on certain repercussions of the Dreyfus Affair, the Narrator thus describes him:

But Swann belonged to that stout Jewish race, in whose vital energy, its resistance to death, its individual members seem to share. Stricken severally by their own diseases, as it is stricken itself by persecution, they continue indefinitely to struggle against terrible suffering which may be prolonged beyond every apparently possible limit, when one already sees nothing more than a prophet's beard surmounted by a huge nose which dilates to inhale its last breath, before the hour strikes for the ritual prayers and the punctual procession begins of distant relatives advancing with mechanical movements, as upon an Assyrian frieze.[10]

This extraordinary paragraph, in which Proust seems to foretell the Hitlerian death-camps, is particularly revealing: *'they continue indefinitely to struggle against terrible suffering which may be prolonged beyond every possible limit . . .'*. The image is not merely dramatic; I feel that it is intensely *personal*. A Gentile could never have written it, nor framed it in a style so moving, cruel and authoritative. Become a prophet himself, the author is, as it were, possessed by the spirit of his persecuted race. His vision arises from a gulf where memory is crystallized and Time suspended, where what has been and what is now merge with what is yet to be. Then the burst of illumination passes, and the novelist can return to the everyday world of appearances; and it is there that he draws his final portrait of his hero, integrated once again into the fugitive social world, in which everything decays and passes.

The moment has come, however, for the novelist to detach himself from Charles Swann. But, before he bids him good-bye, he gives us a last impression of his hero, a pitilessly candid sketch:

. . . All eyes were fastened upon that face, the cheeks of which had been so eaten away by disease, like a waning moon, that, except at a certain angle . . . they stopped short like a flimsy piece of scenery . . . Whether because of the absence of those cheeks, no longer there to modify it, or because arterio-sclerosis, which also is a form of intoxication, had reddened it, as would drunkenness, or deformed it, as would morphine, Swann's punchinello nose, absorbed for long years in an attractive face, seemed now enormous, tumid, crimson, the nose of an old Hebrew rather than that of a dilettante Valois. Perhaps too in him . . . the race was making appear more pronounced the physical type that characterizes it, at the same time as the sentiment of a moral solidarity with the rest of the Jews, a solidarity which Swann seemed to have forgotten throughout his life, and which, one after another, his mortal illness, the Dreyfus case and the antisemitic propaganda had revived. There are certain Israelites, superior people for all that . . . in whom there remain in reserve and in the wings, ready to enter at a given moment in their lives, as in a play, a bounder and a prophet. Swann had arrived at the age of the prophet.[11]

So Swann must die; but genius has brushed him with its wing; and, as the author proudly informs us, he is not destined to complete extinction.

The death of Swann had been a crushing blow to me at the time. The death of Swann! Swann, in this phrase, is something more than a noun in the possessive case. I mean by it his own particular death, the death allotted by destiny to the service of Swann. For we talk of 'death' for convenience, but there are almost as many different deaths as there are people . . . And it is this diversity among deaths, the mystery of their circuits, the colour of their fatal badge, that makes so impressive a paragraph in the newspapers such as this: 'We regret to learn that M. Charles Swann passed away yesterday . . .'[12]

This passage is all the more moving, since we know that it was based to some extent on the real obituary notice that appeared in the newspapers of the death of Monsieur Charles Haas. And, aware of his own value, exercising the divine right that belongs to men of genius, Proust himself addresses this imposing shade:

And yet, my dear Charles Swann, whom I used to know when I was still so young and you were nearing your grave, it is because he whom you must have regarded as a little fool has made you the hero of one of his volumes that people are beginning to speak of you again and that your name will perhaps live. If in Tissot's picture representing the balcony of the Rue Royale club, where you figure with Galiffet, Edmond de Polignac and Saint-Maurice, people are always drawing attention to yourself, it is because they know that there are some traces of you in the character of Swann.[13]

The novelist's object is no longer to mislead us; on the contrary, he shows his cards; and the Narrator becomes Marcel Proust, while, in Tissot's picture of the club, Charles Haas is identified with Charles Swann.

Another proof of Proust's enduring pride is afforded by the recollections of Emmanuel Berl, a writer who has described the novelist better than anyone else. In an autobiographical narrative, *Sylvia*, he records his visits to Proust, and their talks, which were not so much conversations as impassioned controversies. Particularly memorable is Berl's account of how their relationship was broken off, which shows that Proust's loftiness was based on an unshakeable conviction of his own abilities. The two men clashed over a question of love, about which their ideas were very different. The young Berl was going through a painful love-affair; and, while meditating on it, he had arrived at conclusions totally opposed to the views that he heard expressed by Proust. He went to visit Proust one night – it was generally at night they met – and communicated his 'good news':

He heard me out with his customary, his terribly acute attention and, much to my surprise, seemed to find my news disturbing. In his large eyes, shaded by heavy eyelids that failed to deaden their lustre, I thought I saw reflected a bird's-eye-view of the accursed region that lay ahead of me. Immediately confounded, I noted with astonishment that I did not really feel that he was wrong . . . I looked at Proust; newly shaved, his cheeks suggested the substance of a vegetable that had been cultivated in a cellar; his face – that of a discontented Sumerian divinity, though its expression was calm, appeared to refuse the diluted incense curling up beneath his nostrils . . . I said that, according to his manner of thinking, love was no more than a masturbatory hallucination. His face, already so pale, became even paler. His eyes blazed with fury . . . From the *cabinet de toilette* he hurled the most disagreeable phrases that his ingenuity could devise . . . 'You're stupid', he exclaimed, 'stupid! as stupid as' —— and he launched a series of names, some of them names of people rightly renowned for their intelligence. I had no difficulty, however, in understanding what we were supposed to have in common. It was the feebleness of those who have become incapable of recognizing anything that hurts them, of acknowledging a fact, no matter how obvious it may be, if it runs contrary to their system of ideas or upsets their preconcerted attitudes. Clearly, he suspected, with justifiable disgust, that two or three words from a young girl, perhaps a stupid girl, had been enough to make me forget the truths that he himself had taught me. This kind of mental flaccidity revolted him, no doubt, far more than any physical infirmity or moral blemish. Probably he was right. But he grew even angrier; and, descending to the lowest level of vulgarity, I reflected that he found normal love-affairs intolerable because, for him they were impossible ... He divined my thoughts as if they had been spoken aloud; and they served only to increase his scorn and indignation ... 'Get out! Get out!' he cried ... I left his presence, half anxious to make my escape, half driven forth against my will ...

This long passage, better than any attempts at critical dissection, shows the complete reliance that Proust placed upon the value of his own knowledge. To be misunderstood was an insult, not to the writer himself, but to the principle he called 'Truth', of which he acted as custodian. Emmanuel Berl is a Jew. He, too, one day became aware of the fact, when he saw his playfellows whisper and turn aside. Was there a similar incident in Marcel's childhood? Certainly, it was not the Dreyfus Affair that first opened his eyes to his position. At most, the sinister light it threw merely illuminated the anomalies of human nature and his individual loneliness, condemned to tread a path that Milton calls 'the solitary way'. But *consciously* he refused to accept this tabu; and at a time when he took a zealous interest in the Affair, collected signatures and sent Picquart, then suffering imprisonment, a copy of his first book, *Les plaisirs et les jours*, he acted not so much from a sense of racial solidarity as to protest against a wrong that he himself found insupportable. Only a deep Freudian analysis could explain his horror of the mental confusion to which ignorance and injustice lead. It was there that Proust discovered Sin.

Was it because he knew himself to be connected through ties of blood to victims whose martyrdom (as he guessed) had by no means reached its end, that made him alternately sympathetic, furious and over-sensitive? Did he, to some extent, identify himself with the victims? Was it his Jewish origins that would not let him rest? The only reference we have to enlighten us comes in the poetic paragraph I have already quoted, which begins 'But Swann belonged to that stout Jewish race ...' In his *Memories, Dreams, Reflections*, Jung supplies a useful footnote: ' ... We remain ignorant (he writes) of whether our ancestral components find an elementary gratification in our lives, or whether they are repelled. Inner peace and contentment depend in large measure upon whether or not the historical family, which is inherent in the individual, can be harmonized with the ephemeral conditions of the present.'

These are two major reasons why we must perforce admit that Proust was deeply affected by all the lacerating consequences of the Jewish problem – first, the almost exasperated attachment he felt for his mother (from which the novelist does not exempt the Narrator, though he dispenses him from being either a homosexual or a Jew); while the second, a much more secret reason – this, of course, is my own hypothesis – consisted in the fact that the Jewish elements of his psychology refused to allow themselves to be forgotten, but pursued him, as the Furies pursued Orestes, with their ancestral plaints and clamours. There his genius failed him, and he had to confess defeat. This state of affairs, which seems to be established by the novelist's indirect avowals, is doubly pathetic, considering the trouble that Proust had taken to throw his readers off the scent. No pains are spared to suggest that he remains detached, beyond the struggle.

This air of invulnerability, moreover, was not confined to the attitude that he adopts towards the Jewish problem. There is a touch almost of malice, of trickery and teasing deception, in his general treatment of the reader. For example, when he indulges in spying, as he very often does, he never owns up to having played the spy, but always employs some kind of literary subterfuge. It is while pretending to await the appearance of the insect, destined to fertilize a rare plant, that he surprises Monsieur de Charlus passionately engaged with Jupien; and, while enjoying an innocent country walk, that he witnesses the dark scene that takes place between Mademoiselle Vinteuil and her female lover. Finally, it is owing to a war-time hazard that he visits Jupien's brothel and lays bare the sinister and portentous secrets of the homosexual underworld:

> The clients who had wished to leave had collected together in one room ... They were not acquainted with one another, but one could see that they belonged nevertheless roughly to the same world, rich and aristocratic. The appearance of each one had in it something repugnant, a reflection, I presumed, of their failure to resist degrading pleasures.[14]

At this point, another quality, a peculiar attribute of the Jewish race, suddenly emerges in the narrative. That quality is *verve*; and the prodigious and fascinating verve that Proust displays has a highly individual character. He exercises it not only with relish, but with an aggressiveness that is at once joyful and ferocious. It becomes revengeful. He destroys. He mocks to his heart's content. The spirit of derision reigns. It approaches the verge of sacrilege; even innocence does not escape. We read how the baron de Charlus contemplates insulting an old lady who is waiting for the omnibus, or hear him, drunk with an illusory conviction of his own power, pouring ridicule upon the Blochs. Yet Monsieur de Charlus, the Narrator assures us, is good, charitable, delicate; just as both the author and the Narrator are full of noble human feelings. Who utters a sneering laugh in their shadows? This cruel verve is provoked by a feeling of interior panic, by a sense of individual weakness; and, in those whom it afflicts, it may breed a lunatic despair, to which they give rein with a wild abandon. Verve is a means of escape; wit becomes consolation. I mock; therefore I am powerful. It is thus that the offended and persecuted restore their injured self-esteem. Dostoievski provides many examples of this particular situation; and one has also heard of the mordant witticisms pronounced by Jewish humourists at the most desperate moments of their lives. They have the courage to laugh we are told! A frivolous explanation. They are joking to protect themselves – while struggling 'against terrible suffering which may be prolonged beyond every apparently possible limit . . .'

The gift of mockery is their secret weapon – a weapon that may well be bestowed upon the Jewish child before he leaves the cradle; verve is one of the prerogatives shared by most Jews. Proust himself made a masterly use of it; he or his personages often carry it to the point of sacrilege. Even though he was conscious of his own strength, there were times when he allowed himself to be carried away, abandoned any pretence of verisimilitude, and swept ahead with a kind of mad excitement. But the air of madness was apt to be somewhat deceptive. Does he not refer to 'Dostoievski's vision of humanity which is more fantastic than Rembrandt's *Night Watch* . . . Those bufoons of his, how vividly they illustrate important aspects of the human spirit!'

Paradoxical as the statement may seem, Proust, in this vein, occasionally resembles Feydeau.[15] For instance, on the night of an air-raid, when, amid the cataclysmic tumult of earth and sky, Proust and friend Saint-Loup are able to laugh at their strange experiences, and, with the help of a satirical commentary, coolly dominate the situation. They regard the situation as 'a first-rate farce', which might have provided paragraphs for a gossip-columnist. Saint-Loup and the Narrator find amusement in inventing them:

'Seen about town: the duchesse de Guermantes magnificent in a night-dress, the duc de Guermantes indescribable in pink pyjamas and bath robe,' etc. 'I am sure', he said, 'that in all the large hotels you would have seen American Jewesses in their night-dresses, hugging to their ravaged bosoms the pearl necklaces which will enable them to marry a ruined duke. The Ritz, on these evenings, must look like Feydeau's *Hotel du libre échange*.'[16]

In his temporary refuge, the brothel kept by Jupien, Proust assembles the most discordant elements – social elements that were never meant to blend, but are here united by the anguished pursuit of pleasure: soldiers on leave, besotted businessmen, unidentifiable recruits, a priest (whom, at first sight, the Narrator maliciously assumes to be a woman), a deputy, the Narrator's friend Saint-Loup and, finally, the baron de Charlus, wearing the shackles of Prometheus. All these queer associates are busily coming and going, jostling and rubbing shoulders in a sort of crazy dance, which transforms a night of Sodom into a contemporary *Walpurgisnacht*. Proust is saved from alarm or disgust by the satirical verve he owes to his Jewish descent. Like the Narrator, he can afford – or believes that he can afford – to stand aloof. In the guise of ethnologist, he explores the modern Brocken, where, to quote Anna de Noailles's phrase, *'gît ardent, supplicié, invincible, au destin lié, mais tremblant qu'on ne le bafoue, le désir que jamais l'on n'avoue'*. Thus farce neighbours tragedy, and Goya joins hands with Jerome Bosch!

For Proust, it is interesting to remember, 'accursed race' are not the Jews, but these terrible puppets gathered that night at a brothel, an *'hotel de libre échange'*. One of the essays published in *Contre Sainte-Beuve*, and entitled '*La Race Maudite*', sufficiently proves this point. Proust was never confronted with the necessity of being obliged to acknowledge his mother's origins. But the Narrator's unconcern was no more than a literary ruse, a pretence of objectivity. It also reveals his distrust of humanity and his contemptuous attitude towards his fellow men. Proust would only identify himself with the Jews in so far as they were victimized; and then, it was the victim, not the Jew he championed.

On the other hand, it is a significant fact that one of his dearest friends was Jewish – Reynaldo Hahn, who, as the companion of his brilliant youth, had shared his *fous-rires* and his inimitable youthful pastimes. Nor must we forget that the salon where he had his first worldly successes, and gained the friendship of Anatole France, was presided over by a Jewish person, Madame de Caillavet. Proust, however, did not reach the Faubourg Saint-Germain by the road that leads through Israel. He owed his social conquests to the strength of his personality and to his natural desire to please. Throughout, his object, which he pursued with untiring zeal, was the enlargement of his own knowledge; and he was merely concerned with the Jews in as much, like any other component part of the social system, they might advance his lifelong pursuit of Truth. He pretended to accept the existing system that he might the more effectively dismantle it and proclaim its unreality. Moral tabus and patriotic catchwords, religious faith and semitism – all were examined by Proust in the spirit of a scientist. Neither the author nor his Narrator is deterred by sentimental feelings. Proust shows the same verve, the same delighted zest, the same ferocious concentration, whether he is studying the Jews, the servants at a grand hotel or the most magnificent members of the aristocracy. Every detail he absorbs with the same greed and dwells on with the same affection.

In his masterpiece, he rarely exhibits a preference; if he has a personal choice, he keeps it hidden. The energy with which, during the First World War, he fought to save the churches and cathedrals of France was not inspired by his religious feelings. He defended these shrines because they had once enclosed or, rather, had expressed a truth. His position as regards the Christian faith was primarily an *aesthetic* one. Evidently, he was reluctant to become engaged; for the path he followed in his private life gave him access to an inferno very different from that described by any priesthood. Dr Faustus, in a cork-lined alchemist's cell, surrounded by the wreathing smoke of fumigations, he devoted his life to austere researches from which he would rarely tear himself away, except at night sometimes, when he donned his great-coat and had himself driven to the Ritz, there to join a few friends whom he held spell-bound until the dawn had broken. Should he wish to remain in his cell, he might perhaps receive a visitor, and overwhelm him by his knowledge, his kindness, now and then by violent rages, but always by the unerring insight he showed into the secret springs of his visitor's personality.

In Proust's work, however, there is one subject that he never deals with openly – the union of Jews and Gentiles. On the plane of passion, when he is analysing love or friendship, it is a factor that he does not take into account. Swann, a Jew, loved Odette – or, at least, dedicates his life to her; Saint-Loup loves Rachel, the daughter of a Jew; but she does not love him. Even in passing, Proust refrains from any reference to the theme of inter-racial alliances. Yet he himself was the offspring of such an alliance; and it is hard to believe that there was nothing about his parents' marriage that he felt deserved attention. The mixture of classes interested him more than the blending of races and religious faiths, which resulted in equally serious conflicts. Did he think that there were no deductions to be made? Or had he private motives for wishing to avoid the issue? This is a question we cannot hope to answer. All we can say is, that, if the author had been neither a Jew nor half a Jew, he might well have discussed this problem freely – at all events, with the same apparent objectivity of approach that he reserves for homosexuals.

The novelist's silence is all the more provocative since marriages of this kind always roused some adverse criticism. But it was not the kind of problem that Proust would pause to consider, though his own family life might have provided him with valuable evidence. As in the Dreyfus Affair, he adopted an impartial standpoint, seeming to find the marriage of a Gentile and a Jew no different from a marriage between Catholic and Protestant, or a Frenchman and an American. Maybe his peculiar type of sensitiveness made it impossible for him to discuss a problem that involved his parents' memory. Again, we face an unanswerable question. Often, in his great novel, when seeking to answer a question, the novelist throws out a number of hypotheses – explanations difficult to reconcile, sometimes downright contradictory, that the author proposes as tentative solutions, without committing himself to any definite view; and here, no doubt, we should follow Proust's example.

Does a race, or, indeed, a domestic clan ever change its special attributes? I think not; they appear again and again in each of its successive members:

> I had seen the vices and the courage of the Guermantes [writes Proust] recur in Saint-Loup, as also at different times in his single life his own strange and ephemeral defects of character, as in Swann his Semitism. And now I could observe the same phenomenon in Bloch ... As he sat at table in the midst of his family, he was animated by the same wrath against his father-in-law as had animated his own father against M. Nissim Bernard and even interrupted his meals to deliver the same tirades against him ... It seemed to me now that throughout the whole duration of time great cataclysmic waves lift up from the depths of the ages the same wraths, the same sadnesses, the same heroisms, the same manias, through one superimposed generation after another ...[17]

The picture becomes identical, though (the spectator adds) it is 'often not so insignificant, as that of Bloch exchanging angry words with his father-in-law, M. Bloch the elder doing the same ... with M. Nissim Bernard, and many other pairs of disputants whom I had myself never known'.

On the subject of Bloch and the death of his father, Proust refers to 'the strong family sentiments which often exist in Jewish families'. Bloch 'had found his loss unbearable and had had to take refuge in a sanatorium, where he stayed for nearly a year'. This last characteristic, which Proust lends to Bloch, had, however, been provided by a Gentile – the unhappy Henri van Blarenberghe, whose crime I have already mentioned. The death of Blarenberghe's father seems to have driven him to matricide. For Bloch, however, despite his real grief, the consequences were much less serious; and, not without humour, Proust describes the marks that this cruel loss had left upon his personage's character: 'To my condolences he replied in a tone of profound grief which was at the same time almost haughty, so enviable in his eyes was the privilege which he had enjoyed of approaching this exceptional man whose very ordinary two-horse carriage he would have liked to present to some historical museum.'

The novelist's verve suddenly explodes, infiltrating his description of a genuine human sorrow, until it culminates in a burst of derision that sweeps over Bloch's head and covers the whole human race. Bloch may not be the novelist's favourite cock-shy; but, with sympathetic irony, he is perpetually aiming at him. He is never spared because he is always an irritant. If proof be needed, we can find it in the masterly description of his final triumph when, at last, on a certain footing of intimacy, he is received among the Guermantes:

Bloch had come bounding into the room like a hyena. 'He is at home now', I thought, 'in drawing-rooms into which twenty years ago he would never have been able to penetrate.' But he was also twenty years older. He was nearer to death . . . At close quarters, in the translucency of a face in which, at a greater distance or in a bad light, I saw only youthful gaiety . . . I could detect another face, almost frightening, racked with anxiety, the face of an old Shylock, waiting in the wings, with his make-up prepared, for the moment when he would make his entry on to the stage and already reciting his first line under his breath. In ten years, in drawing rooms like this which their own feebleness of spirit would allow him to dominate, he would enter on crutches to be greeted as the 'Master' . . .[18]

One asks oneself whether this passage does not include a shade of indirect self-criticism. For a second, 'The Master' has ceased to be Bloch! But one hesitates in view of the pitiless sketch that Proust has drawn upon an earlier page:

I had difficulty in recognizing my friend Bloch, who was now in fact no longer Bloch since he had adopted, not merely as a pseudonym but as a name, the style of Jacques du Rozier, beneath which it would have needed my grandfather's flair to detect the 'sweet vale of Hebron' and those 'chains of Israel' which my old comrade appeared definitely to have broken. Indeed an English *chic* had completely transformed his appearance and smoothed away, as with a plane, everything in it that was susceptible of such treatment. The once curly hair, now brushed flat, with a parting in the middle, glistened with brilliantine. His nose remained large and red, but seemed now to owe its tumescence to a sort of permanent cold which seemed also to explain the nasal intonation with which he languidly delivered his studied sentences . . . Thanks to the way in which he brushed his hair, to the suppression of his moustache, to the elegance of his whole figure . . . his Jewish nose was now scarcely more visible than is the deformity of a hunch-backed woman who skilfully arranged her appearance.[19]

Such is the descriptive skill of the passages quoted above that one asks oneself why the novelist has not made more of the theme of Israel. But he tells us if we read between the lines. His impassioned quest drives him through all the circles of an inferno, from which he has determined that he will wrest its secrets, even though he is well aware that he may never succeed in obtaining a wholly satisfactory answer. But the search itself lends him the support he requires; through that research he lives and breathes.

It is the vital mechanism of existence that absorbs his attention above all else. He designates, displays it, examines it and comments on it, with amusement, sorrow and surprise, but invariably refuses to disclose any sign of partisanship. In the long-drawn symphony of his great book innumerable themes occur; but, among them, the theme of Israel never occupies a dominant position. Yet it remains a strongly insistent theme. Like '*la petite phrase*' in Vinteuil's sonata, it is a leitmotif that runs through the whole composition:

There was in me a personage who knew more or less how to look, but it was an intermittent personage, coming to life only in the presence of some general essence common to a number of things, these essences being its nourishment and its joy . . . The stories that people told escaped me, for what interested me was not only what they were trying to say but the manner in which they said it and the way in which this manner revealed their character or their foibles; or rather I was interested in what had always . . . been more particularly the goal of my investigations: the point that was common to one being and another.[20]

This, above all, is what interests Proust and explains his attitude towards the Dreyfus case. It is the social phenomenon alone that he observes and he denounces. Once the victim had been rescued, the cause of Israel itself shrinks into the background; his object is to emphasize the phenomenon, and depict the frivolity, hardness of heart and inconsequence that are as marked in the collective social organism as in the existence of an individual. His famous 'detachment', which has often surprised his critics, was derived from his contempt for human nature: 'Dreyfusism was now integrated in a scheme of respectable and familiar things. As for asking oneself whether intrinsically it was good or bad, the idea no more entered anybody's head, now when it was accepted, than in the past when it was condemned. It was no longer "shocking" and that was all that mattered.' And, to illustrate his theory, he adds: 'No one troubled to remember that he had been a Dreyfusard, for people in society are scatter-brained and forgetful and, besides, all *that* had been a very long time ago . . . Brichot himself, that great nationalist, when he alluded to the Dreyfus case now talked of "those prehistoric times".'

One might perhaps venture to draw a comparison with the atrocious spirit of the Nazis, and with the series of social movements to which the Nazi revolution gave rise; after which one must again pay homage to Proust's intuitive and prophetic genius, when he remarks that, during the post-war years, the terms 'Dreyfusard' and 'anti-Dreyfusard' were said to have completely lost their meaning – by the same people who would have been astonished and disgusted if one had told them that, in a few centuries, and, conceivably, even earlier, the word '*boche*' would probably be no more than a subject of historical curiosity, like '*sans-culotte*', or '*chouan*', or '*bleu*'.

As we read these cruelly accurate lines, we are bound to reflect – and the parallel is by no means flattering – upon the conditions of our own period. Did Proust's knack of envisaging the future originate in the Jewish gift of prophesy, or was it the result of a deliberate intellectual process? Possibly our best plan is to follow the writer's lead, and devote our attention to the way in which things are said, rather than to the things themselves. His field of investigation extended far beyond the limits laid down by the conscious mind. And, once his conscious intelligence ceased to function, and his daimon took control, he could enjoy the delights of merely 'seeing', and plunge into the gulf with Gogol and with Dostoievski. Then he could dream of vengeance and sacrilege:

> *Si le viol, le poison, le poignard, l'incendie,*
> *N'ont pas encore brodé de leurs plaisants dessins*
> *Le canevas banal de nos piteux destins,*
> *C'est que notre ame hélas! n'est pas assez hardie.*

To this quatrain from Baudelaire's *Fleurs du Mal*, we may append two lines from Boileau, which the novelist often quoted, and which perhaps supply a key:

> *Il n'est pas de serpent, ni de monstre odieux*
> *Qui par l'art imité ne puisse plaire aux yeux*

In conclusion, as the novelist said himself: 'The man who inhabits the same body as a great genius has very little contact with him.'

Knowing humanity, Proust understood that any attempt to communicate must be couched in a contrived and indirect form. In order to make his discoveries acceptable, they must be transposed and partly hidden. Prudence was another reason – the prudence transmitted by a part of himself that had inherited the memory of unending persecutions. Thus, suddenly, with the 'notions of light, of sound, of perspective, the rich possessions wherewith our inner temple is diversified and adorned', emerges the stream of his ancestral Jewish past. The leitmotif recedes, only to return:

The phrase had disappeared. [Proust wrote in his memorable description of Swann listening to Vinteuil's music.] Swann knew that it would come again at the end of the last movement . . . Swann listened to all the scattered themes which entered into the composition of the phrase, as its premisses enter into the inevitable conclusion of a syllogism; he was assisting at the mystery of its birth . . . Swann knew that the phrase was going to speak to him once again . . . It reappeared, but this time to remain poised in the air, as to sport there for a moment only, as though immobile, and shortly to expire. And so Swann lost nothing of the precious time for which it lingered. It was still there, like an irridescent bubble that floats for a while unbroken. As a rainbow, when its brightness fades, seems to subside, then soars again and before it is extinguished, is glorified with greater splendour than it has ever shewn; so to two colours which the phrase had hitherto allowed to appear it added others now, chords shot with every hue of the prism, and made them sing.[21]

A superficial critic may object that it was not precisely the theme of Israel that formed the subject of Swann's impassioned meditation, as, with intense feeling he listened to Vinteuil's sonata and awaited the appearance of '*la petite phrase*'. But, by a kind of poetic transposition, which may not have been entirely conscious, between the little phrase and the theme of Israel the writer has established a mysterious link. That link, thanks to the legerdemain practised by a man of genius, may give us an allusive answer to the questions we have here been asking.

5

Proust and Painting

I. H. E. Dunlop

NEARLY all the great French writers of the nineteenth century took an active interest in the art of their times. Baudelaire, Balzac, Zola, Huysmans and the Goncourts played an influential part in the artistic life of their century, either by writing art criticism or by portraying the lives of artists. Proust, who is not strictly a nineteenth-century writer, but whose taste and knowledge of painting had been largely formed before 1900, was also keenly interested in art. But, unlike many of his predecessors and contemporaries, he was never an activist; he never championed any of the new movements that came in wave after wave from 1870 to the outbreak of the First World War. He was never an art critic; and his name is not linked with that of an outstanding painter, as, for example, Baudelaire with Delacroix and Zola with Manet and Cézanne.

Proust took more from painting than he gave to it; and, like Flaubert whose style and method correspond so closely with the realists and naturalists of his day, he wrote with an eye that was profoundly influenced by the study of painting in general and the Impressionists in particular.[1] This point of view is to some extent confirmed by Victor Graham in *The Imagery of Proust*.[2] Of 4,578 images, analysed according to sources, 203 are derived from painting, compared with 171 from music. By far the largest number – 944 – stem from nature; and of these 326 are connected with the sea and water. Bearing in mind the Impressionists' preoccupation with outdoor subjects, and particularly with the sea and stretches of water, it is reasonable to argue that Proust's debt to painting is higher than these statistics might at first suggest.

Proust is best known for his searching investigations of social behaviour and of his characters' thoughts and gestures; but, at the same time, he is a visual writer; and part, at least, of his great work could be transformed into film. Some of the nuances of social life would be lost; but any competent art director, with the help of an encyclopedia of painting, could find ways of reproducing on the screen Proust's descriptions of characters, buildings, landscapes, and settings. Similarly, Proust's readers are expected to be familiar with a wide range of artists and their works. For example, it would be a help to have a thorough knowledge of Italian art, from Giotto, Fra Angelico and Orcagna to the masters of the High Renaissance. Flemish and Dutch artists – Memling, Breughel, Hals, Van Dyck, Cuyp, Potter, Rembrandt, Maes, de Hooch, Vermeer and Wouwerman – are mentioned; so too are English artists, notably Turner and the pre-Raphaelites; and almost the whole of French art from the eighteenth century onwards – Watteau, Chardin, Robert, Courbet, Decamps, Gérôme,

Meissonier, Corot, Moreau, Puvis de Chavannes, Détaille, Helleu, the Impressionists, the Cubists, Le Sidaner and La Gandara. Characters in *A la Recherche* are frequently compared to portraits by the Old Masters. The baron de Charlus, for example, resembles a grand inquisitor painted by El Greco; the duc de Guermantes, the Bourgmestre Six by Rembrandt; and Odette Swann recalls one of the daughters of Jethro in Botticelli's painting of the Zipporah.

Almost any of his descriptive passages, chosen at random, points to Proust's visual sensitivity. At Balbec the Narrator looks out at the sea and notices little triangles of 'spray delineated with the delicacy of a feather or a downy breast from Pisanello's pencil and fixed in that white, unalterable creamy enamel which is used to depict fallen snow in Gallé's glass'.[3] On the horizon there is 'a band of red sky over the sea, compact and clear-cut as a layer of aspic over meat, then, a little later, over a sea already cold and blue like a grey mullet, a sky of the same pink as the salmon we should presently be ordering at Riverbelle'.[4] Proust is seldom content to describe something as just red or grey. He goes further and describes an object's colour in differing conditions of light. Before going out to play with Gilberte Swann, the Narrator studies the weather:

It remained dark. Outside the window, the balcony was grey. Suddenly, on its sullen stone, I did not indeed see a less negative colour, but I felt as it were an effort towards a less negative colour, the pulsation of a hesitating ray that struggled to discharge its light. A moment later the balcony was as pale and luminous as a standing water at dawn, and a thousand shadows from the iron-work of its balustrade had come to rest on it. A breath of wind dispersed them; the stone grew dark again, but, like tamed creatures, they returned; they began, imperceptibly, to grow lighter, and by one of those continuous crescendos, such as, in music, at the end of an overture, carry a single note to the extreme fortissimo, making it pass rapidly through all the intermediate stages, I saw it attain to that fixed, unalterable gold of fine days, on which the sharply cut shadows of the wrought iron of the balustrade were outlined in black like a capricious vegetation, with a fineness in the delineation of their smallest details which seemed to indicate a deliberate application, an artist's satisfaction . . .[5]

Here, as in many similar passages, Proust demonstrates that he had the capacity to observe colour and light with the concentration and accuracy of a painter. The inter-relation of colour and light had been established by the Impressionists in the eighteen-seventies and even earlier, but there was no more convincing demonstration of these ideas than the series of exhibitions that Monet held in the eighteen-nineties. In 1891, for example, Monet exhibited fifteen paintings of haystacks, observed at different moments; and, in the following year, he showed six views of poplar trees. His studies of Rouen cathedral, under differing climatic conditions and at different times of the day, were eagerly awaited and eventually displayed to the public in 1895. Proust admired the cathedrals; and he must surely have been impressed by their underlying philosophy as well as by their beauty.

He was in his mid-twenties when he saw these paintings; and, at that stage in his life, he was better acquainted with the Old Masters than with contemporary painting. He made frequent visits to the Louvre; and friends like Lucien Daudet, then studying painting, Reynaldo Hahn and Marie Nordlinger regarded him as an 'incomparable guide'. He was a frivolous companion. Daudet recalled Proust's habit – which was also Swann's – of finding likenesses to people he knew in portraits by the Old Masters. 'Do you see this Ghirlandaio of the little boy and the old man with a polyp on his nose?' he would say. 'It's the very image of the marquis du Lau. Ah, dear boy, it's *so* amusing looking at pictures.'

There was a serious side to this activity. Under the impact of the revolution in taste that had been started by Baudelaire and Manet, critics were beginning to look at the Old Masters in a new light. From 1850 onwards, people began to find parallels to contemporary art in the art of the past: schools and periods were revalued; the Italian primitives were admired after centuries of neglect; and painters who had fallen into obscurity were rediscovered, the two most important being Vermeer and El Greco. Vermeer, for example, began to be noticed in France between 1855 and 1860 by Maxime du Camp, Gautier, and Étienne Thoré, who published a study of Vermeer in 1866. This was followed by books and articles by Henry Havard, Verhaeren and Proust's friend, the art-critic Jean-Louis Vaudoyer, who in 1921, on the occasion of the exhibition of Dutch pictures at the Jeu de Paume, wrote an article for *L'Opinion* that moved Proust to write: 'Ever since I saw the View of Delft at the Museum in the Hague, I knew I had seen the most beautiful picture in the world. In *Du Côté de chez Swann*, I couldn't keep myself from having Swann work on a study of Vermeer. I hardly dared hope that you would render such justice to this wonderful master.' Proust went to see the exhibition; and the effort nearly caused his death.

El Greco, who was first praised by Gautier, and later admired by Huysmans, Montesquiou and Maurice Barrès (one of the originals of Bergotte), received very much the same treatment. Proust was deeply disappointed to miss the El Greco exhibition of 1908.

Inspired perhaps by Robert de Montesquiou's example, and assisted by friends like Marie Nordlinger and Jacques-Emile Blanche, Proust now began to take an interest in contemporary painting. There was a fairly wide range in the homes of his acquaintances. Madame Straus had Boudins and Monets, including his *Bras de Seine, près Giverny*; Antoine Bibesco collected Vuillards; Blanche had Renoirs and Fantin-Latours; and Montesquiou owned Helleus, Boldinis, Whistlers and Monticellis, as well as numerous portraits of himself. Proust was not yet a chronic invalid, and still kept more or less normal hours. He was able, therefore, to go to exhibitions and galleries. With Marie Nordlinger, he visited Durand-Ruel's, where they would look at a Manet, a Lautrec or a new Monet. But, after 1902, when he developed the habit of sleeping by day and working at night, he could no longer move about so freely, and missed seeing important shows by Gustave Moreau, Monticelli, Blanche and Sargent. He only just managed to summon up enough strength to attend the big Whistler retrospective in 1905.

Whistler was a particular favourite of his; and he would not hear a word said against the painter. On 24 June 1905, nine days after going to the Whistler exhibition, he wrote to Marie Nordlinger:

You know that at present the artistic élite of France are having a frightful reaction against Whistler. He is regarded as a man of exquisite taste who, because of it, was able to pass himself off as a great painter when he was nothing of the kind. Jacques Blanche ... has expressed the same opinion with more fairness and some warmth. It is not at all my own. If the man who painted the Venices in turquoise, the Amsterdams in topaz, the Britannies in opal, if the portraitist of Miss Alexander, the painter of the room with the rose-strewn curtains, and above all, the sails at night belonging to Messrs Vanderbilt and Freer (why does one see only the sail and not the boat?) is not a great painter, one can only believe there never was one.

Proust's admiration for Whistler, and also for the painter's arch-enemy, Ruskin, led him to seek some form of reconciliation between the two. In a letter to Marie Nordlinger, he wrote:

Ruskin and Whistler were mistaken about each other because their systems were opposed. But there is one truth, and they both saw it. Even in the action against Ruskin, Whistler said, 'You say I painted this picture in a few hours. But actually I painted it with the experience of my whole life.' But at that very moment Ruskin was writing to Rosetti, 'I prefer the things you do quickly, immediately, your rough sketches, to what you work over. What you work at you spend, say, six months in doing; but what you sketch at one swoop is the expression of years of dreams, of love, and of experience.' On this level the two stars strike the same point with a ray perhaps hostile, but identical.[6]

This interesting letter shows that Proust was familiar with two separate but inter-related theories current among painters and critics in the eighteen-nineties. Firstly, with the gradual acceptance of Impressionism, people began to value the sketch rather than the finished work, and to prefer painterly qualities, as manifest in the artist's quick and apparently careless brushstrokes, to the meticulous finish of Ingres and the academic artists of the Salons. For this reason, the painters of the eighteenth century, Fragonard and Boucher, were reappraised. Secondly, critics tended to emphasize the autograph nature of an artist's painting. Brush-strokes were recognized as an artist's signature; and, as Whistler argued, this effect could only be achieved after a lifetime's experience. Elstir, who resembles Whistler in more aspects than in the sound of their names alone, likes to free himself of all pre-conceptions when he starts a painting. He wants his personality to be unconsciously expressed in his actions and his view-point. Monet, who also contributed to the character of Elstir's art, though not to his character as a human being, expressed a similar opinion when he said to Roger-Marx that 'my only virtue resides in my submission to instinct. Because I have re-discovered the powers of intuition and allowed them to predominate, I have been able to identify myself with the created world and absorb myself into it.'

Proust was probably only dimly aware of the significance of Whistler's and Monet's beliefs, which later critics have seen as the foundation of abstract art and action painting. He never had the opportunity to discuss such topics with the artists themselves. There is no record of his talking to Monet; and he met Whistler only on one memorable occasion. The meeting took place around 1897 in the salon of Méry Laurent, a cocotte who contributed a little to Odette. Whistler maintained that Ruskin knew nothing whatsoever about painting; but Proust was not put off; and in the end, as he later wrote, 'I made him speak a few kind words of Ruskin! And from which occasion I kept his charming grey gloves which I have since lost.'

The major figures in painting at the end of the century – except for Whistler, who must be counted among them, if only because of his influence on painters and writers on both sides of the channel – somehow escaped Proust. But he did get to know a number of minor, and not so minor, painters through the salons that he attended as a young man. He knew portraitists like Helleu, Boldini, Jacques-Emile Blanche; genre painters like Jean Béraud, who was his second in his duel with Jean Lorain; cartoonists and illustrators like Sem and Forain; and the *avant-garde*, as represented by the Nabis and the Symbolists.

His range of acquaintances and friends in the art world was to some extent limited, as he tended to meet artists through society, when reputations were made or in the making, and not as Baudelaire or Zola had done, when artists were still struggling to gain some form of recognition. Thus, during the year in which Proust risked severe illness to attend the Whistler exhibition, Gertrude Stein was attending the Salon d'Automne and striking up friendships with Matisse and Picasso.

Proust believed that the main danger for an artist was not rejection and lack of recognition but too much social success. In the salons he saw writers and painters frittering away their talent, and knew that he himself faced very much the same dangers. When he came to depict the character of a great artist, he made Bergotte choose between society and art, and Elstir break with society in order to realize his ambitions as an artist.

Jacques-Emile Blanche was typical of the kind of painter whom he met in society. They had a common background. Both came from well-off middle-class homes; both went to the Lycée Condorcet; and both had fathers who were successful doctors. Blanche's father, Dr Antoine Blanche, ran a lunatic asylum at Auteuil, not far from the villa inhabited by Proust's uncle. Ten years older than Proust, Blanche had already acquired a reputation as a sharp-tongued young man. After one interchange between Blanche and Proust, Dr Blanche intervened: 'Now Jacques, you must try not to upset him. Pay no attention, my dear boy, keep absolutely calm. Jacques does not mean a word he's saying. Just sip a glass of cold water and count up to a hundred!'

Because of their age difference, Proust and Blanche only began to meet in 1891 at the salons of Madame Straus and Princess Mathilde; and they did not really come to know one another until 1892, the year in which Blanche's famous portrait of Proust was first exhibited. Their friendship was broken by Montesquiou, who picked a quarrel with Blanche; and the different positions they adopted over the Dreyfus case drove them further apart. They came together again, however, after an interval of almost twenty years; and Blanche was among the first to publicize the merits of *A la Recherche*. He also took the risk of persuading Proust to write an introduction to his first volume of *Propos de Peintre*, which was published in 1919. Proust maintained that Blanche's development as an artist had been endangered by his social activities. Only by withdrawing from the social world had Blanche found time for his work, though the consequence was that his talents had not been properly appreciated. Blanche felt that these opinions could be applied more accurately to Proust himself; but he allowed the introduction to appear. In his memoirs he was at pains to point out that he had confined his social activities to England, where he was a frequent visitor, and that in France he had dedicated himself to painting.

Blanche was more than just an able portraitist. He seems to have had a deep understanding of the inner character of writers and fellow painters. His portraits of Proust, James and Hardy, for example, have left their mark; and today it is almost impossible not to think of Proust in the image recorded by Blanche – the young man with the white face, staring black eyes and smooth black hair parted in the middle, an orchid in his button-hole, and the dapper clothes. Blanche's memoirs of painters and writers have proved equally lasting. Unlike Proust, he really knew the great artists of his own time; and Proust must have gained valuable insight into painting from his meetings with Blanche. But they were both too clever, too self-seeking, and too observant of each other's faults to become close friends; and it is safe to assume that Blanche did not contribute much to the character of Elstir as he emerges in the latter volumes of *A la Recherche*, though Proust may have had him in mind when he sketched Elstir as the painter nicknamed 'Biche' by the Verdurins in *Du Côté de chez Swann*.

Among the artists whom Blanche must have talked about to Proust was Degas, in the eighteen-nineties a venerable and awesome figure, respected by young up-and-coming painters and by traditionalists alike, and generally feared for his trenchant criticisms. Perhaps Proust thought of Degas when he wrote of Elstir that, 'failing society that was endurable, he lived in isolation with a savagery which fashionable people called pose and ill-breeding, public authorities a recalcitrant spirit, his neighbours madness, his family selfishness and pride'. Degas exhibited many of these characteristics; but his isolation was caused by old age, failing eye-sight, and mounting dissatisfaction with the changing world around him. He did not, as Elstir had done, choose to isolate himself from society in order to achieve artistic freedom. Degas never had any difficulty in applying himself to his work. From a fairly early age, he built up a protective barrier against intruders, which later earned him the reputation of being a recluse and a misogynist.

That side of Degas's character can be exaggerated. He could, of course, be crotchety and difficult, and was known to have a biting tongue; but he was also a well read, cultivated man, who took a deep interest in the art of past and present, and often showed considerable kindness to his fellow painters. Towards the end of the nineteenth century, he occupied a central rôle in the artistic world, looked up to and admired by such artists as Forain, Blanche, Boldini, Helleu, Lucien Daudet and Tissot, all artists, with the exception of

Tissot, who were known to Proust personally. He moved in a social world similar to Proust's; and they had many acquaintances and friends in common.

For example, Degas knew Charles Haas, Proust's chief model for Swann – friend perhaps is scarcely the right word. In his letters, he refers to Haas as 'an idler', 'a dancer' and 'utterly contrived'. 'Haas may arrive in eight or ten days,' he wrote to his friend Bartholomé, 'and the attitude he adopts towards me, whether to see me or cut me . . . will either be an effort for him or none at all. He knows that my sight is bad and that when I do see him, it makes no difference. Will he have a line of action and the courage to follow it? You know how droll ladies' men are with other men.'[7]

Degas also knew another model for Swann, Charles Ephrusi, the editor of the fashionable and influential art magazine, the *Gazette des Beaux Arts*.

His closest friends were the Halévys; and, before the Dreyfus case erupted, he dined with them so often that he was regarded as part of the family. Daniel Halévy was Proust's contemporary. They were both at the Condorcet; and, while he was still a schoolboy, Daniel began his Boswellian notes of the great painter's conversation. A typical dinner party at the Halévys, like one recorded in December 1896, was liable to include Degas, Blanche, Fernard Gregh, Louis de la Salle, and Robert Dreyfus. The last three were all schoolfriends of Proust and, with Daniel Halévy, all associated in the little review called *Le Banquet*, to which Proust contributed, and which had been born in the salon of the Halévys' cousin, Madame Straus.

Despite his reputation as a misogynist, Degas enjoyed the company of fashionable and intelligent Parisian beauties; and here again his path crossed that of Proust, who in his youth was liable to become infatuated with women far beyond his reach, like the famous cocotte, Laure Hayman. Degas, for example, was as fascinated as everyone else by Madame Howland, a clever and well-born Parisian whose beauty dazzled the salons and whose social success survived an unfortunate marriage to an American. Before she paid one of her rare visits to America, Degas wrote to Ludovic Halévy: 'I just learned from her own lips of the departure of our beautiful friend. But grief was immediately followed by a desire to laugh at your farewell preparations made so far in advance . . . So our beautiful friend is coldly sad and I can guarantee that the three men, who will be at Le Havre to the minute at the appointed hour, will have difficulty in not shedding a tear. But that must not be arranged in advance.'[8] Madame Howland never lacked a male following. She was admired by Haas and Montesquiou; and Proust dedicated to her a sketch that he wrote for the *Revue Blanche*. In

Le Cercle de la rue Royale; picture by James Jacques Joseph Tissot. In the doorway, Charles Haas.

Le Temps retrouvé, the duchesse de Guermantes defends Madame Howland against the snipings of a rival hostess: 'Why, of course, Madame Howland had all the men in her salon, and your friend was trying to lure them to her own!'

In their different ways, Degas and Proust were also devoted to Madame Straus; and, to see her, Degas was prepared to cancel at the last moment an appointment with another friend. 'It is the only day that this person, in demand on all sides, has free,' he wrote apologetically. He had met Madame Straus out shopping; and 'I was dragged along to a fashionable dressmaker,' he explained, 'where I assisted at the fitting of a most effective toilette.' He was on good enough terms with Madame Straus to be critical of her portrait, painted by Elie Delaunay shortly after her first husband's death, which, when exhibited, was widely praised. 'It's studio mourning,' commented Degas. 'She is weeping on the dado.'

Proust was a frequent visitor to Madame Straus's salon, where he must certainly have seen Degas. It seems improbable that they talked much; but Proust evidently used to hear the latest Degas stories. In a letter to Madame Straus he repeats one of the painter's most telling remarks. 'Perhaps you have heard it,' he writes. 'It comes from Degas, reported by Forain (not to me!), and it's about Gustave Moreau: "He taught us that the Gods wore watch chains." I don't, however, find it at all wonderful, and I find that it smacks rather too much of Forain to come from Degas.'[9]

If Proust kept clear of Degas, he had very good reasons. Degas disliked homosexuals and anybody remotely resembling an aesthete; and after the Dreyfus trial he gave up seeing his Jewish friends. Montesquiou, who admired Degas's work, once made the mistake of greeting the painter at an exhibition at the Champs de Mars. He was standing proudly before a pale green bed he had designed with the help of his protégé Gallé. 'Do you think you will conceive better children in an apple-green bed?' said Degas. 'Watch out, M. de Montesquiou; taste is a vice.' 'Taste,' he said on another occasion, stamping his foot, 'It doesn't exist. An artist makes beautiful things without being aware of it. Aesthetes beat their brows and say to themselves, "How can I find a pretty shape for a chamberpot?" Poor creatures, their chamberpots may be works of art but they will immediately induce a retention of urine. They will look at their pots and say to all their friends: "Look at my chamberpot. Isn't it pretty?" No more art. No more art. No more art.'[10]

Whether Proust heard these opinions it is impossible to say; but in a sense, he might have approved of the thought behind them. Proust had taste, or what the French call sensibility; but he was not an aesthete of the type of Huysmans, Montesquiou, Wilde, and Haas. He himself led a life that was the reverse of aesthetic. Though his style might be grand – he stayed at the best hotels, gave dinners at the Ritz, and invariably over-tipped – his own background was confused to the point of ugliness. His clothes became more and more untidy; his rooms were chaotic; and he was an accumulator of souvenirs rather than a collector of works of art. 'If I were rich,' he wrote to Madame Catusse, an interior decorator and antique dealer, 'I should not try to buy masterpieces that I should leave to museums, but those pictures that retain the odour of a city or the dampness of a church, and that, like curios, hold their illusion as much by association with an idea, as in themselves.'

He had no desire to improve the collection of odds and ends that he had inherited from his parents. 'As for pictures,' he wrote, again to Madame Catusse, 'I don't want to see much of any of them except the small and oldish shepherdess with the monstrous, well-bred air of a Spanish infanta, the portrait of Mother, and my portrait by Blanche . . . William Morriss said, "Have nothing in your apartment except things you have found beautiful or which you have judged as beautiful." A chest, a table, even if they are ugly, even if they are useless, still evoke an idea of utility. But a picture that isn't satisfying is a horror.'

Taste, then, was not Proust's vice; and on that subject he would have agreed with Degas. But, when he came to create the great contemporary painter as personified by Elstir, he did not look to Degas as his model, a natural choice, or to Monet, because he did not know him personally, but to more congenial company, to Helleu and Vuillard. This choice was to some extent forced upon him. After the Dreyfus trial, Degas would have been impossible; Monet lived most of the year at Giverny and, in the eighteen-nineties, when his work began to be a commercial success, spent much of his time travelling. Helleu, on the other hand, had reached the peak of his career during the years in which Proust's taste and knowledge of art were formed – roughly 1885–1905 – and was highly regarded by people whose judgements Proust respected[11]; while Vuillard, besides being an extremely intelligent man, was one of the most talented artists associated with the *Revue Blanche*.

Helleu's most influential patron was Proust's mentor, Robert de Montesquiou. They met between 1886 and 1887; and Montesquiou, attracted by Helleu's elegance and his romantic temperament, had introduced his protégé to the Faubourg Saint-Germain. Helleu's portraits – pastels, etchings and drawings –

were immensely popular, particularly with fashionable ladies; and he was never short of commissions, among them being a request by Montesquiou to paint blue hydrangeas for his house at Versailles. In 1913 Montesquiou published a book on Helleu that remains the only full-length study of the artist. 'Man of a sole God: art;' he wrote, 'of a sole master: taste; of a sole woman: the charming model who lends the elegant life of her body to all his compositions ...' Luckily for Helleu, who might have suffocated under too close a relationship with Montesquiou, he had numerous admirers, both among his fellow artists and among art critics and contemporary writers – for example, the Goncourts, Octave Mirbeau, defender of the Impressionists, Huysmans, and Blanche, who devoted a beautifully written essay to him in *Propos de Peintre*.[12]

Here Blanche recalls Helleu's influence on himself and on his fellow art students, Alfred Stevens, Boldini, and Forain:

According to us, young art students, his juniors, he was the cleverest, the most gifted of us all; Manet, Monet and Renoir thought so too. Furthermore, we thought he was as intelligent as he was witty. We were captivated by his verbal outpourings, a mixture of enthusiasm and disdain; we were drawn to this fanatical painter by the sureness of his judgements on art. What wouldn't we have done to have had a chance to see the oil studies he kept in his mysterious lodgings ... where no one was allowed in except those redheads with greenish skins, mistresses and slaves, who used to say, 'If you knew what he has in there. He is a genius. You can't refuse anything to a man like that.'

Though Helleu could be impetuous, quarrelsome, and cruel in his judgements, he won the respect of the artistic world. Boldini, Sargent, Whistler, Sem, Rodin, Monet thought highly of him; so did Tissot, who gave him a diamond for his engravings. Degas admired his draughtsmanship and tried to persuade him to exhibit alongside the Impressionists; and, when fashion had turned against him, Forain did his best to sustain Helleu's belief in himself. Critics and writers treated him with no less respect. Edmond de Goncourt wrote an introduction to his exhibition of 1896; and Helleu's arrival at the salon of Princess Mathilde is recorded in the Goncourts' *Journals*:

At the end of the evening Helleu arrived. Despite the cold he had spent the whole day at Versailles painting the statues half-buried by snow. He spoke of the beauty of the spectacle and the peculiarities of the arctic world. Talking of the craze for painting stained-glass windows, he confessed to having shared this taste and said that he had worked at Chartres, Rheims, and Notre Dame. He had spent every morning there for nearly two years, exploring every corner of the towers where those angels seem to be hanging in the sky and flapping their wings to prevent themselves from falling down. He told us on feast days when the choir had been chanting, the organ thundering, and the bells pealing, he had waved his brush in the air and painted as though he were the conductor of an orchestra, quite mad with excitement.

It was these paintings that led Proust to say that Monet had fixed for ever the exterior of Rouen cathedral, but for interiors he did not know of any so beautiful as those by the great painter, Helleu. Octave Mirbeau was equally impressed and wrote, with typical Gallic flourish: 'The Cathedral of Rheims, serene, peaceful; the pillars rising like prayers . . . A deep religious silence fills the deserted aisles, and the rose-window, at the end of the choir opens out softly.' Other writers began to notice his work; and one of his first pictures to be accepted by the Salon, *La Gare et le Tunnel des Batignolles*, was praised by J-K Huysmans. Monet also liked his work and, to Helleu's delight, asked him for a canvas.

With these admirers to his credit, it would have been surprising if Helleu and Proust had never met. In the event, it was Montesquiou who introduced them at Madeleine Lemaire's. Helleu's taste, his articulateness, and his lively conversation no doubt appealed to Proust. In return, Proust was as usual flattering and almost excessively polite. In 1909, he wrote, rather naïvely, to Madame Straus: 'Fancy me having been indiscreet enough to tell him that a picture of Versailles, a sketch, was the best thing he had done. A few days later it arrived. I am so embarrassed by his kindness that I don't know what to do, and I should like to find something nice that would please him with which to express my gratitude.' Proust's solution of the problem was to return the painting, and then agree to take it back after it had been inscribed with a dedication.

Proust probably saw Helleu most often on his return to Cabourg in 1907, and on his subsequent visits. In a letter from Cabourg, dated 1909, he wrote to Madame Straus that he was glad she was seeing Helleu: 'I know that it makes him very happy and I should think that you would like him. Even physically he is charming, and Montesquiou was right when he said that few descendants of those who were guillotined have as much "breeding" as the descendant of the Convention . . . He has the simple nature of the true artist, and if very few people can make him happy, of those very few, all do.'[13] Proust visited Helleu on his yacht at Deauville; and their discussions formed the basis of the Narrator's talks with Elstir. The subject of their conversations is largely a matter of guesswork – Proust's correspondence with Helleu has not been published; but in a letter to the marquis de Lauris from Cabourg, dated 1907, he wrote, 'Sem and Helleu, both very *intelligent*, have, each separately, tried to convince me that primitive art was no good, that there is no painting prior to Rubens, etc., and I therefore went with one of them to see the Boucher tapestries at Balleroy . . .' As a pupil of Ruskin and a devoted admirer of the Gothic style and early Italian painting, Proust can hardly have agreed with Helleu, but there is no doubt that the painter's manner and conversation were incorporated into the character of Elstir. Both Helleu's intellectual qualities and his rhetorical gifts made him a director of contemporary taste; and he was as much responsible as the Goncourts for reviving an interest in eighteenth-century art. Like Charles Ephrusi, he was recognized as a connoisseur and expert, whose advice was widely sought in questions of decoration. According to Blanche,

Helleu created a style that lasted twenty years . . . He started a revolution amongst the dealers in paintings by the primitives. The Wildensteins were launched on their journeys down the great roads of France in their hunt for treasures guarded by the aristocracy in their castles. The old houses of the Faubourg Saint-Germain let slip their wares and Helleu pushed them into the hands of rich foreigners.[14]

As early as 1866, Whistler had devised colour schemes for interior decoration, and had turned his dining-room into a symphony in blue, and his drawing-room into a harmony of pale yellow and white. Helleu took Whistler's clean, uncluttered interiors a stage further. He banished the damasks and gold-and-red-plush of the Third Empire, and brought back the whites and silks of the eighteenth century. He was deeply fastidious. According to his daughter, Madame Howard-Johnston, he once rubbed soot into a newly-covered chair because its tone was too harsh, and he felt that it needed a patina. Proust once described a visit to Helleu's studio:

One day when our discussions were unfinished Helleu invited me to continue them back at his apartment. He lived in the Rue Emile-Menier . . . in an apartment high up in the building, with windows looking on to the gardens of Thiers Foundation and on to a vast expanse of sky. He worked in a big room bathed in light, decorated with empty eighteenth-century wooden frames, placed along a white wainscoting. An Empire piano on the mahogany of which sprang some butterflies in golden bronze, acted as a prop for card-board boxes and portfolios full of drawings and dry-points. There were some ancient chairs which seemed so fragile and so pure in form that one hesitated to sit on them. A number of canvases were stacked one behind each other, with their fronts to the wall so that one could only see their stretchers. And there was an Empire Jardinier full of wilting roses.[15]

Proust failed to mention the white Saxe porcelain placed against white walls, the white marble chimney-piece with the bust of Marie-Antoinette, the chairs decorated with lyres, the ancient harp, and the eighteenth-century globe which came from the Ministère de la Marine.

Helleu's white spilled on to his canvases. Like Whistler before him, Helleu tended to orchestrate his paintings around a predominant colour, muted with white. In his paintings of the gardens at Versailles, the trees form a copper-coloured background; the statues are painted in a mixture of pale mauves and browns; and there is a Monet-like pale mauve sky. His regattas are characterized by the use of pinks and creamy whites. Blanche noted that 'silver, the metal which reflects colours in all their purity, became for him a symbol'. Helleu wrote of a sitter he was particularly pleased with because she had 'grey hair, grey pearls and a grey dress'; and to Montesquiou he once complained: 'To think that at the Beaux Arts when I was fifteen I was the only one who liked Manet and Monet, until sixty of my friends followed in my footsteps. Now they paint everything violet, but not me.'

A passionate student of French art before the Revolution, Helleu used to say that his ambition was to be, 'a minor master like those of the eighteenth century'. He was particularly fond of Watteau's drawings, notably the ones in the Louvre; and he once etched his wife admiring the drawings from the d'Ymécourt collection. Inevitably, critics began to see his work in eighteenth-century terms. In 1886, an article in *Le Courrier des Consulats* compared his drawings with those by the 'charming masters of the eighteenth century'; Goncourt called him 'our Watteau'; and Degas is supposed to have gone one further, and labelled Helleu a '*Watteau à vapeur*'. Degas solemnly denied this remark, though it is attributed to him by Daniel Halévy and the duchesse de Clermont-Tonnerre amongst others.[16] In any event it is a play on the words '*bateau à vapeur*' or steam-boat, and refers to Helleu's passion for boats as much as to his debt to Watteau. The remark reappears in *A la Recherche* where Saniette argues that he prefers Helleu to Elstir, because Elstir is just a 'steam Watteau'. 'Old, old as the hills,' snorts Monsieur Verdurin. 'I've had that served up to me for years.'

Helleu's talents as an artist are best seen in his drawings and dry-points. His virtuosity, the flourish of his lines, his delicate touch, is indeed reminiscent of the eighteenth-century masters. It is a technique ideally suited to the portraiture of women. His particular 'trick' was to concentrate on the hair and head-dresses of the ladies whom he drew, leaving the rest of their features under-stated. Delicate white faces peer out from under a mass of dark curls or typically broad-brimmed floppy Edwardian hats. He came to be regarded as the arbiter of feminine elegance; and the great couturiers of his day, Félix, Doucet and Worth, used to consult him for his views. It has been said of Helleu that, having seen one of his dry-points, 'young people lengthened their figures, pulled back their hair, studied the supple gestures of the wrist, placing the hand on top of a tall parasol in the manner of Marie-Antoinette'. Society ladies, from the comtesse Greffulhe to Consuelo Duchess of Marlborough, were only too happy to invite him to stay with them and commission him to paint their portraits. Although Edmond de Goncourt noted 'his completely feminine charm, like that of certain scented, lace-trimmed feline dandies', Helleu was no homosexual. Among his fellow artists he had a reputation as a lady's man. When he was a student Blanche recalled, 'Marie Renard who was a model for Manet and Berthe Morisot, posed for him, and Olympia, that strange tubercular and neurotic girl kept house for him, sharing his pleasures and his despairs (for he was never satisfied with himself); darning his silk socks, washing his sleeves and cuffs . . . And he sold nothing. What disinterested labour, thought Olympia.'

In 1886, after a courtship lasting for two years, Helleu was allowed to marry the beautiful sixteen-year-old Alice Guérin. She was his model in many of his drawings and dry-points, her tall thin figure being ideally suited to Helleu's art. In *A la Recherche*, the Narrator is at first rather horrified by Madame Elstir's appearance, and fails to understand what the great painter can see in her. He notes with amusement that Elstir hurriedly hides a drawing of a young actress when his wife enters the studio. Later, the Narrator begins to regard Madame Elstir in a more favourable light; Madame Verdurin, on the other hand, remains notably vitriolic about the painter's wife, calling her a prostitute, though not in so many words, and blaming her for having separated Elstir from 'the little clan'. At this point, however, the resemblance breaks down. Madame Helleu was liked by everyone. Montesquiou was an admirer and his monograph on Helleu is dedicated to her.[17]

Apart from his taste for women, Helleu's greatest passion was for boats. He had been born at Vannes; and his father was a ship's captain before he became a Custom's officer. 'I ought to have been a sailor,' Helleu used to say. 'But I love only Paris; voyages make me home-sick. I am a brute civilized by painting.' Blanche used to imagine him as permanently dressed in sailor's clothes – in his youth, a blue shirt and beret with a red pompom; later, in beach clothes or the oarsman's straw-boater; later still, in the dress of a yachtsman at Cowes. 'I don't care about getting rich,' he used to maintain, 'but if I had a boat I would paint nothing but seascapes.' Eventually, he managed to acquire a boat himself, *L'Etoile*, which he kept at Deauville or at Cowes. One of his proudest moments occurred at Cowes in 1904, when Edward VII, aboard the royal yacht, was the first to raise his hat to Helleu, standing on the deck of his much humbler craft.

During the same year, Helleu was appointed a Chevalier of the Légion d'Honneur. His work was exhibited and praised in London and New York; and among his most notable commissions was to paint the ceiling of New York's Grand Central Station. For one reason or another, Helleu remained dissatisfied with his work. Of his paintings, which he rarely showed, he wrote to Blanche,

If they weren't thrown in the stove or into the sea it's thanks to you, my old friend. You urged me to show my pictures. Pride and the knowledge of the uselessness of trying to make something of oneself these days prevented me. Now that I have become a solitary old man, I think some of my paintings are good. But can one judge one's own worth? You were offended by my criticism of your paintings. If I have hurt your feelings, remember that I was harder on myself than on others.

Proust seems to have understood Helleu's sadness and isolation in latter years. Elstir, we learn, is one of the few people to mourn the death of Monsieur Verdurin. His death 'signified to him the disappearance of one of the last traces of the perishable social framework, falling into limbo as swiftly as the fashions in dress which form part of it – that framework which supports an art and certifies its authenticity like the revolution which, in destroying the elegances of the eighteenth century, would have distressed a painter of *fêtes galantes* or afflicted Renoir when Montmartre and the Moulin de la Galette disappeared'. Whistler and Monet had educated the public to appreciate Elstir's art. When Monsieur Verdurin died, 'it was as though part of the beauty of his work had disappeared with some of that consciousness of beauty which had until then existed in the world'.[18]

Edouard Vuillard's work has withstood the death of his admirers and changes of taste better than that of Helleu, partly because he was a more intelligent artist and partly because he was more modern-minded and less worried about 'taste'. Like Helleu, he is what the French call a *'petit maître'*; and, like Helleu's, his art derives to some extent from Whistler. Whistler's famous portrait of his mother, reduced to a tenth of its actual size, could pass for an early Vuillard. Proust came to know him either through Antoine Bibesco, who was one of his

Proust and Painting

Rouen Cathedral, by Claude Monet. Monet exhibited twenty views of the west façade of Rouen Cathedral at Durand-Ruel's in 1895. The critics were generally favourable and most of the pictures were sold. Pissarro, Degas and Cézanne admired the exhibition. Proust was particularly impressed, partly because of the beauty of the pictures and partly because of the subject's associations.

above: Whistler, by Paul Helleu. A portrait of 1897.
top left: Madame Chéruit, the celebrated dress-designer, in a fur collar; Helleu.

above: Robert de Montesquiou, by Helleu; a dry-point signed and dated 1913.
top right: Madame Helleu looking at Watteau drawings in the Louvre; Helleu.
opposite: Helleu at his easel, by Giovanni Boldini. Helleu and Boldini were old friends and rivals.

An oak-leaf vase by Emile
Gallé, c. 1890, signed. Proust
admired Gallé's work and
mentions him in *A la Recherche*.
He used to commission work
from Gallé's studio as presents
for friends.

Young woman undressing, by Boldini.

above: The Client, gouache by
Jean-Louis Forain.

Madame Helleu and her son
Jean on board a yacht,
by Helleu.

Poster for 'La Revue Blanche', by Pierre Bonnard. After the closure of 'Le Banquet', Proust and several of his fellow contributors were invited to write for 'La Revue Blanche'. Bonnard and Edouard Vuillard were both associated with the *Revue*.

opposite : An interior by Edouard Vuillard.

earliest admirers, or by way of the offices of the *Revue Blanche*. In 1893, after the closure of *Le Banquet*, Proust and a number of his friends were invited to contribute to the *Revue Blanche*, an influential review started by two wealthy Polish brothers, Thadée and Alexandre Natanson. Verlaine, Mallarmé, Barrès, Jean Lorain, Gregh, Léon Blum, Jacques Baignères and the young André Gide all wrote for the review. The Natansons were among the first to take an interest in the Nabis, particularly in Bonnard, who designed the famous poster of the *Revue Blanche*, and in Vuillard, who was commissioned by Alexander Natanson to paint ten decorative panels of children playing in the parks of Paris for his dining-room, which overlooked the Bois de Boulogne. Vuillard, a former pupil of the Condorcet, a spawning-ground of the Nabis, must have met Proust on numerous occasions. In the late eighteen-nineties, Vuillard used to attend the salon of Princess Hélène Bibesco, whose guests had included musicians like Liszt, Wagner and Debussy, writers like Anatole France and Maeterlinck, and painters like Puvis de Chavannes, Bonnard, and Redon. In 1902, when Proust dined with Antoine Bibesco at Armenonville in the Bois de Boulogne, Vuillard made a sketch of the party, which Proust tried to buy. The sketch, he wrote, was 'a unique point of intersection between Vuillard's admirable talent which has so often kindled my memory and one of the most delightful and perfect hours of my life'.

The Normandy coast in Proust's day was the home of many artists; and, besides calling on Helleu, Proust used to visit Vuillard. From Cabourg, in 1907, he wrote to Reynaldo Hahn: 'I went yesterday to see Vuillard, who was wearing a blue workman's overalls (a blue which was a little too delicate)'. Proust thought it was a music-hall outfit; and the comic aspect of the occasion was further underlined by Vuillard's intensity and his manner of speech. 'He would say, "a chap like Giotto, don't you think, or even a chap like Titian, don't you think, knew just as much as Monet, don't you think; a chap like Raphael . . ." He said "chap" once every twenty seconds. But he is a rare being.' Proust remembered Vuillard's colloquial manner of discussing great artists when he described Elstir talking about the sculptures on certain Romanesque and Gothic churches.

Vuillard's parents were less prosperous than Proust's but he, too, came from a home dominated by a tender and affectionate mother. She formed the centre of his life, and appears in many of his early paintings, either seated in an arm-chair or at work, bending over an ironing-board, or occupied with other domestic duties. After her husband's death, when Vuillard was fifteen, his mother took

Salome dancing, by Gustave Moreau. Proust was a keen admirer of Moreau's work. The mythological Elstirs, which the Narrator sees on his first visit to the Guermantes, are based on paintings by Moreau. Proust wrote a long and penetrating study on this painter in *Contre Sainte-Beuve*.

to making corsets. Her father was a textile manufacturer; and one of the artist's uncles was engaged in the same line of business. Thus he grew up surrounded by multi-coloured fabrics, lengths of cloth and ribbons; and it is not surprising that his early pictures should resemble a patchwork quilt, or to use the famous aphorism of Maurice Denis, 'a flat surface covered with colours arranged in a certain order'.

Although Vuillard was full of self-doubts, and would ask his friends whether it was right to earn a living as a painter, he seems never to have had to struggle for recognition. He coasted through life from one fruitful meeting to the next. At the Condorcet he met Denis and X-L Roussell; at the Academy Julien, Sérusier and Bonnard; and through the *Revue Blanche* many future patrons. Lugné-Poe, another ex-pupil of the Condorcet, who founded the *Théâtre de L'Oeuvre* mainly with the view to putting on Ibsen and Maeterlinck, provided Vuillard with a number of commissions. The name of his theatre was supplied by Vuillard, because, says Lugné-Poe, he was 'the most interested in the theatre and the best judge of these matters ... His scenery for Rosmersholm stamped the note of intimacy and distinction on our set. Vuillard surpassed himself in ingenuity and economic invention in creating atmosphere and scenic decoration.'

'The outstanding quality of his painting,' wrote Denis of his friend, 'is intelligence.' Among the Nabis, he was regarded as the most thoughtful member of their group. He used to speak 'little and slowly as though carefully seeking the exact word to express his thoughts', wrote Pierre Veber. Roger-Marx, who knew him well, drew a verbal picture of the artist:

There is noise around us, the noise of conversation, the noise of wind. Yet we are alone. The dialogue is almost a monologue, for when he seems to be answering me, he could be more fairly described as answering himself. Words rise slowly out of the depths of his nature, painfully even, but they are the right ones. He regulates and explains them by gestures. His speech is broken by frequent intervals, so anxious is he to express his true meaning. He twists his fingers nervously or raises his hand to his brow ... around us reign only calm and disinterestedness.[19]

In Proust's portrait of Elstir, there is a good deal of Vuillard's manner, a more measured tone than Helleu adopted. Proust was probably too occupied with society to follow the heated discussions at the *Revue Blanche*, where, as Thadée Natanson tells us:

Sérusier struggled wildly in search of words which could convey even part of his ideas. Vallotton's anger and sarcasm were deep and biting like his woodcuts. Roussel swam into such deep waters that his listeners were not alone in losing their footing. Contrasted with these Vuillard and Bonnard were reserved. Distrusting anybody's influence, including his own over other people, Bonnard loved to contradict. Vuillard took in everything and maintained his good humour, but he could at rare intervals break out into a rage which shook him and made his face as red as his beard.

The Nabis and the Symbolists were the intellectual and artistic avant-garde of Proust's youth; but just how far Proust followed their ideas, or understood their works, is hard to estimate. He was certainly acquainted with Maurice Denis's *Theories*; and in his foreword to Blanche's *Propos de Peintre*, quotes Denis's famous aphorism. Vuillard expressed his views on Proust and art in a letter to Maurice Chernowitz: 'In a worldly manner which took nothing away from his charm, one quickly came to believe in the sincerity of his interest in the arts. I believe he liked painting as much as literature. He seemed to me to really appreciate Vermeer and from several letters I had from him I kept the memory of a person who was attentive and much more anxious to understand than to make clever ironic remarks like the world he frequented.'[20]

Although in later life he seldom went out, Proust showed an uncanny ability to discover what was going on in the artistic world around him. In his letters to Blanche and Walter Berry, he mentions Picasso as a painter 'whose work and person is not unknown to me'. He saw Picasso's cubist paintings almost by accident, late at night, at the home of a Chilean beauty, Madame Errazuriz,[21] and met Picasso himself at a memorable dinner party given by Violet and Sydney Schiff in honour of the Ballet Russe. Among the guests were Stravinsky and Joyce. In his preface to *Propos de Peintre*, Proust wrote of 'the great and admirable Picasso, who has concentrated all Cocteau's features into a portrait of such noble rigidity that, when I contemplate it, even the most enchanting Carpaccios in Venice tend to take a second place in my memory'.

As Juliette Monnin-Hornung has pointed out, this is an astonishing comparison, which throws some doubt on the sincerity of Proust's compliment.[22] Proust, however, had no illusions about his capacity to judge new art, and was well aware how easily one could make a fool of oneself by setting up as an authority. The duchesse de Guermantes shows her lack of sincerity when she observes that 'really the other day I was with the Grand Duchess in the Louvre and we happened to pass before Manet's Olympia. Nowadays nobody is in the least surprised by it. It looks just like an Ingres. And yet, heaven knows how many spears I've had to break for that picture which I don't altogether like but which is unquestionably the work of somebody.'

The Dowager marquise Zélia de Cambremer, who salivates at the mention of anything new, is even more ludicrous. '"I suppose you know Claude Monet's pictures of waterlilies," she asks the Narrator. "What a genius . . ."' On hearing the name of Poussin,

she produced six times in almost continuous succession that little smack of the tongue against the lips which serves to convey to the child who is misbehaving at once a reproach for having begun and a warning not to continue. 'In heaven's name, after a painter like Monet, who is an absolute genius, don't go and mention an old hack without a vestige of talent, like Poussin . . .' 'But, M. Degas assures us that he knows nothing more beautiful than the Poussins at Chantilly' [replies the Narrator]. 'Indeed? I don't know the ones at Chantilly', said Mme. de Cambremer, who had no wish to differ from Degas, 'but I can speak about the ones in the Louvre which are appalling.' 'He admires them immensely too.' 'I must look at them again. My impressions of them are rather distant,' she replied.[23]

Proust was particularly adroit at exposing the hypocrisy of those who pass judgements upon modern art. He warns against a hasty acceptance of the New and, at the same time, points out the danger of rejecting the New merely because it fails to resemble the Old. In several passages, he pleads for open-mindedness:

What artists call posterity is the posterity of the work of art. It is essential that the work . . . shall create its own posterity . . . No doubt one can easily imagine, by an illusion similar to that which makes everything on the horizon appear equidistant, that all the revolutions which have hitherto occurred in painting or in music did at least shew respect for certain rules, whereas that which immediately confronts us, be it impressionism, a striving after discord, an exclusive use of the Chinese scale, cubism, futurism or what you will, differs outrageously from all that have occurred before. Simply because those that have occurred before we are apt to regard as a whole, forgetting that a long process of assimilation has melted them into a continuous substance, varied of course but, taking as a whole, homogeneous, in which Hugo blends with Molière.[24]

This open-mindedness may perhaps be a form of evasion. When he was considering the work of his own day, Proust did not always trust his own judgement. But without his knowledge of earlier painters and paintings his great book might have been very different. The work of Turner, Monet, and Whistler undoubtedly helped shape his vision of the outside world; Blanche, Helleu, and Vuillard combined to produce the character of Elstir; Degas acted as a kind of *deus ex machina* in the world of art where Proust moved; and critics like Ruskin, Mâle and Montesquiou provided some of the aesthetic and intellectual background to the novelist's ideas about art and beauty. In return, he put into words some of the beauties of nature and man with an artistry and clarity that few writers have equalled; he provided insights into paintings and buildings that specialist writers on art can seldom achieve; he recorded the social history of the arts of his time; he created Elstir; and he scattered throughout his novel many observations and thoughts about art that are both original and stimulating.

Proust and the Nineteenth Century

B. G. Rogers

IT WOULD be foolish to attempt to chart the many and various literary influences brought to bear on the author of *A la Recherche du temps perdu*, from
early writers like Chateaubriand to naturalistic authors like Zola, without
turning this short essay into a work almost as long as Proust's novel itself.
What can, perhaps, be attempted is a review of some of the major traditions
that Proust absorbed and adapted; in many respects, *A la Recherche* is a masterly
synthesis of most of the conflicting aspirations of the nineteenth century; and
it is not difficult to catch traces of all the most important 'movements' and
'schools' operating between 1800 and 1900 in the story of Marcel's self-
discovery. Indeed, that long, rich and often anguished study of the growth
of the narrator's vocation to be a writer is achieved precisely through his confrontation with the works of artists both living and dead, and most particularly
with the novelists who preceded him and whom he is finally determined to
emulate.

But if *A la Recherche* is a summing up of the nineteenth century, it also opens
the door to most of the later developments in the novel of our own time. I
can perhaps best illustrate this backward and forward looking quality of the
work by tracing a line between two authors who at first sight seem to have
little in common with each other: the minor novelist and short story writer
Barbey d'Aurevilly, and the experimental novelist of our own day Nathalie
Sarraute. It seems a far cry from the overblown romantic prose of the *Diaboliques*, a set of six stories dealing with love, death and crimes of all kinds in the
Paris and Normandy of the eighteen–sixties, to the meticulous, disembodied
narratives of Madame Sarraute's novels, like *Martereau*, where nothing seems to
happen, where the plot disintegrates deliberately in the final pages, and the narrator asks himself whether all that he has been experiencing ever happened at all.
And yet a line can be drawn between them, by placing Proust in the centre,
and tracing, backwards, his debt to Barbey, and forwards his effect on Nathalie
Sarraute.

Proust made no secret of his liking for the works of Barbey d'Aurevilly;
and his name crops up in the novel in one of Marcel's conversations with
Albertine, where the future novelist turns critic and analyses a distinctive
characteristic which recurs in all the works of that writer. What Proust particularly noted, I think, in Barbey, was his ability to present a seemingly normal
situation and then to turn it inside out, revealing all kinds of hidden secrets,
memories and scandals behind the unassuming façades that he has first established. This preoccupation with the apparent and the real recurs at much greater

length in *A la Recherche*, and in fact becomes one of the major themes of the work, developing into the various characters' interest in lying, jealousy and their double, sometimes triple lives. And it is this very theme which gives animation to the works of Nathalie Sarraute, who takes it one stage further, and develops a theory of 'conversation and sub-conversation', where the meaning given to words has one set of resonances on the surface, and another beneath the surface, so that the apparent banality of a phrase, like the apparent banality of the situation in any one of the stories from the *Diaboliques*, may suddenly reveal another world unexpectedly and dangerously existing at another level.

That example, which it might be profitable to examine more closely in another context, was merely intended to show how Proust was affected by even minor writers in the nineteenth century, deepening themes which they treated, exploring them in relation to his own preoccupations and drawing them into the stuff of his own creation, while at the same time opening up paths for later novelists to explore in their own distinctive ways. So when we come to paint the general picture of Proust's literary heritage from the nineteenth century, we must not forget that he stands at the crossroads, as it were, and also looks resolutely forwards to some of the most original and experimental writing of today.

In one respect, however, I have no hesitation in placing Proust firmly in the nineteenth century. A broad, overall survey reveals it as a period that began in chaos, and which in both its literary and political history attempted to impose order and coherence on that chaos. It was a century which exploded into life with the French Revolution of 1789, saw the birth of romanticism, the school of 'art for art's sake', the realistic novel, symbolism and naturalism, all, in their way, attempts to give meaning and order to man and his aspirations. All of these various searchings for coherence are paralleled by the external history of the time, the quest for political stability, the choice and rejection of various forms of government, all operating against the background of the steadily advancing industrial revolution and the continued rise in importance of money and the bourgeoisie. It is also a period of time dominated by the presence, and subsequently by the memory, of one man, Napoléon Bonaparte; and it is no mere coincidence that the heroic stature of his achievements, and even of his failures, is reflected in many of the writers of that time. Hugo and Balzac are both titanic figures; Hugo attempted, like many others but with a greater measure of success, to write the modern French epic in his *Légende des Siècles*, once again an attempt to explain humanity in relation to its past and its future.

Balzac attempted to sum up all the characteristics of Restoration society in France, another quest for a perspective which would place modern man in an understandable framework, by explaining the forces at work in the new society which had taken the place of the disintegrating empire. His vast, ambitious series of interrelated novels, with their overall title *La Comédie Humaine* is, like Hugo's *Légende des Siècles*, a kind of 'summum', a project which seeks to embrace everything and to place everything in a coherent relationship with everything else. Zola, of course, carries on the same tradition, albeit in a cruder and over-simplified way, with his set of interconnecting novels, which chronicle the lives of a family in the Second Empire, under Napoléon's successor. And finally, not published in entirety until 1927, we have *A la Recherche du temps perdu*, one of whose aims is to paint a picture of the upper bourgeoisie and aristocracy which flourished right up until its virtual destruction, at least in its life-style as Proust records it, with the onset of the First World War. But *A la Recherche* goes further. It attempts to create a coherent set of aesthetic laws within a self-contained, some critics say 'circular', construction which justifies itself. One more link in the chain which stretches, it is not unjustifiable to say, from the centralizing forces of Napoléon's empire building right up to the polarizing 'laws' of Proust's novel of social, aesthetic and psychological observation. And in this respect, Proust is unquestionably a man of the nineteenth century.

Among his other literary forebears, I should briefly in this context mention Baudelaire and the Symbolist poets, one of whose central preoccupations was to map the hidden affinities connecting all phenomena, and to sum up the individual consciousness and experience in those terms. Indeed, the shift from a mainly socially orientated edifice like the *Comédie Humaine* to a mainly aesthetically preoccupied quest for order and explanation in, for example, Baudelaire's *Fleurs du mal* is itself reflected in Proust, whose own work merges the two, and presents Marcel's slow elaboration of an aesthetic code against the background of a chronicle of the social changes of his day. But what I wish to emphasize is the nature and stature of the attempt, the great, vaulting ambition behind all of the works I have been mentioning, an ambition, as Proust himself remarks when discussing Balzac, that gives a greater value to the novels as a whole than to any one of them taken individually, the whole, if you like, being greater than the sum of its parts. Now, Proust's novel was never conceived as a series of parts; but the desire to embrace the totality of his experience is very akin to the recurrent obsession of nineteenth-century writers to be all-embracing in one or another field. And in my opinion, Proust is the greatest of them all, since he comes nearest to achieving that aim.

ANOTHER tradition, not originating in the nineteenth century, but fostered and developed by it in the writers of the romantic period, is the preoccupation with the self, a tradition of introspective self-observation and examination, that stems largely from the *Confessions* of Jean-Jacques Rousseau. When one opens the novel at its first page, and reads the famous lines on sleep and the strange, evocative world which lies somewhere between sleep and waking, it is clear that we are entering a world that has been partially shaped by the great romantic tradition, by introspective writers like Chateaubriand, Lamartine, and the Hugo of the *Contemplations*. And yet it is a devastatingly lucid world of self-analysis, not suffused by the soft, hazy glow of, say, Lamartine's *Méditations*, although often sharing the lyricism and poetry of the early romantics. Proust has taken the century's preoccupation with the self, with the relationship existing between the self and the outside world, and its later development into a quest for the clarification of the relationship between the artist and society – he has taken this preoccupation and merged it into the framework of his own self-discovery. One might say that the whole tide of self-analytical prose, which includes the novels of analysis like *Adolphe*, by Benjamin Constant, or *Dominique*, by the painter Eugène Fromentin, culminates in the novel that searches for the identity of the self in past time.

IN SPEAKING earlier of the nineteenth century in general terms, I attempted to emphasize one of its major characteristics, namely that of seeking again and again, in varying ways, to impose order on the increasingly complex world of modern man. One of the most disappointing aspects of these attempts, and one which has had a profound effect on our own times, since we have blindly inherited the major thesis to which many philosophers and writers held towards the end of the century, is the increasing trust that was placed in science and materialistic philosophies. When we think of the writings of Hippolyte Taine, the philosopher, historian and critic, and recall the widespread influence of his thought on thinkers and writers, including perhaps the greatest and most imaginative of the later novelists of the century, Zola, we have little difficulty in forming some idea of the general intellectual climate of the eighteen–seventies, the period in which Proust himself was born. Underlying most of Taine's writings is the notion that the human being is the product of a predetermined equation between physical and psychological phenomena, a theory that owes not a little to the equally widespread positivistic ideas also current in the second half of the century. In the field of literary creation, Zola's famous preface to the Rougon-Macquart cycle of novels distinctly echoes this theory, along with those of Lucas and Claude Bernard.

Thus it was on a wave of naturalistic literature that Proust came to maturity, although he also read widely in the literature that preceded it. If, therefore, we are justified in seeing Proust as the greatest in a chain of writers who all indulged in the nineteenth century's '*péché mignon*' of attempting to explain the universe in terms of God, society, history or art, it is no less valid to see *A la Recherche* as a conscious, and indeed at times violent, reaction away from the materialism and positivism with which that century finally came to a close. The novel is an attempt to chronicle a certain kind of social milieu at a given moment in time. It is also an attempt to create a self-contained framework within which the hero-narrator may give unity and coherence to the world around him. But the means whereby this coherence is to be achieved are to be found precisely in the rejection of too complete a reliance on the intellect, in the refusal to accept as final the information that pure reason feeds into our minds.

As all readers of Proust know, the most striking passage, if we exclude the poignant description of the child's anguish at bedtime, in the early sections of *Du Côté de chez Swann,* is the scene where Marcel makes the chance discovery of the importance of pure sensation in the discovery of the past, and through the past, of the inner recesses of his own personality. The *madeleine* episode, however, despite the importance given to it for purely aesthetic reasons at this stage of the novel, has always seemed to me to be inferior in impact to the three much more climatic revelations of involuntary memory in the final section of the work, *Le Temps retrouvé*. There, three times in rapid and increasingly moving succession, Marcel is transported back to different periods in his life, resurrected, as it were, from his futile and barren existence surrounded by decaying and morally decadent figures, by the intervention of an impression so completely all-embracing that his life is henceforward completely transformed.

The careful shaping of the first *madeleine* passage is necessary in the general scheme of the novel the architecture of which arises from a sustained 'flash-back' technique, which introduces the 'double vision' of the narrator's observations about life, and allows the final revelations retrospectively to incorporate a whole aspect of existence which Marcel's intellect had been unable to grasp, but which he had intuitively stored up in the recesses of his mind, only to be liberated by the sensations which restore his past to life, and free him from the death menacing his contemporaries. But the three manifestations of this same power, compared by Proust to the magic sign which the heroes of the Arabian Nights' Tales suddenly discover at critical moments in their lives, these three later manifestations carry with them the whole accumulated weight of the preceding volumes, and evoke in us, the readers, a memory (however literary) in precisely the same way that is described as taking possession of the narrator.

In *Du Côté de chez Swann* this accumulated experience of Marcel's life does not exist; it is presented to us *after* the revelation. But the fact that makes the final pages of the novel so moving is that Proust has contrived to make us participate, however much at one remove, in the blinding revelation that memory, and the sensations which call up memory in all its fulness, are the one true guide to the recapture of all that has gone before. Thus we can see that Proust's substitution of the imagination and the irrational workings of mind and senses for the dryness and barrenness of the intellect alone is worked into not just the stuff of the novel, but into the very form which that novel must inevitably take. Studies of Proust's earlier and abortive work, called nowadays *Jean Santeuil*, but never published in Proust's lifetime, reveal clearly that it was for the lack of just such a form and all its resulting techniques that the ideas contained in the final novel, and already existing in more than embryonic shape in *Jean Santeuil*, took so long to be formulated in their fullest and most complete form. It was only by finding a form of construction which itself embodied and spontaneously expressed in non-analytic and non-rational terms the kernel of Proust's thought, that the author's accumulated experience could be most authentically presented to the reader.

It would be naïve of us to imagine, however, that Proust was the first to heed the warnings of an over-reliance on reason and materialism. Baudelaire and the Symbolists, in the second half of the century, had already pioneered the way towards a more acceptable recognition of the complexity of man's reactions to his environment. The interreaction of colours, sounds and scents, to which Baudelaire constantly refers, is an earlier manifestation of Proust's own attempts to give importance to the irrationality of authentic impressions, involving a mixture of all the senses. Let us, for the sake of clarity, somewhat simplify the situation as it existed towards the end of the nineteenth century, and postulate two antagonistic currents of thought; the first is that which tries to come more closely into line with the very way in which the industrialized society of the time was moving, and has continued to move. The second is that which reacts strongly to the increasing materialism of our civilization and tries to withdraw, in some cases, into a pure world of wholly aesthetic purity. (Mallarmé is a good illustration of this tendency taken to an extreme point.) As usual Proust manages to avoid the worst excesses of both viewpoints.

While he stresses the importance of sensations, he also accords the intellect an importance that Mallarmé would have been loth to admit. While he abhors the naturalistic novels presenting a 'slice of life' – all externals and no profundity – he combines the search for the 'essence' of the moment, for the hidden meaning of each passing second (which is not to be found simply by rational means), with a decidedly concrete and totally convincing presentation of the externals as well. Once again, we can see how true it is to regard Proust as standing at the cross-roads between the nineteenth century and our own times, since it is this very insistence on the subconscious, and the recesses of our inner life, which have subsequently been taken up in a multitude of different ways, in philosophy, in literature and even in modern theories of psychology, where Proust and Freud, along with his successors, come remarkably close to one another.

IN HIS rather flowery preface to Proust's early collection of stories and essays entitled *Les Plaisirs et les Jours*, Anatole France referred, not unjustifiably, to their 'hothouse atmosphere', where 'the strange, sickly beauty of wise orchids draws its nourishment from sources other than the earth'. That deliquescent, over-refined quality which marks so much of the final years of the nineteenth century, with its Des Esseintes, its Oscar Wildes and its conscious aestheticism, could not fail to leave a mark on a writer as sensitive as Proust. While Proust's aesthetic creed was much more profound than the often empty posturings of figures like Robert de Montesquiou, we can today easily detect something of the same note not only in the very style in which *A la Recherche* is written, but also in the kind of universe which it unfolds.

The characters described by Proust belong, by and large, to a fairly wide spectrum of the social scale; but the great majority of them inhabit the comfortable middle and upper-middle classes which Proust knew and to which he himself belonged, together with the moneyed, international aristocracy with which he was, for a time, on fairly close terms. And along with these leisured and over-refined people (though not necessarily intelligent or even remotely artistic), the world of their servants and hangers-on is analysed in minute detail, the sub-world of pimps, parasites and courtesans; we should look in vain, despite the opening sections which are set in Combray, for the invigorating air of the countryside, the world of peasants, country lawyers, farmers and shopkeepers, which constituted by far the greatest majority of people living at that time. What we do find, however, is the world of Parisian town mansions, sea-going yachts, expensive restaurants, private concerts and elaborate parties. And the great theme of love, and its attendant, jealousy, likewise refract this steamy, hothouse light, as Proust relentlessly pursues his characters through their painful and minutely analysed love-affairs.

It is only right to add that the gradual moral decay which creeps slowly through a surprising number of the main characters is artistically worked into the overall scheme of the book, whereby the narrator contrasts the vanity of the world around him with the high and pure ideals of art. But of the number of marriages described in the course of the novel, how many are even remotely happy? Leaving aside the deliberately idealized family pattern at Combray (but from which even the father is ruthlessly edged out as time goes on), most of the webs of human relationships are warped where they are not specifically perverted. The long, sincere but over-emphasized descriptions of male and female homosexuality, of neurotic jealousy and unreasonable possessiveness, of lying, cheating, backbiting and internecine struggle, whether in elegant salons or in the franker atmosphere of the theatre green room, seem to me to belong to that world that produced *Lady Windemere's Fan* and the *Portrait of Dorian Gray, Les Nourritures terrestres* and *Si le grain ne meurt*, besides all the worthless contributions from poets and novelists who could all be summed up as having in their make-up, as Proust himself did, something of the spirit of Count Robert de Montesquiou. Indeed, anybody wishing to be initiated into the social and literary ambience of the '*fin de siècle*' would do far better to read *A la Recherche*, where it is vividly re-enacted for us, than to read those novels of Zola's where he talks so much about it, but cannot make us feel it as Proust can. In some respects, Proust catches the final, self-tormenting, life-weary picture of the last romantics, parading their refinement and their *ennui* in a world made all the more tragic in that they could have no idea that it was soon to be swept away.

But it is all presented, if not with the gusto of Balzac, at least with his penetration and ill-concealed enjoyment. There can be no doubt that if Proust owes more to one individual source than to any other, it is to Balzac.

When Balzac came to read Sir Walter Scott's *Waverley* novels, he soon reached the conclusion that the unity implied in their progressive resurrection of a remote way of life would have been greatly enhanced by allowing characters appearing in one novel to reappear in another, perhaps in a different context and seen in a different light. From this discovery it was but one step to the elaboration of that famous technique, which gives such interest and depth to the *Comédie Humaine* as a whole, a technique which consists of reintroducing familiar characters from one novel into many of the others, where they play sometimes a subsidiary role, sometimes a major one, but always giving the reader the impression that he is dealing with a familiar, existing world, which in literary terms parallels more closely than any other his knowledge of whatever society he is himself personally familiar with.

This aspect of the *Comédie Humaine* was to have a profound effect on Proust. With definite ideas about the deforming power of time – time that can change a character out of all recognition; with definite ideas, too, about the different *profiles* that each individual presents to different people, and to different circumstances – ideas which may briefly be summed up in the celebrated phrase: 'our social personality is a creation existing in the minds of other people'; with all these ideas, each of which required a specific technique to illustrate it graphically in the novel, Proust adapted the Balzacian idea of reintroducing characters in different situations, allowing the passage of narrated time to emphasize the fluidity of their personalities, and their presence in different social and psychological situations to underline their ambiguity and complexity.

Let us take the well-known example of Odette to illustrate both of these aspects; she is the enigmatic and morally dubious 'lady in pink' whom the narrator meets as a small boy at his uncle Adolphe's apartment in Paris; she next appears as the wife of Marcel's friend Charles Swann, and then assumes a slightly different rôle in the boy's life as the mother of his beloved Gilberte. In the semi-independent section dealing with Swann's great affair before his marriage to her, she is presented as the friend of the pseudo-artistic Verdurin clan, Odette de Crécy. After Swann's death she gradually rises in the world, and eventually becomes Madame de Forcheville, only to reappear in the narrator's life much later at Balbec in the guise of an ambiguous portrait painted by Elstir.

By an amazing cross-fertilization, she moves from the Swann, or bourgeois, side of the novel to the Guermantes, or aristocratic, side, through the marriage of her daughter Gilberte to the Guermantes Robert de Saint-Loup. She later becomes the mistress of the duc de Guermantes himself; and, in a masterly revelation towards the end, Proust takes us right back to her origins as an unknown 'cocotte'. When he makes his periodic visits to the Verdurins, now immensely rich and also moving ruthlessly into high society, Marcel meets a ruined old aristocrat, whose former wife had bled him of every penny. He turns out to be none other than a Monsieur de Crécy, with the result that what Marcel had taken to be a '*nom de guerre*', adopted by Odette when she was still unknown, is revealed to be a hidden part of her past, and yet another manifestation of the multiple personality which Proust goes on to explore almost right up to the last pages of the work.

Another similarity to Balzac that appears in *A la Recherche du temps perdu* is the deliberate juxtaposition in the works of both authors of characters who are wholly fictional and others who were historical figures of the time. Thus, in the course of Marcel's initiation into society, we catch glimpses of Princess Mathilde, hear allusions to the Prince of Wales, to the comte de Paris, and, among others, to prominent politicians and statesmen of the day. So intricately are real, fictional and semi-fictional characters woven into the texture of the narrative, that one is sometimes surprised to discover that a character like the princesse de Luxembourg turns out to be wholly fictitious, so indistinguishable is she in 'tone' from historical figures like Napoléon 1's niece, Princess Mathilde. And just as Balzac continued to revise, edit and modify his characters' names, in order to give later creations a fictional past originally attributed to somebody else, so Proust, in his constant revisions of the middle and later sections of the novel, continually inserted allusions and characteristics into the unpublished manuscripts, until it is virtually impossible now to distinguish reported fact from original creation. The nearest that we are ever likely to come to doing so has been absorbingly set out by Mr Painter in his brilliant biography of Proust; and anyone wishing further to pursue this line of inquiry cannot be too strongly urged to consult that work.

To continue this short parallel between Balzac and Proust, it is necessary (perhaps surprisingly) to introduce the theme of money. If Balzac can be said to have elaborated a set of laws which implicitly regulate the hidden fluctuations of modern society, then pride of place among those laws must be given to the importance of money. To take but one example, in Balzac's powerful study of commercial bankruptcy *César Birotteau*, the author plots the financial ruin and subsequent rehabilitation of a businessman in Paris. He is shown to be the victim of larger financial concerns who use him as a pawn, as well as of his own ambition and the sudden bankruptcy of his unscrupulous lawyer. One of the most interesting aspects of this novel, which might so easily have turned into a dull, over-technical case-book of a phenomenon that must have been very familiar to the readers of that time, is the curious way in which the life-blood of the central character, Birotteau – indeed, not just his life-blood, but his very personality – seems linked to his professional and financial status. Without money, Birotteau simply does not exist; and it is only through titanic efforts that he recovers not only something of his former life but also something of his previous self. Nowhere else in the *Comédie Humaine* is the equation between money and identity so rigorously demonstrated.

Now, in Proust's study, both of the laws regulating the society of his own day, and of the laws regulating the workings of passion, love and jealousy, money plays a part the importance of which is seldom sufficiently emphasized. In *Un Amour de Swann*, the whole basis of Odette's decision to become Charles's mistress is, at the outset, the desire to be made financially secure. He is merely one in a series of wealthy patrons who included in the past not only Marcel's Uncle Adolphe but an unnamed Grand Duke, who provided her with a supply of foreign gold-tipped cigarettes. As I have already mentioned, her earlier, undisclosed marriage to Monsieur de Crécy had only lasted for as long as there was money to be had from him.

Similarly, in the laws directing the sometimes ponderous changes in the make-up of society, Proust takes into account a number of factors, including great, accidental upheavals like the Dreyfus case and the First World War, or artistic revolutions like the arrival in Paris of the Russian Ballet, that helped to spur on Madame Verdurin and some of her coterie in their efforts to climb the social ladder. But one of the most bitterly ironical revelations of the latter part of the work is that concerning this same Madame Verdurin's ultimate success. By a dazzling series of metamorphoses comparable with those of Odette herself, this odious woman becomes successively the duchesse de Duras and then the princesse de Guermantes herself through a series of convenient and providential deaths and remarriages. And it is precisely through her vast and seemingly increasing fortune that she achieves such triumphs, the Guermantes, who were partially German, having lost a large part of their investments owing to the war, and Madame Verdurin simply amassing even more thanks, no doubt, to France's armament drive.

Her prodigious rise in fortune is perhaps the best illustration of the Balzacian side of *A la Recherche du temps perdu*. Like some female Rastignac, although not starting with his disadvantages, she relentlessly pursues her aims, using anyone and anything which might further her cause. On a vastly extended scale, she is almost a Proustian version of one of Balzac's monomaniacs, although she is presented with far more awareness of the complexities and inconsistencies of character than, for example, Hulot or Claes, and the amount of time that passes between her first appearance as a slightly raffish and pretentious artistic hostess and her elegant 'soirée' in the Hôtel de Guermantes, with which the novel closes, must be in the order of forty or fifty years. Indeed, Marcel's increasing revulsion from society, and the perceptible darkening of the later stages of the novel, are both not a little bound up with the author's cynical exposure of the rôle of money and the exploitation which accompanies it in the world he sees around him.

The unscrupulous violinist Charles Morel bleeds the homosexual Charlus unmercifully; Charlus himself is ultimately reduced to paying boys to carry out his perverted rituals. The ultimate degradation of the once golden Robert de Saint-Loup is connected with the discovery, during the darkest days of the war, of a male brothel where he too pays for his hidden pleasures. It is one of the novel's most masterly strokes that the purifying message of the narrator's intuitive certainty in the eternal validity of art should come precisely in the second princesse de Guermantes's salon, paid for with money accrued during the war, and immediately after an encounter with the now enfeebled Charlus being wheeled along by his pimp and former lover Jupien.

There are other, more technical and probably more subtle links between Proust and his great predecessor which there is no space to go into here. But my few observations may perhaps give some idea of the immense debt that the later novelist owed to the author of the *Comédie Humaine*, a debt of which, it is only fair to emphasize, Proust was himself very well aware.

PROUST'S various other debts to Flaubert, Stendhal and Baudelaire in particular have been examined and recorded by scholars of the nineteenth century; and, in his valuable work entitled *Proust and Literature*, the American critic Walter A. Strauss has summed up Proust's own observations on most of his literary predecessors. During the course of that work, however, he raises a question that may throw light on our present review of Proust's attitude to the nineteenth century in general. It is a surprising fact that of the literature of the preceding three hundred years, Proust makes little or no mention of the sixteenth and eighteenth centuries, but couples the classical period of the seventeenth century, symbolized for him principally by Racine, with the more varied, but for him equally 'classical' period of the nineteenth century. The eighteenth century, with its exciting developments in the field of the novel in particular, is almost totally excluded. *Why?*

Part of the answer may be found in studying the very form and construction of *A la Recherche du temps perdu*. It is well known that the original plan of the work was to have been severely symmetrical, consisting of three parts; *Du Côté de chez Swann* was to have been balanced by a Guermantes section, and the two were intended to amalgamate and form a conclusion in a third part called *L'Adoration perpétuelle*. Many traces of this former symmetry remain throughout the novel, particularly in the earlier sections. But during the course of its preparation, and especially during the war years when Proust was unable to publish, the work proliferated; and, while the essential construction was able to contain the additions without being severely distorted, the almost perfect shape of the original underwent modifications. Nevertheless, despite these considerations, it is generally agreed that the sense of form, indispensable in any work of art, is not only strongly communicated to the reader, but, as I have already pointed out, also plays a major rôle in the spelling out of Proust's beliefs in the importance of anti-conceptual experience.

Now, in both the seventeenth century and the nineteenth century, the concept of shape, form and pattern as an integral part of the substance of the work was paramount. A mathematician, I am sure, would experience a sense of delight in the perfect form of a play like Racine's *Andromaque*. In this study of thwarted love and passion, which was one of Proust's most cherished plays, and to which he often refers, a crucial meeting between Andromaque, who is pursued by King Pyrrhus, and Hermione, to whom Pyrrhus is officially betrothed, changes the whole course of the tragedy and precipitates all the events that eventually bring down disaster on Pyrrhus's court. That almost casual scene contains the crux of the tangled emotional relationships between the various characters, and – and this is the point I would like to emphasize – occurs almost with mathematical precision in the very centre of the third and central act.

Many more examples of this rigorous and beautiful symmetry and form could be found in all the great literature of this period. In the nineteenth century too, despite the vagaries of romanticism, an overriding sense of form and pattern makes itself continually felt; and I have already referred to Proust's admiration of the overriding importance of form in Balzac, which transforms each individual novel into something part of a thing immeasurably transcending it. But, if we may make so sweeping a generalization, it seems to me that precisely what is lacking in the eighteenth century is this sense of form. The rigorous pattern of classical tragedy may be found, it is true, in the lifeless neo-classical imitations of Voltaire's interminable works for the theatre. But the most important characteristic of truly representative eighteenth-century litera-ture is its discarding of conventional forms.

The eighteenth century in France is the vast and sprawling *Encyclopédie*; it is the proliferation of all those subversive dictionaries and works of classifica-tion with which writers of true insight attacked the conventions of their day. Indeed, the very fact that existing frameworks were insufficient to accommo-date the mass of contradictory ideas, discoveries and scientific advances of the Enlightenment is an essential part of the literature of the time. It is not by accident that *Candide* basically follows the loosest of all novelistic patterns, by which I mean that of the picaresque tradition. Nor is it a coincidence that the influence of their ideas was spread by writers like Rousseau, Voltaire and Diderot in pamphlets and correspondence, the latter by its own nature, being the epitome of the absence of form.

It seems not unreasonable to suppose, then, that Proust was temperamentally and artistically biased in favour of writers from the past who, like himself, quested after the ideal form in which to express themselves. It is true that Proust did not hold Flaubert in very high esteem, except mainly for his experi-ments in language which were connected with new aspects of the presentation and communication of time; and this at first sight seems surprising when we consider that author's painstaking search for the *mot juste*, the one, perfect way in which to communicate an impression or an idea. But, as Proust himself explains, it was the banality of Flaubert's intelligence that he despised; and he was not far from equating the great novelist, in this respect, with some of his own most unprepossessing creations, like Frédéric Moreau in *L'Education sentimentale*. But the satisfying, underlying unity in Baudelaire's *Fleurs du mal*, for example, struck a responsive chord in Proust, as did the overriding form of Hugo's *Légende des siècles*. Both seventeenth and nineteenth centuries were, for him, 'classical', and classical in the French definition of that term, which among other qualities inevitably includes a conscious and unconscious pre-occupation with form.

INDEED, this preoccupation with form, which can be traced in Proust's love of the seventeenth and nineteenth centuries, and in the very construction of his own work, is partially the result of another series of trends that marked the second half of the nineteenth century. In the works of artists of all kinds from the middle years of the century onwards, there gradually evolved the notion that all manifestations of artistic expression shared something in common. The Symbolist poets for example became obsessed with the relationship between poetry and music, and attempted to evolve a transmutation of pure musical expression by applying it to the printed word. Similarly, in the realm of music itself, former boundaries were being overthrown; and particularly in the work of Wagner, which in so many respects parallels that of Proust, poetry, legend, opera and the drama were all being fused to support a vast superstructure with philosophical and even metaphysical implications.

Proust's fictional artists in *A la Recherche du temps perdu*, Elstir, the painter, Vinteuil, the composer, Bergotte, the novelist and even La Berma, the great actress, are all perceived by the Narrator as he grows in stature and maturity to be separate but connected manifestations of a power of vision which embraces them all. The common denominator linking them all – although why this should apply to an interpretative artist like an actress I have never understood – is their ability to communicate in various languages, but with the utmost sincerity and discipline, their own, individual versions of a permanent beauty, which results from their ability to construct an inner, coherent universe which is a translation of the world around them, refracted through the lens of their own characters and personalities.

Thus all great art, in whatever medium it is expressed, depends upon a number of factors; but these factors are common to every medium. Art is the consequence of experiencing reality in its totality, with a freshness and individuality that can only come from the most delicate and perceptive observation. It is, too, the consequence of being able to relate subconsciously and consciously all the fleeting impressions and observations that pass through the mind (and which for Proust constitute the true essence of our contact with the world), until they form another world within us, possessing a unity and clarity which the outside world can never possess. And, finally, it is the consequence of being able to find or invent a new language which will transmit this inner world, both in its outline and its substance, faithfully and painstakingly accurately, to others. Proust's own work is both the explanation of this belief, and its demonstration. His style is the necessary instrument for the communication of the author's delicate and subtle perception of his vision of reality. His characters and their various lives reflect his personal interpretation of the world in which he lived. And the long thin line that links all the aspects of the novel is the slow discovery of the Narrator's vocation, a vocation which can only be fulfilled once this comprehension of the rôle of art has been fully explored.

I have attempted, so far, to restrict this essay to a consideration of general tendencies and influences, singling out only Balzac as a central figure from the past to illustrate Proust's debt to the nineteenth century. But it would be unfair not to lay some emphasis on Proust's great involvement with the music of Wagner, and briefly to point out certain similarities between the two artists. While Wagner's central belief in the purifying rôle of love hardly coincides with Proust's own bitter denunciation of it, both artists construct edifices, the *Ring*, *A la Recherche*, on a belief in the interdependence of different manifestations of artistic expression. But we can go further, and liken *A la Recherche*, in some important respects, to a prose version of Wagner's four music dramas, seeing both as separate but connected manifestations of something common to all art, just as the paintings of Elstir are intimately connected with the music of Vinteuil. When we look at those charts of the different leitmotifs in the *Ring*, we see how the composer, who begins by using them sparingly in the earlier sections, gradually begins to multiply them, to expand them and finally in *Götterdämmerung* to elaborate them further and bring them all together, catching up all the strands of the sections that have preceded, until the final scene restores order and unity to the world, symbolized by a return to the first theme representing the eternal, ever-flowing Rhine, with which the work began.

It is not fanciful to draw a parallel here between the construction of the *Ring* and that of *A la Recherche*. Proust does not use a plot in the conventional sense of the word, but relies far more on the recurrence of passages of description, analysis and reflection all similar in tone, all somehow related to each other, which begin with the anguish of the child at bed-time (an anguish which later migrates to his tortured love and jealousy), which continue with the discovery of sensation in the *madeleine* episode, which are more richly explored in the *Combray* section and the passage on the two 'ways', and which continue to beset the Narrator all through his life, in Paris, in Doncières, at the seaside in Balbec, in railway trains, salons, churches, restaurants, culminating in the three great dramatic, one might almost say operatic, revelations of involuntary memory in the final stages of the last volume, which open the path to the rediscovery of the past, and the return to the certainties and beliefs with which the work had opened.

The complicated sub-sections of the *Ring* find an echo in the often tortuous

explorations into characters' lives and surroundings in *A la Recherche*; but the overall unity common to them both contains them masterfully, thanks to the flexibility and comprehensiveness of both structures. In short, Proust's real love of Wagner's music may be seen once again to be the expression of a close affinity between himself and another artist preoccupied with themes similar to those which interested him, but also, as in the case of Balzac, the means whereby he was able to adapt, from one medium to another, formulae and techniques which helped him to express himself with the great precision necessary in all great works of art, and to find that personal language without which *A la Recherche* could never have been written.

IF I HAVE strayed outside the limits of the nineteenth century's literary traditions by these remarks on Wagner, it is because artists in that century had become unconscious of national boundaries more than ever before, and because the relationships between different art forms were beginning to preoccupy many thinkers. I have had no space to deal with the multitude of writers whose influence on Proust is indisputable, including important foreign influences like Ruskin's and George Eliot's. What I have been able to do, perhaps, is to show how Proust, like all artists, is the product to some extent of his environment, of the past which has contributed to form the climate in which he lives, rather than some unexplained phenomenon which bursts into life with no regard for the future or the past. Of all the great novelists of recent times, Proust was certainly one of the most widely read, one of the most profoundly literary. I am sure that if he had not had the spark of genius which turned him into a great creative writer he would have become one of France's most acute and sensitive literary critics. But in *A la Recherche du temps perdu* Proust's love and acceptance of his literary ancestors is grafted on to his own, original creation, building on to what had gone before, gratefully accepting help and advice from the greatest of his predecessors, but transforming his literary patrimony into a treasure house probably richer than that of anyone else in recent times.

7

Proust as a Soldier

Anthony Powell

THE CAREERS of writers under arms arouse conjecture. What were they like as soldiers? Tolstoy is to be envisaged without too much difficulty as a Gunner officer; Lermontov, anyway within his own terms of reference, as a Hussar. In contrast, Dostoievski in the Engineers can never have been a run-of-the-mill Sapper subaltern, even if later, with the 7th Siberian Regiment of the Line, on the Chinese frontier, his saluting is recorded by the Chief Bugler as punctilious. One can picture Rilke (always, it appears, in parade uniform) silently ruling his parallel lines for the account books of the Imperial and Royal War Office. Poe, on the other hand, even in a rank that proliferates unusual characters, defies speculation as Regimental Sergeant-Major to the 1st United States Artillery. For that matter, during his four days' embodiment, did Kierkegaard give physical expression to the dread interrogatory *Either/Or?* by mounting a charger, himself wearing the bright yellow coatee, enormously plumed black helmet, of the Danish Royal Horse Guards?

At the age of thirteen, Proust's favourite painter had been Meissonier, that somewhat facile master of the lonely cavalry piquet or off-duty troopers playing cards; and, as it happened, he continued throughout life to be keenly interested in military affairs. Indeed, treatment of soldiers and soldiering in Proust's work deserves fuller examination than that accorded in the present brief survey. The army also provides a clear-cut background from which to present examples of how Proust operated when he 'put people into his book'. His own fairly well-documented interlude with the French 76th Regiment of infantry, makes an appropriate introduction to the subject.

The mood is set by the Narrator's comments during the visit to Saint-Loup, then serving as *sous-officier* in the small garrison town of Doncières, where the roof of the Louis XVI cavalry barracks was surmounted by a weathercock. This was no doubt the sort of edifice, conjured up in *Jean Santeuil*, that had attracted the attention of 'a poet accused of espionage because he spent two hours looking at the changing colours on a barrack building at sunset'; suspicious behaviour that caused his judges to shrug their shoulders. A Proustian touch is added to this hypothetical situation by the Judge not only failing to see what can be beautiful in a barracks, but adding that he, too, from time to time writes poetry. The Judge's view, aesthetic or contemplative, was in no sense Proust's.

The silence, though only relative, which reigned in the little barrack room where I sat waiting was now broken. The door opened and Saint-Loup, dropping his eyeglass, dashed in. 'Ah, my dear Robert, you make yourself very comfortable here,' I said to him; 'How jolly it would be if one were allowed to dine and sleep here.'

And to be sure, had it not been against the regulations, what repose untinged with sadness I could have tasted there, guarded by that atmosphere of tranquility, vigilance and gaiety which was maintained by a thousand wills controlled and free from care, a thousand heedless spirits, in that great community called a barracks where, time having taken the form of action, the sad bell that tolled the hours outside was replaced by the same joyous clarion of those martial calls, the ringing memory of which was kept perpetually alive in the paved streets of the town, like dust that floats in the sunbeam; – a voice sure of being heard, and musical, because it was in command not only of authority to obedience but of wisdom to happiness.

As it turns out, Saint-Loup has, of course, already approached the Squadron Commander (Captain de Borodino, of whom more will be said later), and obtained permission for the guest to lodge in barracks overnight. This arrangement so much delights Marcel that, long afterwards in the narrative, he compares its legacy of content with the famous occasion – almost the corner stone of *A la Recherche* – when his mother allowed him as a child to spend the night in her bedroom.

It might very reasonably be urged that there is a big difference between being temporarily housed by a soldier friend – in possession of quarters decorated with Liberty hangings, eighteenth-century German stuffs and photographs of superlatively smart relations – and compulsory existence as an 'other rank', in a draughty barrack room, on a straw palliasse, between intervals of drill or fatigues, in a world where scepticism as to 'authority to obedience' bringing 'wisdom to happiness' might easily result in transference to the *Bat. d'Af.*; desert sands and Saharan forts taking the place of rotating weathercocks and classical pediments. The poet of the barracks might continue to argue that that were merely to exchange Fragonard and Hubert Robert for Delacroix and Fromentin, pastoral days for Arabian nights. Certainly Proust showed himself equally appreciative of his own service in the ranks, where, anyway for a season, he found moral and mental relief in being told what to do for most of the time.

Even though he wrote later of his months in the army as a 'paradise', there must have been bad moments as well as good, physical and temperamental discomforts, notwithstanding an understanding Commanding Officer who excused early morning parades, and jumping ditches during training in equitation. Those who have had any direct contact with the French army are familiar with an excellent tradition – on the whole to be admitted superior to our own – of having a good time when a good time is on offer. None the less British army regulations lay down certain basic standards of comfort pooh-poohed by the

French. For example, the French ratio of man-to-room space is – or was – a modified version of the Black Hole of Calcutta; and, eighty years ago, in Proust's day, sanitary conditions in barracks may have been less than ideal. In this last connection, when, with incredible appropriateness, Alfred Jarry was appointed latrine orderly during his military service, he remarked of such duties: 'It is no mere bow to rhetoric to designate with the word "brush" these objects known in civilian life as brooms. They are, in reality, exceptionally suited for sketching decorative designs on the ground . . .', so that cloacal deficiencies may have been amply compensated by the graphic art of the author of *Ubu Roi*. That, however, was a year or two after Proust's own tour of duty.

Jarry was, of course, a conscript; Proust, a volunteer. George Painter – to whom the writer of this essay, like all Proustians, owes a considerable debt – gives a lucid account in his biography of Proust's military circumstances. They were not at all unfavourable. In 1889, the year he joined the army, administrative changes were taking place in the law governing conscription. Hitherto, service had been in theory for five years; in practice, few, if any, of the conscripts being retained so long. To make absolutely sure the period was no more than a year, it was possible to 'volunteer'; such an opening being available only to those of baccalaureate level in education, together with ability to call on a sum of about sixty pounds to pay for uniform.

If Proust had wished to avoid the army entirely, he could no doubt have done so simply on the grounds that he was taking a university education. The additional fact of bad health, put forward through his father, a doctor with imposing Civil Service connections, would certainly have provided adequate grounds for exemption. At the same time, this was the last year of the volunteer system. It was, therefore, a question of moving quickly; doing a year, or arranging to keep out of the army altogether. Proust chose to join.

Volunteers served in the ranks, but were treated more or less like officer-cadets. It might be remarked *en passant* that in Great Britain that would have meant being given a much tougher time. In France things seem to have worked differently. For instance, volunteers, at least unofficially, were allowed to employ a comrade-in-arms to look after their uniform and equipment. If their period of training was satisfactory, they passed out in the rank of *sous-officier* of the Reserve, of which there is no precise British equivalent. This was apparently the status of Saint-Loup (who was preparing for a course at the Cavalry School of Saumur), when Marcel stayed with him in barracks. An annual calling-up for training was subsequently required, with possibility of promotion to lieutenant, captain or even higher rank. Saint-Loup's circumstances are not, in fact, absolutely clear, but we shall return to them.

The 76th were stationed at Orléans. Rather surprisingly, Proust does not mention that the Battle Honour 'Solferino' decorated their regimental Colour, as to which one would have expected at least a short dissertation on the purplish tint dedicated to that battle, in contrast with Magenta's brilliant crimson. Some of the life Proust lived with his regiment is described in *Jean Santeuil*; an inchoate work of great interest to those concerned with the technique of novel writing, on account of the manner in which the army material, and much else of a directly autobiographical nature, is there presented; then, after more thorough digestion, remodelled in preferable form for *A la Recherche*, or excluded altogether from the narrative.

If Proust looked back with pleasure on his year in the ranks, that was certainly not because he was cut out to be a soldier. No doubt the duties were considerably less arduous than those of a wartime army, not such a grind and more leave; but there must nevertheless have been tedious moments. Later, Proust compared his inability to grasp the abstruse phraseology of a pretentiously 'modern' critic with his own former efforts to perform the exercise known in army gymnastics as the 'bridge-ladder', for which he 'never received any marks'. The 'bridge-ladder' sounds uninviting. Such occasions are not great fun at the time.

At one moment, he was appointed clerk at a Divisional Headquarters but – 'not without reason', he says – the Chief of Staff could not tolerate the novelist's handwriting; and he lost the job. One likes to think of Part II Orders covered with the elaborate, spidery corrections of a Proustian manuscript; but that would probably be to expect too much of life. For the last few months of his service, as a matter of form, he was posted to the instruction squad for promotion to *sous-officier*; passing, George Painter tells us, sixty-third out of sixty-four or, according to Maurois, seventy-third out of seventy-four. One cannot help speculating about the candidate at the bottom of the list.

As against such stresses, and those that must have taken place on the square and in the field, were champagne parties given by the volunteers in rooms hired in the town – a practice expressly forbidden, but, in fact, watched rather enviously by less affluent officers, who were sometimes invited in to take a glass. In spite of such diversions, one feels there was justification when, a Confession Album having put the question: *What event in military history do you most admire?*, Proust wrote down: *My own enlistment as a volunteer.*

Military
Life

As a soldier;
there were times
when Proust
considered that
he might
become
'passionately
interested in the
military art'.

The barracks at Orléans where Proust was called to the colours on July 15th, 1889.

above: 1914: troops on the march.
top left: Lieutenant comte de Cholet,
an officer under whom Proust served.
top right: Reynaldo Hahn at the front.

opposite : The degradation of Captain Dreyfus, January 1895.

Le Petit Journal

Le Petit Journal
CHAQUE JOUR 5 CENTIMES

Le Supplément illustré
CHAQUE SEMAINE 5 CENTIMES

SUPPLÉMENT ILLUSTRÉ
Huit pages : CINQ centimes

ABONNEMENTS

	TROIS MOIS	SIX MOIS	UN AN
PARIS	1 fr.	2 fr.	3 fr 50
DÉPARTEMENTS	1 fr.	2 fr.	4 fr.
ÉTRANGER	1 50	2 50	5 fr.

Sixième année   DIMANCHE 13 JANVIER 1895   Numero 217

LE TRAITRE
Dégradation d'Alfred Dreyfus

left: Major Georges Picquart, whose heroic intervention in the Dreyfus Case brought about his own imprisonment.

The Dreyfus Case: Maître Labori defending Zola on trial for libel, 1898; Clémenceau behind.

Allégorie

Par autorité de Justice

above left: The Jewish interest, masked and manipulated by Germany;
Forain caricature.
above right: The Flag on sale; anti-Dreyfusard caricature by Forain.
top: Rennes, 1899; Dreyfus arrives at the gaol.

There was enough leave to allow him to make a habit of attending the Paris salons of hostesses like Madame Arman de Caillavet, in whose drawing-room, in blue *capote* rather too big for him, red epaulettes and red trousers, Proust would be seen somewhat embarrassed, clutching several parcels and his *képi* when he said good-bye. A photograph shows him in this turn-out, a figure from the albums of Caran d'Ache, whose comic genius so well expressed itself in military subjects of the day. Madame Arman (who contributes something to Madame Verdurin) had rather unwillingly added 'Caillavet' to her name, a decision of her rich husband, who owned a vineyard *château* of that name; and their son, a great friend of Proust's, was known simply by this additional latter half of the family surname. When Proust volunteered for the army, Gaston de Caillavet was already doing his service as a Gunner. Since he is one of the models for Saint-Loup, he may have played a part in persuading Proust to take the plunge.

These labels attached to Gaston and his mother – that he gave something of Saint-Loup, she of Madame Verdurin – raise a big subject, at which a glance may now be taken. Captain de Borodino, mentioned earlier as Saint-Loup's Squadron Commander, is one of the characters in the novel drawn from life. His prototype was Captain Walewski, a Company Commander in the 76th, grandson of Bonaparte by a Polish lady, an affair well known to history. As it happened, the Captain's mother, in addition to his grandmother's imperial connections, had been mistress to Napoléon III. That such a figure, with origins, appearance and behaviour all crying out for chronicling, should turn up in Proust's regiment illustrates one of those peculiar pieces of literary luck which sometimes attend novelists. Borodino represents the most extreme example of 'putting in' – that is to say, no doubt whatever exists as to his identity, owing to the exceptional nature of his background. At the same time, he is only an extra on the Proustian stage. He takes no emotional or dramatic part in *A la Recherche*. In fact, the manner in which he is 'put in' is organically different from that which applies to the always multi-composed characters who dominate the narrative.

If Captain de Borodino represents the furthest extremity of the process in his unequivocal perceptibility and lack of vital rôle, General de Froberville, also a minor character, is somewhat nearer the centre of the stage. He is less essentially a portrait, and plays some small part in the story. Froberville had, for example, put up Swann for the Jockey, and seconded him in more than one duel. General de Froberville's prototype in real life was General de Galliffet, a

The Dreyfus Case: Mercier, the War Minister (left), confers with members of the military court at Rennes, 1899.

well-known personality in the world with which Proust deals. Galliffet, who had led the cavalry charge at Sédan, suppressed the Commune with an almost Communist savagery, and (though not a Dreyfusard) insisted on a revisionist approach to the Dreyfus case, was also a wit and a womanizer. Mr Painter mentions several stories about him: the silver plate covering the wound in his abdomen (received in the Mexican campaign) alleged to lend physical subtlety to his many love-affairs: the distinguished lady archaeologist, rather masculine in dress, who insisted on joining the men after dinner, at which the General took her by the arm, with the words: 'Come along, my dear fellow, let's go and have a pee.' Froberville is allowed no such knockabout stuff. A novelist less disciplined than Proust might have devoted much more space to him as a comic character. Indeed, so far from Froberville being a caricature of Galliffet, Galliffet is a caricature of Froberville; the real man, far the more exotic creation.

Froberville first appears, an eyeglass jammed in his face like a shell-splinter, at a party of Madame de Saint-Euverte's. It is true that he tells Swann, also present, that he would rather be husband of Madame de Cambremer – whose appearance has taken his fancy – than be massacred by savages (a phrase that recalls a similar one used later by Dr Cottard in similar circumstances); but that is mild enough compared with what Galliffet himself would probably have said. The distinction with which Swann had served in the Franco-Prussian War, where (in the same regiment as Forcheville, his successor as husband of Odette) he had won a *légion d'honneur*, had perhaps played a part in General de Froberville's regard for him. Swann had never bothered to wear the decoration in civilian dress until the time of the Dreyfus case, when he took to carrying its red ribbon in his buttonhole.

Froberville's aid had been sought by Monsieur de Charlus to obtain a *légion d'honneur* of a rather different kind for his protégé Morel, in recognition of the musical talent of the violinist for whom he had conceived so deep a passion. Again, it is possible to imagine all sorts of witticisms from Galliffet; while, if he gave utterance to any at all, none by Froberville are recorded. A slip has been made on the subject by one of Proust's American translators, not without an aspect that might have appealed to General Galliffet's enjoyment of comic situations.

The efforts of Charlus to procure the *légion d'honneur* for Morel were unsuccessful; but, when the war came in 1914, the violinist, after a chequered opening to his military career, behaved courageously in the line, and was awarded the *croix de guerre*. The Narrator comments: '*Il s'y conduisit bravement, échappa à tous les dangers et revint, la guerre finie, avec la croix que M. de Charlus avait jadis vainement sollicitée pour lui, et que lui valut indirectement la mort de Saint-Loup. J'ai souvent pensé depuis, en me rappelant cette croix de guerre égarée chez Jupien . . .'*[1]

There is some obscurity in this passage, if it is not known that certain citations for the *croix de guerre* automatically carry with them a *légion d'honneur*. The translator, for some reason supposing that to render '*la croix*' simply by 'the cross' would be insufficiently understood, goes out of the way to substitute the words '*croix de guerre*', making nonsense of the sentence. Admittedly, the author is a little confusing by dragging in the incident of Saint-Loup losing his own *croix de guerre* in Jupien's homosexual brothel; but a moment's thought might have suggested that – however much awards for bravery were appropriate for those who frequented Madame Verdurin's salon – even Monsieur de Charlus would hardly have had the temerity to press General de Froberville for a *croix de guerre* to be conferred on his favourite merely for playing the violin. Nevertheless, Morel's situation was by no means that of Ludwig II of Bavaria, to whom, as a French newspaper said when he visited Paris in 1874, no patriotic objection could be raised, as during the hostilities of '70 he had 'accompanied his troops only on the piano'.

Froberville/Galliffet therefore occupies a place similar to that of Borodino/ Walewski, though more closely integrated into the novel. Both differ not only in degree, but in kind, from Saint-Loup/Caillavet. The divergence of these types of 'putting in', often misunderstood, cannot be too much emphasized. Since Saint-Loup's origins happen to be particularly complicated, we may turn for a moment from Proust's military characters, the better to pinpoint this matter. Some of its aspects are well exemplified in Philippe Jullian's biography *Robert de Montesquiou*.

From M. Jullian's book it may be seen that Proust, in his construction of Charlus, uses not only incidents and characteristics taken more or less directly from Montesquiou's life, but also – so at least one strongly suspects – includes large chunks of Montesquiou's actual conversation in Charlus's dialogue. At the same time, the biography makes it perfectly clear that the real Montesquiou, morally and physically, when closely examined, was hardly at all like Charlus. A glance at any of Montesquiou's innumerable portraits – say, the Boldini – at once confirms the latter.

To assert there is no resemblance is, of course, an exaggeration. Both were homosexual (Montesquiou with considerable reservations), cultivated, possessed of insane family pride; but there were many contrasts even in these respects.

Montesquiou was quite a different sort of homosexual from Charlus, possessed a frenziedly 'fashionable' taste in the arts that would have appalled the Baron; and the Montesquiou dukedom dated only from the Restoration (in spite of the antiquity of the family), a fact about which Charlus felt particularly snobbish. Contemporaries are apt to be chiefly interested, when reading a novel, in the question 'Who is this meant to be?'; and in this case even the victim himself remarked: 'Shall I have to change my name to Montesproust?' In spite of that, comparisons and contrasts are, in truth, beside the point, almost frivolous, simply because Charlus is so effectively conceived as a character within the novel. The occasional resemblances borrowed from Montesquiou – if you like, the many resemblances to Montesquiou – are totally unimportant. In Charlus a new figure emerges; one that lives entirely on its own. The same is, of course, not true of Borodino, though had he not existed, an officer of illegitimate Napoleonic descent, serving obscurely in a regiment of the Line, would certainly be a happy conception in a novel. Froberville, again, is perfectly imaginable without Galliffet, though the knowledge that Galliffet was frequenting the *beau monde* at the Guermantes period, for readers who like a stiffening of social history, gives an authenticity to the narrative.

In the making of Saint-Loup, a far more formidable list of contributors has been put forward. There is Gaston de Caillavet mentioned above, Bertrand de Fénelon, Louis d'Albuféra, Jacques d'Uzès, George de Lauris – even Boni de Castellane and Lieutenant le comte de Cholet of the 76th, who presented Proust with a signed photograph 'from one of his torturers'. Again it may be said categorically that, in his fictional essence, Saint-Loup has nothing to do with them. He too, like Charlus, and the other main figures in *A la Recherche*, whatever has gone to the building up, emerges simply as a living figure in a great novel.

At Doncières, Saint-Loup and his friends in the regiment discuss the art of war with the Narrator. The aspect of Staff Duties that immediately catches Marcel's imagination is that concerned with Order of Battle. Saint-Loup explains:

If it is not the first time an operation has been attempted, and if for the same operation we find a different Corps being brought up, it is perhaps a sign that the previous Corps have been wiped out or have suffered heavy casualties in the said operation; that they are no longer in a fit state to carry it through successfully. Next, we must ask ourselves what was this Corps which was now out of action; if it was composed of shock troops, held in reserve for big attacks, a fresh Corps of inferior quality will have little chance of succeeding where the first has failed. Furthermore, if we are not at the start of the campaign, this fresh Corps may itself be a composite formation of odds and ends with-drawn from other Corps, which throws light on the strength of the forces the belliger-ent still has at his disposal and the proximity of the moment when his forces shall be definitely inferior to the enemy's, which gives to the operation on which this Corps is about to engage a different meaning, because, if it is no longer in a condition to make good its losses, its successes even will only help mathematically to bring it nearer to its ultimate destruction . . .[2]

Saint-Loup, who could hold his own as a talker, continues for several pages in this strain. His remarks about German theories of attack were, of course, written by the author after the First World War had taken place; but Saint-Loup's comment that the 'break-through in the centre at Rivoli' would crop up again, was 'no more obsolete than the *Iliad*', is not without bearing on tactics in the Second World War. In rather the same way, although he may in one sense have been wrong in disparaging *Field Service, 1895*, for its doctrine that cavalry was only useful for moral effect, in another he was right to foresee the mobile striking force of armoured vehicles that were to take the place of cavalry in attack. There are indications that, even for Marcel, Saint-Loup went on talking about his military theories rather too long, and when he got on to the subject of tactics and strategy, may have been regarded as a bit of a bore in the mess.

Was he at this time planning to make a career of the army? This is hard to decide. After his marriage, whenever homosexuality was discussed, Saint-Loup would remark: 'I have no ideas about such things. I am just a soldier, nothing more. I am as little interested in these matters as I am deeply interested in the Balkan War.' He would then go off into one of those rather pedantic disserta-tions on the great flank-turning attempt at the Battle of Ulm – to some extent personifying that tactical movement himself by changing the subject from one too near home for his own taste – finding parallels for this operation in the contemporary campaign in the Balkans.

These words seem to indicate that Saint-Loup was a Regular; but perhaps it was merely a whim of his to pose as such. In spite of the professional talk there, the Doncières interlude does not suggest a very serious attitude to the army on Saint-Loup's part. One pictures him as about the same age as the Narrator, possibly a shade older. In any case he would have been in his forties by the time of the Balkan War, and might be expected to have become a major or lieutenant-colonel though it might be argued that promotion tended to be slow in European armies before 1914. When the First World War came, he could even have been given command of a battalion. Perhaps he was. All we are told is that, finding the cavalry unlikely to be employed in action (in spite of his own earlier prophecies that the *arme blanche* was by no means out of date), he exchanged into the infantry, then again to the *Chasseurs à pied*; perhaps the equivalent of a posting to the Reconnaissance Corps in the Second World War.

Someone of Saint-Loup's background might be expected to have gone to Saint-Cyr, like young Létourville (relation of the duchess of that name), who had just graduated from the military academy, when Marcel met him, soon after the war. He seemed just the acquaintance to take the place formerly filled by Saint-Loup, another specialist who would talk amusingly about military matters. Like so many similar reminders of the ravaging of Time brought home at the princesse de Guermantes's party, was a note received from Létourville signed 'your young friend' – emphasizing a difference in their ages that had never, until then, struck Marcel. Perhaps the solution of the question is that Saint-Loup had retired early in a junior rank, but always continued to look upon himself as a professional soldier. That would fit in with his romantic side. Had he served continuously until he married Gilberte, something would probably have been said, at least in retrospect, about homosexual difficulties within his unit.

Saint-Loup's aristocratic and military affiliations did not prevent him, at the Doncières period, from being a Dreyfusard; mention of the case – an important underlying theme of Proust's novel – being avoided in the mess for that reason. Later, when the injustice done to Dreyfus was used without much scruple by the Left, to serve less worthy political purposes, and attack the army in a general way, Saint-Loup and others, who had faced the dire disapproval of friends and relations for their support of Dreyfus, to some extent withdrew into the background. The feeling that vilification of the army, as such, had gone too far, even resulted in General de Froberville's nephew, Colonel de Froberville (married to a distant cousin of the Guermantes), receiving some unexpected invitations to grand parties, merely because, although impecunious and not much 'asked out', he was a professional soldier.

The Dreyfus case, one of the most extraordinary cauldrons of human behaviour ever put on to stew, containing ingredients, moral and material, of almost every known variety to attract the interest of a writer, lacks, so far as I know (though I am at any moment prepared to find this incorrect) an element of homosexuality. So much of *A la Recherche* turns on that particular axis that it is perhaps unexpected that Proust did not allot an aspect of inversion to haunt one of the byways of the *Affaire*. In *Jean Santeuil* he does, however, devote a good deal of space to Colonel Picquart, another good instance of Proust's approach to army matters, and also his technique for absorbing 'real people' into his writing.

Picquart's story should be briefly recalled. An Alsatian, sixteen years old when Alsace was annexed by Germany, he was regarded as an ambitious and very promising officer. Although no mention of him is made in *A la Recherche* in connection with Froberville, he had served on Galliffet's staff, been present at Dreyfus's court-martial, and, in due course, put in charge of the Secret Service Section – an outstandingly ramshackle one – at the French War Office. On taking over, Picquart re-examined the Dreyfus file held by his Section, coming to the conclusion that something had gone badly wrong in the Court's acceptance of evidence. He drew this fact to the attention of his superiors, with the consequence that he was himself posted to North Africa (stationed where there was a good chance of death in action) then, when he persisted in making further representations about Dreyfus, put under arrest, imprisoned, and placed in the running for condemnation to five years in a fortress.

All this is striking enough; but when it is added that Picquart, if not a rabid antisemite, was decidedly unfriendly towards Jews, he will at once be seen to be building up the sort of character upon which a writer likes to get to work. When Dreyfus was cleared, Picquart refused to meet him; and, when, in due course, Picquart rose in rank and was in a position to be of some assistance in Dreyfus's professional rehabilitation in the army, he would take no step to make things easier. Clemenceau, in a slapstick mood, appointed him his Minister of War, a post Picquart filled without great distinction, behaving rather badly to officers who had merely been carrying out orders issued by former anti-Dreyfusard superiors. Picquart remained unmarried all his life; dying, in consequence of being thrown from his horse, when in command of an Army Corps, about six months before the outbreak of war in 1914.

Even this very truncated summary conveys some idea of the complexity of Picquart's character, and of the attraction it could exercise for a novelist. Conrad, for example, would surely have been in his element in dealing with its contradictions and Picquart's ups and downs of fortune. At the same time, the Dreyfus case, unique in itself, was something too extraordinary, too earth-shaking, to allow any real fictional parallel to be contrived. Proust was certainly aware of that. If Picquart was to be handled at all, he must be handled as himself. He does not appear in person in *A la Recherche*, although we are told that Madame Verdurin's guests flocked to see Stravinsky and the dancers of the

Russian Ballet, just as they had once come to goggle at Picquart, when invited to her parties as a 'lion'. In *Jean Santeuil*, on the other hand – an instance of material omitted in the more mature work – Proust gives an account, even if a trifle romanticized, probably as good a one as exists, of Picquart's appearance in court. It includes some of Proust's own musings on the state of being a soldier.

... Jean had now made his way into the Courtroom and was listening to Colonel Picquart.

The Colonel was a friend of Monsieur Beulier, Jean's professor, and like him a man whose life, in spite of his sky-blue uniform, had been spent in seeking the light of reason, while he turned his horse at a corner, or was on his way to the barrack square for an inspection, the truth of everything which might, with some urgency, involve a degree of self-examination.

One cannot help noticing the Jamesian tone here – perhaps on account of the phrase 'with some urgency' – on the whole rare in Proust, in spite of his own involutions of expression.

... As though he had only just dismounted, and still retained even on his feet the quick, light movement of a Spahi, walking quickly straight ahead, with that free and easy carriage which a man might show who had just dropped his reins and unbuckled his sword, and with a look of mild bewilderment on his face advanced to the President's seat, where he came to a stop and saluted, not in military fashion, but with a mingled air of timidity and frankness, as though his every gesture was free of all formality or merely external significance but was overflowing like his walk, the sideways carriage of his head and as would soon be apparent, his well-bred voice, with the elegance and warmth of his personality.

Picquart, under arrest at the time, appears sometimes to have attended the court *en civil*, because Jean noted, during the interval, when people were eating their sandwiches, that his rather superb top-hat was worn at an angle.

Colonel Picquart was a philosopher, whose thoughts, while he moved ahead of his men, were ceaselessly employed in trying to get a clear view of the problems with which they were engaged ... And so in an assembly where Jean, himself a philosopher, found himself surrounded by some two hundred persons with nothing of the philosopher about them, he could not help smiling sympathetically when he recognized the true philosophic note in Colonel Picquart's voice, and heard him answer, 'Do you mind if I don't say anything more about that now? I will come back to it later'. ...
We think of a colonel as of somebody cold-blooded and solemn, only to find a brother of whom to make fun at a distance, have as it were a game with, joking about his

failings, about the way he wrinkles up his nose when he talks, but always with an undercurrent of true sympathy, so that should anyone want to do him a hurt, we should be prepared to give our life for him.

As not seldom in Proust, the picture trembles on the verge of absurdity; yet the balance is somehow preserved, and the effect is oddly telling. That the writer was prepared to sacrifice himself in a war is not to be doubted.

Proust's own earliest experiences of warfare had been during the siege of Paris, before his mother gave birth to him. Prenatally, he must have been familiar with the thud of artillery fire. When invasion took place again, he was in his middle forties; and naturally the subject of the army comes once more to the fore. It is the army in Proust's life and work that is being examined here, rather than the general circumstances of war; but, of course, in the novel these circumstances had important consequences in showing the contradictions and paradoxes of human nature. Professor Brichot, for example, one of Madame Verdurin's 'faithful', an aggressive French patriot before the war, finds himself disapproving of 'militarism' after war breaks out, because 'militarism' has to be German. He praises a Swiss novel, because it ridicules a picture of two children admiring a dragoon. This irritates Monsieur de Charlus, who not only considers a dragoon a beautiful object, but welcomes the variety of exotic military personnel to be found in wartime Paris, especially representatives of Highland regiments wearing the kilt, and Sengalese with high red tarboosh.

The Allied armies fallen back; a German headquarters staff, followed by a 'regiment' – that is to say a German brigade – was quartered at Tansonville. Gilberte was full of praise in a letter for the 'correctness' of their behaviour. Saint-Loup himself wrote the kind of letter that would certainly have been drastically treated by the censor in the Second World War. Still pondering his own tactical theories, he pointed out that the old idea of a 'break-through' had been modified by the necessity for devastating by shell-fire the ground held by the enemy; how, having achieved that, it was impossible for infantry and artillery to advance over such terrain honeycombed with shell craters. 'War,' he wrote, 'does not escape the laws of our old friend Hegel. It is a state of perpetual becoming.'

Marcel was disappointed at this too meagre discussion of military problems. He would have liked to go into the situation far more thoroughly, being particularly annoyed by the fact that names of generals were not allowed to be mentioned in letters. Geslin de Bourgogne, Galliffet, Négrier were dead – and, it must be admitted, even if alive, would be getting a shade old for active service – and Saint-Loup had never discussed with him their replacements, new commanders like Joffre, Castelnau or Pétain. Incidentally, Saint-Loup held in peculiar horror the use of the term '*poilu*', near equivalent in French for 'tommy', dear to the popular Press of the period.

Speaking of the intellectually stimulating effect the war seemed to have had on Saint-Loup, the Narrator makes one of those comments that, from time to time, show how much Proust was child of his age, unable – or unwilling – to advance far into the world of the 'Modern Movement'. This is already clear from his approach to pictures in *A la Recherche*; but the firmness with which he sets his face against changes that were taking place elsewhere is well illustrated by the comment that 'soldier poets' describe the war just as they would have done ten years before, '*vol frémissant de la victoire*', and so on. No doubt there were 'soldier poets' of this sort; but, if worth mentioning, they should surely be contrasted with the very different school, in this category, that almost immediately developed. The label is certainly untrue of, say, Apollinaire, and utterly inappropriate as to what was soon to be written by the 'soldier poets' of our own country. The examples are, in short, not at all representative of the way war poetry was shaping. This is an interesting facet of Proust's approach. If such objections had been raised, possibly he would have taken a stand on his own point of view – finding its conservatism in itself absorbing – just as Marcel was unable to believe that he had grown old, yet only too aware of age and decay in others.

These musings on 'intellectual' soldiers recall to the Narrator an incident involving Colonel du Paty de Clam. This officer, who had played an unattractive part in the Dreyfus case, resigned from the army, and, in 1914, was offered a lines-of-communication appointment. He refused, and enlisted in the *Chasseurs à pied*, Saint-Loup's chosen corps. Subsequently, given the command of an infantry battalion, he died of wounds received in action at the age of sixty-three. Proust's reference to the quintessential military anti-Dreyfusard recalls the occasion at Zola's trial when du Paty de Clam, one of the witnesses, passed the violently Dreyfusard Symbolist poet, Pierre Quillard (whom du Paty did not know), and immediately recited some lines to him from Quillard's own play *La Fille aux Mains Coupées*.

In the old days, the sound of cavalry stationed at Combray going out for a military exercise had been a matter for great local excitement, the gardener's daughter overturning an orange tree in its tub, cutting a finger and breaking a tooth, in her anxiety that no one should miss any of the show. Françoise used to dissolve in tears at the sight – 'Poor boys, to be mown down like grass in a meadow' – while the gardener, to 'draw' her, would remark: 'A fine sight, isn't it, Mme Françoise, all these young fellows not caring two straws for their lives.' The helmets glittered, their horses scraped against the walls of the houses, the whole town was thrilled.

Now it was no exercise. Troops going into action moved through Combray all the time. The battle for Méséglise lasted more than eight months. The big field of corn there became Hill 307. The French blew up the bridge over the Vivonne, for eighteen months holding one half of Combray, while the Germans held the other.

When the Narrator met Gilberte at the princesse de Guermantes's party, where everyone had suddenly grown so old, they talked of Saint-Loup, and the subject of his obsession with strategy and tactics again cropped up. His final words spoken to Marcel, when they said good-bye for the last time, had been that he expected to see Hindenburg, '*général napoléonien*', fight a Napoleonic sort of battle, try and drive a wedge between the French and British armies. Saint-Loup had compared battles with plays, in which it is not always easy to know what the author has intended, probably because he himself changed his mind in mid-campaign. Marcel reflects – with great truth – that, as every critic can re-fashion a play or a campaign in his own way, there were some who saw the Hindenburg offensive as the prelude to a lightning attack on Paris; others who thought it meant a series of unco-ordinated hammer-blows against the British Expeditionary Force.

Gilberte appears to have been just as keen on these matters as her late hus-band, recollecting the time when he said that aircraft would make every army 'a hundred-eyed Argus'. This classical allusion leads to Xenophon, and to the campaigns in Mesopotamia, where the British Command had used the long narrow boat – the gondola of the country – that dated back to the time of the Chaldeans at the very dawn of history. It is not surprising that here, within about a hundred pages of the end of the novel, the question of place-names, playing such a part in the earlier sequences, arises finally in a military connection. The case in point is Kut-el-Amara (a British disaster, where, of 14,000 prisoners-of-war, 3,000 survived), the name meaning 'Kut-of-the-Emir'. This was to be compared with villages the curé of Combray used to speak of, such as Vaux-le-Vicomte or Bailleau-l'Evêque. General Townshend and General Gorringe find themselves named here in *A la Recherche* beside the Caliphs and Sinbad the Sailor.

Proust's own health was naturally far too precarious for there to be any question of serving again in the army. That did not prevent the routine requirements of medical boards, which he accepted – one recalls the great to-do D. H. Lawrence made in similar circumstances – as inevitable consequence of a world war. All the same, there was one aspect of them that was exceedingly troublesome to Proust – the time the boards took place. He dreaded these orders to present himself, merely because they threatened the hour or two's sleep he could achieve only during the daytime. By one of those clerical errors endemic to military administration, certainly a classical one, he was ordered on one occasion to report to the Invalides for medical examination at 3.30 a.m., instead of the same hour in the afternoon. To many people such an instruction would have been disturbing. Proust was charmed. This nocturnal summons seemed just another example of how accommodating the military authorities could sometimes show themselves.

The World of Fashion
J. M. Quennell

IN *A la Recherche du temps perdu*, fashions, flowers and food contribute many of the recurring symbols. Interchangeable as the colours and shapes in a kaleidoscope, they suggest all those forms of art and experience which the novelist wished to recreate. One is used to heighten the effect of another.

Albertine compares the ices she eats at the Ritz to obelisks of pink granite 'rising here and there in the burning desert of my thirst'; while the porphyry of Venetian churches is compared to frozen strawberries. Similarly, Odette remarks that the orchids she is wearing resemble 'scraps of silk and satin'; and Oriane de Guermantes's red dress is likened to a 'great blood-red blossom'. Again, when Proust is describing the marvellous succulence of the asparagus that Françoise cooked, he remembers that they were 'tinged with ultramarine and rosy pink which ran from heads, finely stippled in mauve and azure, through a series of imperceptible changes to their white feet, still stained by the soil of the garden bed . . .' Just as a flowering tree sometimes reminds him of a beautiful woman in a ball-dress, the splendid vegetable in Françoise's kitchen assumes the charm of human flesh and blood.

Proust's references to the clothes his female personages wear, and to Fashion as a dynamic social force, are particularly numerous and vivid. Indeed, were they collected, they would fill the pages of a small anthology. But, in his text, they are never employed merely as a type of literary ornament. 'In the novels of Balzac,' he points out, 'we see his heroines purposely putting on a dress to suit the visitor they are awaiting, or to express the wearer's own mood.' Proust had always been deeply devoted to Balzac; and among the stories that may have inspired this reflection were *Les Secrets de la princesse de Cadignan* and *La Femme Abandonnée*. In the latter, the severe elegance of Madame de Beauséant's long black dress, and the beauty of her aristocratic brow, are set off by her lofty coiffure: '*Ses cheveux, abondants et tressés en hauteur au-dessus de deux bandeaux qui décrivaient sur ce front de larges courbes, ajoutaient encore à la majesté de sa tête. L'imagination retrouvait, dans les spirales ce cette chevelure, dorées, la couronne ducale de Bourgogne. . . .*' As for the mysterious princesse de Cadignan, when she is expecting d'Arthez, she devises, we are told, '*une toilette de l'ordre supérieur, une de ces toilettes qui expriment une idée et la font accepter par les yeux . . . Elle offrit aux regards une harmonieuse combinaison de couleurs grises, une sorte de demi-deuil, une grâce pleine d'abandon, le vêtement d'une femme qui ne tenait plus à la vie que par quelques liens naturels . . . et qui s'y ennuyait.*'[1]

Proust's philosophy of fashion, on the other hand, seems to have been derived from Baudelaire. In his magnificent essay, *Un Peintre de la Vie Moderne*,

Baudelaire had announced that he found all fashions 'delightful – *relatively* delightful, that is to say'. It was the topical quality of fashion that fascinated him, beauty (he had decided) being composed both of an *eternal* element and of a relative, *circumstantial* element, '*qui sera, si l'on veut, tour à tour ou tout ensemble, l'époque, la mode, la morale, la passion*'. Therefore, all that adorned a woman, all that served to illuminate her grace, was an integral part of herself, an extension of her personality; and in *Les Fleurs du Mal*, he devotes an admirable poem to the wearer of a modern crinoline:

> *Quand tu vas balayant l'air*
> *de ta jupe large,*
> *Tu fais l'effet d'un beau vaisseau*
> *qui prend le large,*
> *Chargé de toile, et va roulant*
> *Suivant un rythme doux et paresseux,*
> *et lent . . .*

It was fashion and the fashionable use of cosmetics that, according to Baudelaire, raised a woman from the ranks of the domestic animals. '*Elle était entourée de sa toilette*', writes Proust in *Du Côté de chez Swann*, '*comme de l'appareil délicat et spiritualisé d'une civilisation*'. All Proust's fashionable heroines at length achieve this state of grace.

Those heroines are Odette de Crécy, who begins life as an expensive demimondaine, but gradually climbs the social scale; the duchesse and princesse de Guermantes, who have been born to high position; and Albertine, the middle-class girl whom Marcel encounters at the seaside, and subsequently, once she has become his prisoner, initiates into the mysteries of art and elegance. Possibly Odette is the most interesting; for, when she meets Swann, he is not particularly impressed by her face or body. As a woman, Odette is not 'his type'. Nor does she improve her looks by the slavish pursuit of what she believes to be the latest fashion. Her coiffure is a disaster; it makes her face seem 'thinner and more prominent' than it really is:

As for her figure, and she was admirably built, it was impossible to make out its continuity . . . for the corset, jutting forwards in an arch, as though over an imaginary stomach and ending in a sharp point, beneath which bulged out the balloon of her double skirts, gave a woman, that year, the appearance of being composed of different sections badly fitted together; to such an extent did the frills, the flounces, the inner bodice follow, in complete independence, controlled only by the fancy of their designer,

La Mode

Sale of linens; Art Nouveau poster by H. Thiriet, January 1900.

above: Dress of 1898; 'the preposterous bustle had disappeared'.

above left: Dress of 1890, with ribboned toque.

left: Tea-gown by Paquin, 1901. Among those who employed Madame Paquin were the Queens of Belgium, Spain and Portugal, and the rulers of the demi-monde.

opposite: Afternoon-dress, 1905, by Redfern, the famous English designer, who, like Worth, enjoyed a great success in Paris. He was particularly noted for his sports clothes.

above : Bicycling fashions of the 1890s; in the foreground
(left) the three great demi-mondaines, Liane de Pougy,
la Belle Otéro, Cléo de Mérode.
top left : Girl reading a newspaper, 1890, by L. Anquetin.
top right : Mademoiselle Yvonne De Bray, 1905.

Fashions at Auteuil, 1912.

5e Année
N° 18
20 Juin 1913

PRIX :
2 francs
52 Pages

COMOEDIA

ILLUSTRÉ

Mme IDA RUBINSTEIN
Créatrice de " La Pisanelle "
Habillée par Worth

Portrait par De La Gandara.

above left: Lady in a feathered hat, by Drian, 1912.

above right: 'Rien qu'un nuage'; design for an evening-dress by Chéruit. From *Bon Ton*, 1914.

top left: 'Lassitude'; robe de dîner by Paul Poiret, a disciple of Doucet. Under Poiret's liberating influence, whalebone was discarded and the feminine silhouette became more fluid. From *Bon Ton*, 1912.

top right: 'Le soir tombe'; evening-dress by Doucet, one of the dressmakers recommended by Elstir to Albertine. From *Bon Ton*, 1912.

opposite: Ida Rubinstein, an actress whom Robert de Montesquiou greatly admired, in a dress by Worth.

or the rigidity of their material, the line which led them to the knots of ribbon, falls of lace, fringes of vertically hanging jet, or carried them along the bust, but nowhere attached themselves to the living creature.[2]

Swann, like the Narrator in his relationship with Albertine, becomes an infatuated tutor-lover; and it is he who educates his mistress. Her conception of fashion is that of a woman who knows little of the fashionable world, who sees nothing of its origins, and therefore employs the second-hand ideas that have already been discarded by the architects of style. Odette de Crécy does not appreciate the immense distinction between being fashionable and being 'in the fashion'. The simple elegance of Madame Elstir or the *grande toilette* of Madame de Guermantes, described by Proust on later pages, have no part in Odette's untutored world, where things are quaint and cosy and cluttered, chosen for their sentimental appeal rather than for their intrinsic value. Proust's description of the contents of her drawing-room, in the little house where Swann visits her, suggests the hoard of an hysterical magpie – Japanese silk cushions; screens upon which are fastened photographs; fans and bows of ribbon; Chinese ornaments; Turkish beads and oriental draperies. Odette has heard that exoticism is stylish, and plunges in with a lack of restraint that would have appalled an Elstir or a Charlus – and Swann, too, had he not been in love with her. When she wears black velvet, she displays the same talent for destroying its possible effect by superfluous decoration:

She had in her hand a bunch of cattleyas,[3] and Swann could see, beneath the film of lace that covered her head, more of the same flowers fastened to a swansdown plume. She was wearing under her cloak a flowing gown of black velvet, caught up on one side so as to reveal a large triangular patch of her white silk skirt, with an 'insertion', also of white silk, in the cleft of her low-necked bodice in which were fastened a few more cattleyas.[4]

Swann's pupil was undoubtedly slow, compared with the Narrator's youthful and inquiring mistress. Odette has the special obstinacy of an egocentric woman, sure of 'her type', flattered and spoiled by lovers, content to keep within the safe limits of her warmly quilted world. Even when she emerges as Madame Swann, she finds it impossible to question her own taste, and therefore difficult to accept her lover's judgement:

Swann had a wonderful scarf of oriental silk, blue and pink, which he had bought because it was exactly that worn by Our Lady in the *Magnificat*. But Mme Swann refused to wear it. Once only, she allowed her husband to order her a dress covered

The new silhouette; walkers in the Bois.

all over with daisies, cornflowers, forget-me-nots and campanulas, like that of the Primavera.[5]

She seems unwilling to allow any detail that reflects Swann's past experience to impair her carefully self-constructed image. So it is with enormous tact and gentleness that Swann enlightens his love, sending her exquisite presents, admiring those garments which more nearly accord with 'his style', hanging his own paintings upon her crowded walls, suggesting to his friend Charlus, a man famous for his taste and knowledge, that Odette would welcome an occasional visit.

The strange architecture of the clothes that Odette had been wearing when she and Swann first met had now 'made way for the inflexion of a body which made silk palpitate as a siren stirs the waves, gave to cambric a human expression now that it had been liberated, like a creature that had taken shape and drawn breath, from the long chaos and nebulous envelopement of fashions at length dethroned'. Yet Madame Swann finally achieves a certain style almost *because* of her habit of including some unfashionable feature. 'She need only "hold out" like this for a little longer; and young men, attempting to understand her theory of dress, would say, "Mme Swann is quite a period in herself, isn't she?"'[6]

She has still a lingering interest in what she feels is 'done' and 'not done'; and we recognize a sense of outraged propriety when the Narrator suggests that she should wear the crêpe-de-chine wrappers – 'old rose, cherry-coloured, Tiepolo pink, white, mauve, green, red or yellow, plain or patterned' – that seem to him more beautiful than any of her elaborate dresses, as 'outdoor clothes'. She also apologizes for possessing so many 'at home' gowns, perhaps a reminder of her previous life, but then defends them on the grounds of comfort.

Becoming in the end comparatively relaxed and secure, Madame Swann can afford to dispense with rules and learns to pay a Charlus-like attention to her own well-being that, far from diminishing her elegance, actually increases it: 'When spring drew round and with it the cold weather, during an icy Lent and the hailstorms of Holy Week, as Mme Swann began to find it cold in the house, I used often to see her entertaining her guests in her furs, her shivering hands and shoulders hidden beneath the gleaming white carpet of an immense rectangular muff and a cape, both of ermine, which she had not taken off on coming in from her drive.' When the Narrator, having fallen in love with Gilberte Swann, meets the beloved's mother in her own house, her clothes already express the changing aspects of her personality:

La Maison Doucet, rue de la Paix,
by Béraud.

Jean Béraud.

I would find her dressed in one of her lovely gowns, some of which were of taffeta, others of grosgrain, or velvet, or of *crêpe-de-Chine*, or satin or silk, gowns which, not being loose like those that she generally wore in the house but buttoned up tight as though she were just going out in them, gave to her stay-at-home laziness on those afternoons something alert and energetic. And no doubt the daring simplicity of their cut was singularly appropriate to her figure and to her movements, which her sleeves appeared to be symbolizing in colours that varied from day to day: one would have said that there was a sudden determination in the blue velvet, an easy-going humour in the white taffeta, and that a sort of supreme discretion full of dignity in her way of holding out her arm had, in order to become visible, put on the appearance, dazzling with the smile of one who had made great sacrifices, of the black *crêpe-de-Chine*.[7]

Her philosophy of fashion has changed. Though unaware of Swann's subtle direction and the influence of his friends, Odette Swann develops into the poetic and regally beautiful inspiration of the Narrator's dreams:

It was enough to fill me with longing for country scenes that, overhanging the loose snow-drifts of the muff in which Mme Swann kept her hands, the guelder-rose[8] snow-balls (which served very possibly in the mind of my hostess no other purpose than to compose, on the advice of Bergotte, a 'Symphony in White' with her furniture and her garments) reminded me that what the Good Friday music in *Parsifal* symbolized was a natural miracle which one could see performed every year, if one had the sense to look for it.[9]

True to some of her earlier fancies, she has replaced cattleyas by other flowers of an identical colour. She would appear 'displaying around her a toilet which was never twice the same, but which I remember as being typically mauve; then she hoisted and unfurled at the end of its long stalk, just at the moment when her radiance was most complete, the silken banner of a wide parasol of a shade that matched the showering petals of her gown'. And, tucked into the little bows of ribbon or fastening a sable scarf upon her bodice, lies a bunch of Parma violets.

Meanwhile, she has discovered pale shades of lilac silk, pansy-coloured velvets reminding her of those flowers that had trimmed her straw bonnets when she first visited Swann, orchid-hued satin and the pinkish grey pigeon's-breast taffeta. These are the stuffs of her new wardrobe. Its magic is perceptible only to a few admirers, among them, naturally, her friend Marcel, who, seeing the blouse beneath her jacket, would note

a thousand details of execution . . . like those parts of an orchestral score to which the composer has devoted infinite labour albeit they may never reach the ears of the public;

or in the sleeves of the jacket . . . I would drink in slowly, for my own pleasure or from affection for its wearer, some exquisite detail, a deliciously tinted strip, a lining of mauve . . . just as delicately fashioned as the outer parts, like those gothic carvings on a cathedral, hidden on the inside of a balustrade eighty feet from the ground . . .[10]

The moment has now come when Proust can describe his heroine's dress in terms of music and architecture. She can help him conjure out of time some of the experiences he most values. Finally, she gives the Narrator the same sense of aesthetic reality that he enjoys when he is visiting the duchesse de Guermantes:

Her clothes were connected with the time of year and of day by a bond both inevitable and unique. I felt that the flowers upon the stiff straw brim of her hat, the baby ribbons upon her dress had been even more naturally born of the month of May than the flowers in gardens and in woods; and to learn what latest change there was in weather or season I had not to raise my eyes higher than to her parasol, open and outstretched like another, a nearer sky, round, clement, mobile, blue.[11]

In the centre of Proust's Faubourg Saint-Germain stands the duchesse de Guermantes, supported by her husband, her cousin and brother-in-law, the baron de Charlus, and the prince and princesse de Guermantes, surrounded by carefully chosen fellow-souls. Related by birth, position, money and a kind of intelligence that strikes an outsider as both imaginative and cabalistic, this matrix of society is endowed by the novelist with an almost supernatural prestige. He continues to accept their dictatorship, as an hereditary right they exercise, until the discoveries he makes at the end of the narrative eventually close his lips in lines of bitter disillusion.

The duchesse de Guermantes, however, unlike Odette and Albertine, needs no help from Elstir, Bergotte, or anyone else outside her private world. Indeed, she takes so little interest in Elstir's paintings that she has hung them in an obscure bedroom. It is only when she learns their value that she removes them to one of her drawing-rooms, so that they may reflect her own perspicacity and good taste.

Yet, like all Proust's characters, she is many-sided; and there are times when the 'First Lady in the Faubourg St Germain, the smartest woman in Paris' displays a 'mythological oblivion of her natural grandeur'. 'She looked to see whether her veil was hanging properly, smoothed her cuffs, straightened her cloak, as the celestial swan performs all the movements natural to his animal species, keeps his eyes painted on either side of his beak without putting into them any glint of life, and darts suddenly after a bud or an umbrella, as a swan would, without remembering that he is a god.'

Because, despite her inborn arrogance, she is not completely aware of her beauty and distinction, she is occasionally anxious about her ensemble, and thinks Fashion a strange beast that other people seem able to capture and tame. She will look at an actress with interest or will study the toilette of an ordinary passer-by, in which she thinks she recognizes signs of an elegance that she herself lacks. Straightforward, absolved from pretension by a sense of her own social rank, and protected by the same concern for her personal comfort and amusement that regulates her cousin's life, Oriane is accustomed to standards that seem to her as unsurprising as the inherited furniture and porcelain in the Hôtel de Guermantes.

Proust's system of chronology is often difficult to understand; and two episodes, widely separated in time, are frequently employed to form a single passage. He had been infatuated with Madame de Chevigné (one of the so-called 'originals' of Madame de Guermantes) about the year 1892, whereas his description of the duchesse and princesse at the opera was taken from his visit to Madame Greffulhe's box in 1912. As an historian of fashion, therefore, he is somewhat unreliable; but he refers by name to a series of famous dressmakers who flourished between 1890 and the outbreak of the First World War. Each of the most distinguished Parisian dressmakers was celebrated for some speciality. The Callot sisters created ravishing tea-gowns and indoor dresses, made of different stuffs, georgette over silk over satin, lace over muslin over taffeta; modesty vests with slotted and ribboned lace edges; long skirts with fantails; loose jackets with hanging sleeves and sable borders. Daughters of an antique dealer, they also invented lace blouses and evening dresses in gold and silver lamé. Among their apprentices was the future Madame Vionnet, who, when she had founded her own business, won great success by producing individual models to suit her clients' taste and personality.

Madame Paquin, who opened her establishment in 1891, and whose clients included the Queens of Belgium, Spain and Portugal, provided the grand *robes de bal*, the heavily encrusted satins and velvets worn at court receptions and diplomatic parties, as well as the extravagant dinner dresses in which the princesse de Guermantes or Madame Swann would preside over their salons. The duchesse, however, who was more concerned with cut and disliked garments that suggested any hint of 'dressing up', never looked so well as in the traditional black velvet and the Guermantes diamonds. For Oriane, her clothes belonged to the same category as the other possessions that were hers by right; and she maintained the only standards that she knew without emphasis or ostentation. We may assume that she patronized Jacques Doucet, who designed the sumptuous cloaks, 'Tiepolo red' or pansy-coloured, that could be slipped over a simple indoor dress; Doucet's clothes had a practical line that appealed to Oriane, who always considered herself a busy woman.

The Doucet family had long been concerned with fashion. The dressmaker's grandfather had opened a shop in the Rue de la Paix for men's linen; to which he attached a laundry that specialized in washing and starching the complicated ruffles and frills that decorated masculine shirts at the beginning of the nineteenth century. Beau Brummel and comte d'Orsay had been among his well-known patrons. Doucet's grandmother sold exquisite hand-made lace in a smart little shop further along the Rue de la Paix.[12]

Their grandson, a man of taste and a great connoisseur, who admired the fashions of the eighteenth century and collected the paintings of Watteau, Chardin and Latour, kept his professional career entirely separate from his social life; and many of his friends would have been surprised to learn that he was the couturier of the same name. Carefully dressed in white spats and matching waistcoat, with scented beard and red carnation, he was perhaps the smartest dressmaker in Paris. He was the first to treat fur as a fabric, cutting otter coats, which resembled those worn at the time by Prussian officers.

The Narrator, speaking of Madame Swann at home, tells us that she had discarded the Japanese wrapper as old-fashioned, and now received her friends 'in the bright and billowing silk of a Watteau gown whose flowering foam she made as though to caress where it covered her bosom and in which she immersed herself . . .' No doubt it had been created by Doucet and inspired by a painting in his collection. Like Fortuny, Doucet worked with actresses to design clothes for the stage. His friend and client, the actress Réjane, often lent her name to a new style – for example, to a coat in velvet and pleated satin, à la 'Réjane'.

Doucet was among the four dressmakers recommended by Elstir to Albertine. It was he who perfected the French *tailleur* originally created by Worth, making it both practical and comfortable for the long sight-seeing journeys that were now à la mode.

Among Doucet's disciples was Paul Poiret, who, from 1910 to 1914, exercized a liberating influence on women's clothes. The fierce whalebones were discarded, to give way to less restricting corsets; and the feminine silhouette became more fluid. Poiret, an admirer of Diaghilev, borrowed (though he often denied it) many exotic details from the Russian Ballet, adapting some of the costumes worn in *The Firebird* or *Schéhérézade*; while from the Far East he took silken and cotton kimonos, as brightly coloured as the canvases of Raoul Dufy and the Fauves.

The charming veils that completed many of the toques and hats of the period had been invented by Caroline Reboux. Chinchilla, straw, feathers, ribbons and tulle were swathed in misty veiling that gave the wearer's face a peculiarly romantic look. Some form of headdress was always worn by famous beauties when they attended the theatre. Oriane's cousin, the princesse de Guermantes, sits in her box as if in a sea cave. The sofa is 'red as a reef of coral'; and

at once plume and blossom, like certain subaqueous growths, a great white flower, downy as the wing of a bird, fell from the brow of the Princess along one of her cheeks, the curve of which it followed with a pliancy, coquettish, amorous, alive, and seemed almost to enfold it like a rosy egg in the softness of a halcyon's nest. Over her hair, reaching in front to her eyebrows and caught back lower down at the level of her throat, was spread a net upon which those little white shells which are gathered on some shore of the South Seas alternated with pearls, a marine mosaic barely emerging from the waves and at every moment plunged back again into a darkness in the depths of which even then a human presence was revealed by the ubiquitous flashing of the Princess's eyes.[13]

When she moves out of the shadows towards the front of the box, to watch Berma in the opening act of *Phèdre*, the Narrator uses a new set of images:

Not only the colour but the material of her adornments change. And in the box, dry now, emerging a part no longer of the watery realm, the Princess, ceasing to be a Nereid, appeared turbanned in white and blue like some marvellous tragic actress dressed for the part of Zaïre, or perhaps of Orosmane; finally, when she had taken her place in the front row I saw that the soft halcyon's nest which tenderly shielded the rosy nacre of her cheeks was downy, dazzling, velvety, an immense bird of paradise.[14]

The late and triumphant arrival of the duchesse in white muslin – a material perfectly attuned to the air of simplicity, shyness and confusion she affected as she greeted old friends who had stood up when she entered during the middle of the performance – assures the Narrator of the subtlety and restraint of this first lady of the '*gratin*'. She admires her cousin, but criticizes the Princess's 'exaggerations'. Perhaps to teach her a lesson in good taste

the Duchess wore in her hair only a simple aigrette, which rising above her arched nose and level eyes, reminded one of the crest on the head of a bird. Her neck and shoulders emerged from a drift of snow-white muslin against which fluttered a swans-down fan, but below this her gown, the bodice of which had for its sole ornament innumerable spangles (either little sticks and beads of metal, or possibly brilliants) moulded her figure with a precision that was positively British.[15]

Although the cousins' tastes may differ – the Princess finding Oriane's toilette a little too cold and austere – they are still able to appreciate one another's sense of style, and together help to maintain the barriers that hold the vulgar world at bay. It was their circle – not the dressmakers and milliners who served them – that created new fashions; and Oriane, like Charlus, often launched a fashion merely because it happened to suit her personal convenience. Her independence, for example, becomes clear, when at a performance of a new play she refuses a box and is seen 'sitting by herself, in black, with a tiny hat[16] on her head, in a stall in which she had arrived before the curtain rose'. Why? Because she has decided it was a play worth listening to, and finds this easier if she arrives early and sits close beneath the stage. Soon it is considered more fashionable to watch the beginning of a play rather than dine with a party of friends, go on somewhere else, and arrive in time for the last act. Oriane's self-assurance gives her a physical grace; her bird-like head and beaked nose, her azure eyes and shining fair hair, her tall figure and distinguished carriage, announce the presence of a '*grande dame*', the personification of Proust's ideal woman.

Albertine, the youngest of Proust's heroines, although she possesses an instinctive feeling for beauty of line, quality of cloth, cut and colour, has had neither the experience nor the money to provide herself with the kind of luxuries that she recognizes as being truly elegant. But, once she has become the Narrator's captive, both he and she devote themselves to indulging her delight of finery – silk sunshades, long scarves of tulle, *crêpe-de-Chine* wrappers, cloaks and furs, toques and veils, slippers and gloves, thus transforming the pert young leader of the little group at Balbec, the rakish bicyclist, black polo cap tilted over one eye, into Albertine the woman of the world.

Madame de Guermantes is frequently consulted as to the origin of certain garments or accessories that have been glimpsed and admired by Albertine as the duchesse hurries across the courtyard on her way to luncheon. Albertine's lover pays particular attention to Madame de Guermantes's indoor gowns when he calls upon his old friend. He may find her 'swathed in the mist of a garment of grey *Crêpe de Chine*', exhaling an atmosphere 'like that of certain late afternoons cushioned in pearly grey by a vaporous fog'; or perhaps it will be

'Chinese with red and yellow flames'; and he gazes upon it 'as at a glowing sunset'. No matter what Madame de Guermantes wears, it seems so irrevocably right, and so well suited to the circumstances of their meeting, that her taste, creates 'a definite and poetical reality like that of the weather, or the light peculiar to a certain hour of the day'.

On the duchesse's advice, he orders Albertine a wrapper from Fortuny that causes her immense delight. During one of his discreet visits to Madame de Guermantes, he had asked about an indoor dress 'with such a curious smell, dark, fluffy, speckled, streaked with gold like a butterfly's wing'; and she had told him that she had many, and that they were created by that same Fortuny of whom the painter Elstir had already spoken. For Proust, the great contemporary dressmakers, Callot Soeurs, Paquin, Chéruit and Doucet were part of life in the Faubourg Saint-Germain; and he recognized the contribution they made to the society that he depicts. But Fortuny made a different and much deeper impression. Proust describes his gowns and cloaks in poetic detail. Here he had found a creator of enormous imagination, whose sense of beauty and sense of history corresponded to his own.

Fortuny was the son and (through his mother) the grandson of distinguished Spanish painters. Fortuny *père* had worked mostly in Rome and Paris; and Proust had probably seen his portrait of Madeleine Lemaire in her house. Mariano, or Marianito, the Fortuny with whom we are concerned, suffered from hay-fever and found that Venice suited his health. He, therefore, obtained the post of Spanish Consul, but pursued his other activities with even more enthusiasm. Very cultivated, a keen collector of works of art, he had the appearance and habit of a *grand seigneur*. With his great height, distinguished aquiline features and fine white beard, he is also said to have resembled a noble leader of the Carbonari. He dressed in white knickerbockers, white gaiters and boots with cross-lacings up the side and a short draped mantle over one shoulder. Fascinated by the forgotten fabrics he saw in the canvases of the Venetian masters, he set to work, in his vast studio at the Palazzo Fortuny, to recreate them. By means of careful research and experiment, the blending of dyes, the reproduction of certain textures and weights of cloth, and the use of ancient printing blocks, he produced his own medium, like a modern painter who mixes his paints according to rules laid down by Michelangelo or Leonardo da Vinci.

Silks, fine lawns, and muslins, pearly satins, shining clouds of gauze, deep Tiepolo-toned velvets and metal-threaded brocades were the basis of Fortuny's

Venetian models. We are told by Proust that the clothes were not fancy dress, but –

like the theatrical designs of Sert, Bakst and Benoist who at that moment were recreating in the Russian ballet the most cherished periods of art – with the aid of works of art impregnated with their spirit and yet original – these Fortuny gowns, faithfully antique but markedly original, brought before the eye like a stage setting, with an even greater suggestiveness ... that Venice loaded with the gorgeous East from which they had been taken, of which they were, even more than a relic in the shrine of Saint Mark suggesting the sun and a group of turbaned heads, the fragmentary, mysterious and complementary colour.[17]

The unique character of each garment, probably seen and admired by Proust in the wardrobe of Madame Greffulhe or Madame Straus, and later described as he recalled it, encouraged him to analyse the poetic quality of a woman's clothes, their significance for the woman herself and the imaginative effect they produce upon her audience. The dresses offer themselves; and, by her choice, she clarifies and crystallizes her own personality at that particular moment of her life. For the Narrator, seeing Albertine in her new Fortuny dress is a poetic experience:

The Fortuny gown which Albertine was wearing that evening seemed to me the tempting phantom of that invisible Venice. It swarmed with Arabic ornaments, like the Venetian palaces hidden like sultanas behind a screen of pierced stone, like the bindings in the Ambrosian Library, like the columns from which the Oriental birds that symbolized alternatively life and death were repeated in the mirror of the fabric, of an intense blue which, as my gaze extended over it, was changed into a malleable gold, by those same transmutations which, before the advancing gondolas, change into flaming metal the azure of the Grand Canal. And the sleeves were lined with a cherry pink which is so peculiarly Venetian that it is called Tiepolo pink.[18]

The fabric described here must have been one of Fortuny's brocades, with their contrasts of light and shade, their matt and shining surfaces, or an elaborate design on silk. One of his favourite techniques was to apply stencilling to velvet, at the best of times a difficult stuff to work with. Golden leaves, shaded to give them relief, were repeated over the cloth, giving it a glowing look of autumn. Long silk dresses, pleated from neck to hem, simple and clinging in line, caught round the waist with a chain or a rope of pearls, like the garments of Egyptian ladies painted on the walls of tombs in the Valley of the Kings – these were Fortuny's great achievements. Classical creations, they are still worn by a few elegant and imaginative women. For Proust, their attraction was obvious; they combined the present and the past. They harmonized with his ideas of modern beauty, and recalled, in undiminished splendour, the magnificent world of Carpaccio, Tiepolo and Veronese.

Fortuny himself incorporated many qualities that Proust admired – a gentleman, a connoisseur, an autocratic eccentric, but, above all, an artist who had the same predilection for the art of former days. Madame Fortuny, moreover, might well have been a Proustian character, a shy and sober lady who seldom left her house without her imposing husband, and, when she did, appeared in a dress that he had designed for her, elaborately coiffed and exquisitely jewelled. From the windows of the Palazzo Fortuny she commanded a view of the local brothel opposite, from which she was sometimes deeply shocked to see Fortuny's friends emerging, after an innocent chat with the madame, a particularly intelligent and popular woman. Fortuny's great days were the latter part of the nineteenth and the beginning of the twentieth centuries. He also produced theatrical costumes and decors, and worked with D'Annunzio to create new and highly successful forms of stage-lighting. The Spanish Civil War dealt him a heavy blow; and he eventually lost his fashionable public. He died at the age of eighty. Among his last projects was a design for the catafalque and funereal hangings of his friend the Duke of Alba.

Albertine had what we should now call a 'good eye' for fashion, to which she added a keenly acquisitive nature. We have already described her link with Madame de Guermantes. One of Albertine's pleasures during her imprisonment was to sit at the drawing-room window, watching life in the courtyard below and, when the Duchess appeared, noting any article of clothing that she found particularly stylish. The Duchess's slippers and shoes were especially appealing; and the Narrator was dispatched to find an identical pair, perhaps like the black shoes studded with brilliants that Françoise indignantly described as 'pattens'. Indoor slippers were made of soft leather or fur; and, on one occasion, in answer to a request for information about some shoes that accompanied the butterfly-wing Fortuny dress, the Duchess explains that 'they are made of some gilded kid we came across in London, when I was shopping with Consuelo Manchester. It was amazing. I could never make out how they did it, it was just like a golden skin, simply that with a tiny diamond in front.' Detailed information of this kind was quickly repeated to Albertine, who, with the help of her captor and agent, was soon the possessor of just such a pair of slippers.

Her single-mindedness in the pursuit of these luxuries confirmed her independent spirit. 'A particular toque, a particular sable cloak, a particular

Doucet wrapper, its sleeves lined with pink, assumed for Albertine, who had observed them, coveted them and thanks to the exclusiveness and minute nicety that are elements of desire, had at once isolated them from everything else in a void against which the lining or the scarf stood out to perfection ... an importance, a charm which they certainly did not possess for the Duchess ...'

In Albertine's education, however, the deepest and most lasting influence is that of the great contemporary artist Elstir, who finds her a bright and sympathetic pupil, to whom he is able to communicate his own graceful and sober taste. Albertine's knowledge of architecture, her collection of old silver, her own attempts at painting and her elegant wardrobe are greatly advanced by Elstir's lively conversation. On the question of dress, the master is eloquent and precise. Being a man 'of exquisite taste, singularly hard to please, he would isolate some minute detail which was the whole difference between what was worn by three-quarters of the women he saw, and horrified him and a thing which enchanted him by its prettiness'. His abhorrence of the second-rate permitted him to recommend only four French dressmakers: 'Callot – although they go in rather too freely for lace – Doucet, Chéruit, Paquin sometimes. The others are all horrible.' Albertine, answering the Narrator's ingenuous question, 'is there a vast difference between a Callot dress and one from an ordinary shop?', replies with the authority of a budding connoisseur: 'Why, an enormous difference, my little man! I beg your pardon! Only, alas, what you get for three hundred francs in an ordinary shop will cost two thousand there. But there can be no comparison; they look the same only to people who know nothing at all about it.'

Albertine has arrived at the same conclusion that the duchesse de Guermantes expresses in different terms when she offers to lend her own dresses to the Narrator, so that he may have them copied, first warning him that, 'if you have things from Callot's or Doucet's or Paquin's copied by some small dressmaker, the result is never the same'. She adds that it is a question of handiwork, of style; and any present-day leader of fashion will support this theory, and tell you that to copy exactly a dress from Balenciaga or Givenchy, the two last great exponents of traditional *haute-couture*, is virtually impossible. Elstir describes an enchanting little white hat and the sunshade worn by Mademoiselle Léa at the races, and defines its quality and distinction, 'quite tiny, quite round, like a chinese umbrella' – a jewel of a sunshade that Albertine notes with envy. The painter's choice of colour and line is austere; he prefers a simplicity of dress that enhances its surroundings and, at the same time, gains from them.

Poster of the Théatre de la Renaissance, one of the theatres at which Sarah Bernhardt appeared; by Alphonse Mucha.

The relationship between women's clothes and the landscape or seascape about them should produce the satisfying sense of reality that Elstir finds essential. The hat that has escaped the limits of sanity, the huge yacht that has lost its point and become a liner – exaggerations of this kind Elstir thinks revolting. At the race course, at a regatta, attending the opera or a great reception, he believes that well-dressed women should enlarge the scene but not disturb it. On a yacht, the clothes that enchant him are 'those light garments, uniformly white of cloth or linen or nankeen or drill, which in the sunlight and against the blue of the sea show up with as dazzling a whiteness as a spread sail'.

Albertine accepts Elstir's principles, discovering that they coincide with hers; and she is sharply critical of her young acquaintances who do not understand that suitability is one of the first rules for the fashionable woman. To play golf in a silk frock is her idea of total absurdity and lack of taste; and ostentation without knowledge is, in her eyes, just as serious an offence. It is the painter's wife whose appearance she most admires: 'Look at Madame Elstir,' she says; 'there's a well-dressed woman if you like'. The Narrator, often naïve in these matters, has only observed her great simplicity; and Albertine is quick to correct him: 'She does put on the simplest things, I admit, but she dresses wonderfully, and to get what you call simplicity costs her a fortune.' Now the roles are reversed. And when Elstir orders a great many sunshades, hats and cloaks for his wife, besides consulting his own taste, he invokes the help of Albertine, whom he is beginning to recognize as an important authority on fashion.

Another adviser is Monsieur de Charlus. He, we are told, apart from Elstir, is 'almost the only person capable of appreciating Albertine's clothes at their true value; at a glance, his eye detected what constituted their rarity, justified their price; he would never have said the name of one stuff instead of another, and could always tell who had made them. Only he preferred – in women – a little more brightness and colour than Elstir would allow.' In one of his last detailed accounts of Albertine's appearance, Proust shows us the high degree of subtlety that she has achieved, and describes her own confident addition of colour that delights the Baron.

Indeed, meeting over her skirt of grey *crêpe-de-chine*, her jacket of grey cheviot gave the impression that Albertine was dressed entirely in grey. But, making a sign to me to help her, because her puffed sleeves needed to be smoothed down or pulled up, for her to get into or out of her jacket, she took it off, and as her sleeves were of a

Scottish plaid in soft colours, pink, pale blue, dull green pigeon's breast, the effect was as though in a grey sky there had suddenly appeared a rainbow.[19]

Charlus responds as he would to the final touches applied to a picture by an artist he revered: 'Now we have a ray, a prism of colour. I offer you my sincerest compliments.' High praise from Proust's autocratic and insolent example of France's double-dyed nobility, a man who, in his youth, had been an arbiter of elegance, and had set the tone and laid down laws with a contemptuous disregard for current fashions. Saint-Loup remarks that his uncle had 'acted entirely for himself; in any circumstances he did what seemed pleasing to himself, what was most convenient, but at once the snobs would start copying him. If he felt thirsty at the play, and sent out from his box for a drink, the little sitting-rooms behind all the boxes would be filled, a week later, with refreshments.'

The fashionable world waited for Charlus to produce some new expression of his practical but epicurean taste, whether in manners or in clothes: 'One wet summer, when he had a touch of rheumatism, he ordered an ulster of a loose but warm vicuna wool, which is used only for travelling rugs, and kept the blue and orange stripes showing. The big tailors at once received orders from all their customers for blue and orange ulsters of rough wool.'

His common-sense, together with a noble appreciation of comfort and his own pleasure, reinforced by his birth and position, made him a formidable dictator of style. 'If he had some reason for wishing to keep every trace of ceremony out of a dinner in a country house where he was spending the day, and to point the distinction had come without evening clothes and sat down to table in the suit he had been wearing that afternoon, it became the fashion, when you were dining in the country, not to dress.' In Proust's world, the fashionable man, though less often described, is scarcely less important and attractive than the fashionable woman. Charlus's garments are austere; but there is a compelling vivacity about their cut. Saint-Loup, we are told 'dressed in a clinging, almost white material such as I would never have believed that any man would have the audacity to wear ... His eyes, from one of which a monocle kept dropping, were of the colour of the sea. Everyone looked at him with interest as he passed, knowing that this young Marquis de Saint-Loup-en-Bray was famed for the smartness of his clothes.'

Saint-Loup's dancing eye-glass is a detail that can never be forgotten; it corresponds to something in his nature that still remains with him when he has lost his youth and, at the same time, much of his charm and innocence. Similarly, Albertine's polo cap, which the Narrator sees her wearing on the beach, tilted impudently across her forehead, is as essential a part of her portrait as her rosy cheeks, and shining glance. Neither detail is supplied for purposes of decoration, to lend colour to the story's background. Both enlarge and heighten our understanding of an individual character. Fashion, for the novelist, is a delicate and sensitive carapace, that not only corresponds to the spirit of an age but moulds a human personality.

9

Proust and Cocteau: A Note

Francis Steegmuller

ROUST – a languid, precious, even pathetic young snob who astonished everyone by writing a masterpiece; Cocteau – a brilliant, precociously gifted, immensely promising young charmer, whose production proved to be fragmentary: that is a contrast, between two writers who were friends, that was voiced more frequently in the past than it is at present, when certain of Cocteau's 'fragments' – the poems in *Plain-chant* and *Opéra*, the novels and the films, the drawings, the ballet *Parade*, *La Voix Humaine* – are more often seen to make an astonishingly impressive whole. But, if the contrast seems increasingly inappropriate – its falsity has been most especially emphasized by W. H. Auden in a few paragraphs praising Cocteau's multiplicity – there remains the just as commonly drawn parallel; the picture of Proust and Cocteau as two not dissimilar Parisian worldlings of the arts, frequenters of the salons and the Ritz, of the theatre and the ballet, of princesses and the smarter *plages*, but with the great difference that Proust (the older of the two by eighteen years) 'renounced all that' and shut himself up 'to work', whereas Cocteau glittered until the end, or nearly the end, living most of his last decade on the star-studded peninsula of Cap Ferrat.

Certainly, large portions of the lives of both these writers were passed in atmospheres tinged by the perfumes of the *grand monde*; each was for long periods quite self-admittedly *mondain*; and it is not uninstructive, perhaps, to seek out, in the words of each of them to and about the other, a few of their own considerations on this aspect of their own and each other's careers.

Recently, about a dozen hitherto unknown letters from Proust to Cocteau were published by Gallimard in a volume called *Cahiers Jean Cocteau I*, the first of them apparently dating from 1908, the year the two men met, introduced by Lucien Daudet and perhaps Reynaldo Hahn. In this early note the thirty-seven-year-old Proust, who had not yet even dipped into his tea the slice of toast that was to become the famous *madeleine*, sends to Cocteau, who at nine-teen had just made his poetry-reading début on the stage of the Théâtre Femina under the aegis of the actor de Max, the address of his friend, the poetess Anna de Noailles. The correct way to address the lady, Proust reminded Cocteau, was 'Comtesse de Noailles, and no longer Comtesse Mathieu de N., her brother-in-law having become Marquis'. With the note Proust enclosed some of Madame de Noailles's verses that she had written out in her own hand as a present for Cocteau, who had asked Proust to ask her for them; and Proust offered some advice as to how Cocteau could best thank her: 'Write to her immediately –

Diaghilev and Bakst; sketch by Cocteau.

that would please me – and since she says that she was glad to do it for you I think that if you express very warmly what her poems mean to you she would not be indifferent to what you say. Were you to speak coolly, and for discretion's sake say only a quarter of what you think – this might seem in good taste to Monsieur de Sacy – it would not get through to her. She is at once divinely simple and sublimely proud.' Nothing, one might say, if not a lesson in *mondanité* from an elder expert.

The next letter contains a passage that strikes a different note and refers to Cocteau's work:

Mon ami . . . I have been thinking about you from time to time, and with the presumption characteristic of friends and philosophers have formulated certain futile wishes: such as, for something to happen that would isolate you and wean you from the pleasures of the mind, so that after a sufficiently long period of fasting you might again

Stravinsky and *Le Sacre du Printemps*; by Cocteau.

really hunger after those beautiful books, beautiful pictures, beautiful countries that you now skim over with the lack of appetite of someone who has spent all New Year's Day making a round of calls, each complete with *marrons glacés*. This, according to my prognosis – I am sometimes right concerning others, though powerless to help myself – is the stumbling block that you, with your marvellous and sterilized gifts, must be wary of. But the life that I should wish for you would scarcely be pleasant to you, at least in so far as at present your desires may be shaped by a life of a very different kind. And so my wishes will fortunately prove to be futile, and nothing will be changed, thus assuring the continuation of everything that pleases you most – and perhaps without causing you any harm. For, intellectually as well as physiologically, any diet we may follow counts for less than our temperament: some people walk ten hours a day without losing weight and others eat five meals without gaining a pound . . . I am sending you some mistletoe for Christmas.

189

And yet, in the third of the letters *mondanité* is called quite the opposite of a sin:

I never meant to say that you are a flibbertigibbet or *mondain*. To be the latter I consider a virtue, and you are not at all the former. Even if I thought you were, I hope you don't think me so ill-bred as to say so to you. I will try to explain what I meant. It was all admiration: for if, the other evening, speaking of something else, and confronted with a choice between two admirable traits, I preferred to be lacking in respect – *debetur reverentia* – as proof of confidence, nevertheless I have great respect for your extraordinary talent.

The letters that follow touch on various matters – Proust's enjoyment of Cocteau's writings in the wartime paper *Le Mot*, his sympathy on the death of Roland Garros, his congratulations on the success of *Parade*, his inability to give Cocteau anything for *Les Editions de la Sirène* because he is tied by contract to Gallimard, for whom he is rewriting 'the last three volumes of *Swann*'. (Other letters from Proust to Cocteau, previously published, contain his praise for *Le Coq et l'Arlequin*, the sparkling 'little book on music', as Cocteau called it, and a courteous but very just critique of the long poem *Le Cap de Bonne-Espérance*.) The last of the newly published letters, apparently written close to the end of Proust's life, hints in musical terms at past disagreements and welcomes reconciliation: he has one remark to make, he says – 'A single bar – for no reason, really'; and then, '*da capo*, back to friendship'.

Cocteau's letters to Proust have disappeared, at least for the time being – there must be numbers of them lurking somewhere – and his remarks on Proust are to be found here and there throughout his works, most especially in his *La Voix de Marcel Proust* printed in the Gallimard volume *Hommage à Marcel Proust* (1927) and in a section of his book *Opium* called 'Nous Deux Marcel: Notes sur Proust (Retour de la Mémoire)' and written in the Clinique de Saint-Cloud in 1929 after reading princesse Marthe Bibesco's *Au Bal avec Marcel Proust*. (Both Cocteau articles are reprinted in his collection of *Poésie Critique*.) He recalls the earliest part of their friendship in a passage in *Journal d'un Inconnu* (1953), where he says: 'I often visited Marcel Proust when I was scarcely older than he had been when he wrote *Les Plaisirs et les Jours*, and I noticed something that I then found perfectly normal – that he treated me as though I had skipped that stage, and was already on the arduous path that one day I would really take, and that he himself was already following. Doubtless Proust, unmatched in the art of reading the blueprint of a man's life, knew more than I about my future, still completely hidden from me . . .' It sounds almost as though Cocteau, writing those words ten years before his own death, had in mind Proust's early letters to him of many years before. Perhaps it was precisely that 'art of reading the blueprint of a man's life', Proust's early penetration of the promise and risk that the future held for Cocteau, that accounts for a certain wariness that one senses throughout Cocteau's references to Proust.

On the subject of *mondanité*, however, Cocteau and Proust are at one. It is a mistake, Cocteau says in *La Voix de Marcel Proust*, 'to think that Marcel Proust's life is divided between his *vie mondaine* and his *vie solitaire* – his "first and second periods". Proust's *vie mondaine* could never be considered by him as a frivolous existence, something to be given up. Only his illness kept him secluded. That *vie mondaine*, which he cherished above all else, and which some critics mistook for mere diversion, was the very centre of his rose-window ["*le milieu même de sa rosace*"].'

Later, in another passage in the *Journal d'un Inconnu*, when in the course of a penetrating analysis of Proust as novelist Cocteau finds a flaw in his friend's work, it is not the flaw of *mondanité*: 'There is no doubt that Proust perceived *real* time – the false perspectives that it affects, and our possibility of imposing new ones upon it. But Proust is too greedy, too obsessed with an eglantine, a hotel table, a particle, a dress, to really launch out on the open sea. Doubtless this is legitimate, since his real purpose is to go beyond realism.'

Such, in brief, is the spectacle of two writers who mingled much with the *monde*, writing – one *to* the other, and one *about* the other – concerning the significance it held for each of them. Proust's acceptance of the young Cocteau's *mondanité* is total and quite casual, and with his expertise in the 'art of reading the blueprint of a man's life' he saw that *mondanité* as an integral, essential part of his friend's life as an artist; and Cocteau's mature defence of Proust's *mondanité* is also less a defence of *mondanité* itself than of its appropriateness, its necessity, to Proust's great work. It was only when Proust feared for his young friend's future work that he warned him; it was only when Cocteau, now much older, felt that Proust might have been even more subjective in his work than he was, that he made a specific reservation.

One longs for the discovery and the publication of the younger man's letters to the elder: we would then have, in all its *élan*, and doubtless mingled with much else of great fascination, a unique interchange of views on *mondanité* in the world of the arts by two artists best qualified to speak.

10

Triumph over Time

Pamela Hansford Johnson

IT HAS been held by those who have read it imperfectly that *A la Recherche du temps perdu* is a depressing book. Nothing could be further from the truth. The ending tells of a great discovery, of major significance to the artist: that Time the destroyer can be overcome by its preservation through art, and that, through art, no matter what our fate has been, not a sorrow nor a joy, a triumph or a tragedy, need be irretrievably lost, but may be written or painted or sung into art itself to be preserved for ever in its first freshness and dew.

In the Fitzwilliam Museum at Cambridge, there is a painting by Ruysdael, a view of Amsterdam from the river Amstel. It expresses not a single afternoon hundreds of years ago, but a particular, selected moment in that afternoon. It has been raining – the fields glisten with rain in the pallid light – and it will rain again. The tender and sallow sun, streaming through a sky patched with black cloud and cineraria blue, touches a few sails on the river: soon they will be shadowed again. It is an interim between storms. This painting is the essence of *Le Temps retrouvé*: so it was once, in the artist's recording eye and so it will ever be, netted, captured, the moment for ever sparkling, outside of Time because Time has been conquered.

A la Recherche du temps perdu concerns the anxieties of Time. Once there was a great passion. Where is it now? Drowned in oblivion. Once there was a beautiful woman. Where is her beauty now?

'On [the cheeks] for instance, of Madame de Guermantes, in many respects so little changed and yet composite now like a bar of nougat, I could distinguish traces here and there of verdigris, a small pink patch of fragmentary shell-work, and a little growth of an undefinable character, smaller than a mistletoe berry and less transparent than a glass bead.'

Where, now, is Oriane, duchesse de Guermantes, blonde, bird-nosed and lovely, repository of the essence of the family wit? We have just seen her at the beginning of decay. Yet she remains for ever still young, still sparkling, still malicious – with her electric eyes – in the pages of Marcel Proust, never to age.

Once there was a great composer, made to suffer torments through his lesbian daughter, laid in an obscure grave followed only by a few neighbours and by Monsieur Swann in his black top hat. Where are his few joys, his many sorrows, now? In his music, sublimely preserved. In his sonata, with its leitmotif for the love of Swann and Odette, of Marcel and Albertine, and above all in his superb septet, resuscitated from odd scraps of paper by the devoted labours of his daughter and her friend. Vinteuil and his whole life live in his music.

But let us consider the situation in the last section of *Le Temps retrouvé*. Marcel, as he is called only once in the book, has been spending long years in a sanitorium and has only just returned to the social world of post-war Paris [the 1914-18 war]. He is, in fact, making his first venturous return to that society. He is a middle-aged man, and his past, vertiginous to those who look back down the dreadful cliffs of fall, has come to seem meaningless, destined for the scrap-heap. Once he had literary ambitions: they have come to little or nothing. He was born in Combray, a country town, into a prosperous middle-class family. By random chances, he came to know the world of the Faubourg Saint-Germain. On his visits to the seaside town of Balbec, with its 'Persian church', the idea of which had for so long allured him, he came to know the elusive girl Albertine, to fall in love with her, to waste years of his life upon her, as his friend Swann had wasted years of his life over Odette de Crécy. Once the whole world had sung to him: a line of trees, constantly changing aspect as he passed near them in a carriage, the three spires of Martinville, mysteriously changing place on the horizon, a ravishing milk-girl glimpsed only for a moment when the train stopped for the attentions of the wheel-tapper, a lovely young duchess, tart of tongue, with hair like golden lichen, a proud homosexual nobleman of dilettante interests, a sunset from the windows of the middle-class *salonnière*, Madame Verdurin, the poppies and cornflowers in her vases imitating the lovely country beyond.

Once, all this sang. And now, returning to Paris after the upheaval of war, it seems as though nothing will ever have power to sing to him again.

'Trees,' I thought, 'you no longer have anything to say to me. My heart has grown cold and no longer hears you. I am in the midst of nature. Well, it is with indifference, with boredom that my eyes register the line which separates the luminous from the shadowy side of your trunks. If ever I thought of myself as a poet, I know now that I am not one. Perhaps in the new, the so desiccated part of my life which is about to begin, human beings may yet inspire in me what nature can no longer say. But the years in which I might have been able to sing *her* praises will never return.'

Any artist, ageing, knows what that means. The withdrawal of light behind the drab clouds, never to shine out again. The presentation by nature of something which no longer seems the essence of herself, pristine and glittering as once she was, but which more closely resembles art. And when nature has made her own stiff art, there is nothing left for the artist to do. His inspiration and his spontaneous joy have deserted him, leaving him barren.

Thus, believing that his life is a total failure, Marcel goes to the afternoon party given by the princesse de Guermantes.

On his way there he meets an old friend, the baron de Charlus, nearly senile, who cannot be left for long alone by his devoted and disreputable attendant Jupien, keeper of a male brothel where it was once the baron's delight to be tied up and flogged. Time was, when Monsieur de Charlus was the proudest and most arrogant man in Paris. How often had he abused Madame de Sainte-Euverte, in her hearing, with cloacal metaphors! Now, told by Jupien that here comes somebody he knows, he takes off his hat, releasing a great spouting of King Lear-like white locks, and bows to her with every appearance of deference, as if she were a queen. The baron de Charlus, brought so low, so humbled. Surely time past is time gone for ever? Yet he comes to live, for ever, in all his panache, his monstrous pride, in *A la Recherche*, that book which Marcel, on a single afternoon, learned how to write.

Before the party, everything is there, everything is in a state of readiness, waiting to welcome and inspire him. But Marcel feels no readiness. He feels nothing. Lingering in the ante-room till the programme of music has come to an end (for the princesse has ordered the doors to be closed until it does), he is dead inside: or almost. For earlier that afternoon he had a premonition of joy. Avoiding a carriage, he had stumbled back upon an uneven paving-stone, which brought him sharply back to the time when he had stumbled in the Baptistery of St Mark's, in Venice, and for a lightning second, the past has flooded back. Time regained. Yet he needs more than a single experience, and in that ante-room – the place is symbolic – more experiences of the same kind come to him. A waiter brings him refreshment, and a highly starched napkin. The touch of the napkin to his lips brings back Balbec: the great hotel sweltering in the sunshine, all cool within the dining-room, all blazing on the promenade outside. A careless waiter lets a spoon tinkle on a plate. At once Marcel is back in the train taking his youthful self to Balbec, where there was a brief wait while the wheel-tapper went to work.

All so little, and so much: just as the taste of a madeleine dipped in lime-flower tea had once brought back the whole of his youth in Combray. When the drawing-doors were at last thrown open, Marcel was ready again. For what? He had just experienced a sequence of analogous recognitions. He was to experience a sequence of others, though of a different kind.

What is this? A fancy-dress ball? The experienced costumier knows what a difference a white wig makes in changing appearances. All these people, or nearly all, wore white wigs, as to a masquerade. (It has to be remembered at this point that, due to the recognitions in the ante-room, Marcel has begun to live again, his senses once more alert.)

The Prince himself, as he stood receiving his guests, still had that slightly unreal look of a king in a fairy-story which I had remarked in him the first time I had been to his house, but to-day, as though he too felt bound to comply with the rules for fancy dress which he had sent out with the invitations, he had got himself up with a white beard and dragged his feet along the ground as though they were weighted with soles of lead, so that he gave the impression of trying to impersonate one of the 'Ages of Man'. (His moustaches were white too, as though the hoar-frost of Hop o' my Thumb's forest still lay thick upon them. They seemed to get in the way of his mouth, which he had difficulty in moving, and one felt that having made his effect he ought to have taken them off.)

So many 'disguises', so many recognitions: and then a shock of recognition bestowed by genius upon the reader himself. This old woman with silver hair streaming back from her protruberant temples – it does not sound in the least like the radiantly beautiful Marie-Gilbert, princesse de Guermantes, whose temples never were, in fact, mentioned to us. But the temples of someone else were, and our memory stirs. The fact is that this princesse de Guermantes is not Marie-Gilbert at all, who is dead. It is our old friend Madame Verdurin who, twice widowed and having passed through several social avatars, immensely rich, has 'caught' the Prince for her third husband. This is one of Proust's most splendid *coups de théâtre*, the trick for once having been played upon ourselves, as so many were played upon Marcel.

Meanwhile, Marcel is in two minds. One is occupied by the physical recognitions (how does Odette, now last mistress of the aged duc de Guermantes, manage to preserve her youth, even allowing for the effects of paint and dye?) and one by the revelations which have come to him through 'madeleines' recognitions, that is, the phenomena of involuntary memory. Something is happening to him, which is to change his whole life.

As, in some people, memory is awakened by a scent – say, of wallflowers or of hay – so his has been awakened by the memories of taste, sound, texture, by the stumble on the uneven paving-stone. And all these experiences are magical because they are *outside of Time* – free from it, free to come and to go, to inspire, or to rest in non-recognition. Outside of Time entirely, and therefore infinitely potent.

Here, I think, Proust has been a little specious. The single experience of this sort – most of us have known it, and it has gone deep into the springs of self-knowledge. But to know a series of such experiences, during the course of a single afternoon – this is to speak of miracles, and it is in our own self-knowledge to determine that such miracles come far less frequently to most of us than to Proust's Marcel.

In all, an unforgettable afternoon, bearing the keys not only to Time past but to Time to come. It is a little hard for us to believe in it, hard for us to credit that we are not being subjected to the trickery of genius. Perhaps we are. I suspect it is so. But it is a wonderful, glittering trick, the unlocking of the secret of a novel a million words long. Without it, there could have been no more than despair, the despair of a wasted life. So much time wasted on the social ladder, wasted on a long and tormenting love which ended in death and, worse, oblivion. So much heartache, headache, the ache of the bones, and to no purpose. But here is the purpose. This is what all of it, from the most trivial to the most sublime, from the most ridiculous to the most delicate and sore, was all about. To few of us it is given to sense such a purpose: but to the artist, perhaps, yes.

How was it to Ruysdael, when he looked back upon his painting and saw a moment of the weathers caught for ever? How much to Rembrandt, when he looked back upon a portrait of an old woman and found he had put the whole map of her life into her face? How much to Debussy, when he heard a performance of *L'Ile Joyeuse* and found that all love, its ravishments and its mischiefs, was there? Blessed is the artist, for he shall regain Time.

What was the secret of the series of recognitions which had caused Marcel such joy and had even banished the fear of death?

This is the key-passage.

. . . another inquiry demanded my attention most imperiously, the inquiry . . . into the cause of this felicity which I had just experienced, into the character of the certitude with which it imposed itself. And this cause I began to divine as I compared these diverse happy impressions, diverse yet with this in common, that I experienced them at the present moment and at the same time in the context of a different moment, so that the past was made to encroach upon the present and I was made to doubt whether I was in the one or the other. The truth surely was that the being within me which had enjoyed these impressions, had enjoyed them because they had in them something that was common to a day long past and to now, because in some way they were extra-temporal, and this being made its appearance only when, through one of these identifications of the present with the past, it was likely to find itself in the one and only medium in which it could exist and enjoy the essence of things, that is to say: outside time. This explained why it was that my anxiety on the subject of my death had ceased at the moment when I had unconsciously recognized the taste of the little madeleine, since the being which at that moment I had been was an extra-temporal being and therefore unalarmed by the vicissitudes of the future. This being had only come to me, only manifested itself outside of activity and immediate enjoyment, on those rare occasions when the miracle of an analogy had made me escape from the present. And only this being had the power to perform that task which had always defeated the efforts of my memory and my intellect, the power to make me discover days that were long past, the Time that was Lost.

This passage explains Proust's challenge to Sainte-Beuve that instinct must be rated higher than intellect – though Proust himself was a man of the most formidable intellect. It links, too, with the famous 'flash-back', *Un Amour de Swann*, near the beginning of the entire work.

Charles Swann, a rich man about town, is also a dilettante, for ever vaguely at work upon a monograph upon Vermeer of Delft. He falls passionately in love with the courtesan (it is the only word to describe her) Odette de Crécy, once the wife of an elderly nobleman (her name, incredibly enough, really is Crécy) whom she has contrived to ruin, and for whom Marcel, at a much later date, finds himself buying much-needed dinners. Their long love-affair is marked by a torment of jealousy on Swann's part, a series of betrayals on hers. It foreshadows the protracted and tortured affair later between Marcel and Albertine. Swann wears himself out upon Odette, upon the struggle to find out who she really is, what she is really like, until one morning he awakens cured, crying aloud that he has wasted years of his life, has longed for death, for the sake of a woman 'not in his style'. Yet he marries her, for they have a young daughter, Gilberte (with whom Marcel will one day be in love) and becomes a passionless but uxorious husband, proud of her for her beauty, proud of her, ironically, that she can attract so many men to her 'days', jealous now for the style, the fashionableness, of their household. He becomes, for her sake, a little vulgar, a name-dropper: he, who used never to mention his intimate friendship with the Prince of Wales. Yes, he has wasted his life: and to him, because he is only a dilettante, not a true artist, no extra-temporal recognitions come.

The scheme of the entire novel is circular. Marcel's childhood home lay between his two favourite walks, Swann's way, and the Guermantes's way. The two ways seem irreconcilable: yet Gilberte, Swann's child, marries that most enchanting of Guermantes, Robert de Saint-Loup, and Odette becomes the

*Among
Friends*

Anatole France;
portrait by Kees
van Dongen.

above left : Reynaldo Hahn, one of Proust's oldest friends, and probably the closest.

above right : Bertrand de Salignac-Fénelon, chief of the brilliant young men whose features Proust combined in Saint-Loup.

top left : Montesquiou by James McNeill Whistler: '*Je suis le souverain des choses transitoires*'.

top centre : Boni de Castellane; with whose misfortunes, after his divorce from Anna Gould, Proust deeply sympathised.

top right : Robert de Billy, the future ambassador who helped to launch Proust into fashionable life.

VIII₂

above: Madame de Chevigné, who lent her azure eyes and her bird-like profile to the duchesse de Guermantes.

The comtesse Greffulhe; she had never been 'really understood save by you and by the sun', she told Montesquiou.

left: The princesse de Caraman-Chimay, née Clara Ward, to whom Charlus refers as 'my dishonoured cousin'.

left: The poetess Anna de Noailles, with whom Proust kept up an affectionate correspondence.

left: Madame Straus (centre) among her friends; on the left stands Charles Haas, better known as Charles Swann.

above left: Liane de Pougy, the famous courtesan with whom one of Dr Adrien Proust's colleagues had had an unfortunate liaison.

above right: Laure Hayman, a distinguished member of the demi-monde, who supplied Proust with hints for Odette de Crécy.

top left: Louisa de Mornand, the gifted actress with whom Proust, as a young man, claimed to have been on terms of voluptuous intimacy.

top right: Réjane as the duc de Sagan; she did not altogether return Proust's perfervid admiration.

Clairin

above: Madeleine Lemaire; she had created more roses, declared Alexandre Dumas, than 'anybody else since God'.

left: Reynaldo Hahn at the piano; with Montesquiou (extreme left), Madeleine Lemaire and Frédéric ('Coco') de Madrazo.

opposite: Sarah Bernhardt at home; portrait by Georges Clairin, 1876.

duke's mistress in his old age. And, linking the ways for ever, Gilberte at the Princess's final party presents to Marcel her lovely young daughter – Robert's child.

And now Mlle de Saint-Loup was standing in front of me. She had eyes that were deeply drilled and piercing, and a charming nose thrust slightly forward in the form of a beak and curved, perhaps not in the least like that of Swann's but like Saint-Loup's. The soul of that particular Guermantes had fluttered away, but his charming head, as of a bird in flight, with its piercing eyes, had settled momentarily upon the shoulders of Mlle de Saint-Loup, and the sight of it aroused a train of memories and dreams in those who had known her father.

She is like the diamond drop which completes the necklace, the jewel gleaming with the numberless refractions of Time Past. She is yet too young for the tarnishings of change, and so Marcel sees her now as he had seen her parents in youth, shining with the same almost-forgotten radiance.

Marcel's world has changed, radically: the result of the Dreyfus case, which brought about so many extraordinary social mutations, and of the Great War, which threw up Madame Verdurin and Albertine's vulgar aunt, Madame Bontemps, to the pinnacle of busybody wartime society. 'The Faubourg St Germain was like some senile dowager now, who replies only with timid smiles to the insolent servants who invade her drawing-rooms, drink her orangeade, present their mistresses to her.'

Madame Verdurin, the exhibitionist *salonnière*, who was nevertheless possessed of an unfailing instinct for the arts, is the reigning hostess over the Faubourg these days, since Oriane, duchesse de Guermantes, has long ago lost interest in Society. Ironically enough, she has frittered away her position by taking a Verdurin-like interest in poets, musicians and painters. Oriane is old now: and she startles Marcel by claiming him as her 'oldest friend'. Can it possibly be that he, too, is old? Yes it can. (Though in fact, according to such chronology as can be drawn from the book, he is no more than fifty years of age.) Her claim – for was he not the nervous young cit so awed by her invitations? – shocks him, certainly; but not for long. The parade of physical degeneration has lost the power to frighten him. He has, at last, work to do.

If at least, Time enough were allotted to me to accomplish my work, I would not fail to mark it with the seal of Time, the idea of which imposed itself upon me with so much force to-day, and I would therein describe men, if need be, as monsters occupying a place in Time infinitely more important than the restricted one reserved for them

Jean Cocteau, by 'Coco' de Madrazo.

in space, a place, on the contrary, prolonged immeasureably since, simultaneously touching widely separated years and the distant periods they have lived through – between which so many days have ranged themselves – they stand like giants, immersed in Time.[1]

This is the way the book ends. It ends in a glory of decision, born out of the triumph over Time. For me, it is the greatest ending of any novel ever written. It has to be borne in mind that the true title of the work, in English, is not *Remembrance of Things Past*, the poor choice of a great translator and misleading: it is, *In Search of Lost Time*. It is the story of a great quest which actually succeeds. Thomas Wolfe strove to make communication in 'the incommunicable prison of this earth'. He failed, and felt he had failed. Proust communicates the way in which we may recover and fix, as under a glass, the whole of our lives.

The analogous 'recognitions' are contributions to the entire structure. Another contribution is the phenomenon of the *false recognition* – things are not what they at first seem. This idea Proust took from his master, Dostoievski. At first sight, the baron de Charlus appears to Marcel as a shady character, perhaps an hotel detective watching for thieves or for dubious couples. Marcel believes Madame de Villeparisis to be the greatest among great ladies, though in the eyes of Society (though not of her own family circle) she has been declassed by marriage and by *louche* behaviour in her youth. The 'little band of girls' on the *plage* at Balbec might possibly be the juvenile mistresses of racing cyclists. Impressions form, are dissolved, reform into other and stranger shapes. All things seem inconstant as the sea itself, which is one of the book's most powerful symbols, and at the core of them all is the smiling or sullen Albertine, herself mutable as the sea, in her being the vast disturbing secrecies of love. Albertine, the arcane, the temptress and tormentor, never to be recovered in her essential truth (if truth is in her at all), upon whose memory, after she is dead, the Narrator conducts a hideous autopsy. Here Marcel was perhaps less fortunate than Swann, for once, who, when passionate love had died, could see Odette as she really was without ceasing to support and encourage her. She was essentially commonplace. As Proust says, life had given her some good parts, but she could not play them. At the final party where, in her paint and dye, she still looks much as she ever did, we are given a flash-forward to her in senility, mumbling, nervous, almost stone deaf. This is one of those blows Proust deals us when we are least expecting them.

But for Marcel himself, the artist both intuitive and highly conscious, there is the splendid 'happy ending' which turns the whole work into a Divine Comedy. We have been with him in the earthly Paradise of childhood and Combray, walking between the hedges of pink and white hawthorn, crying out – 'Zut! Zut!' in a vain struggle to express the beauty of a cloud shadow upon water: have been with him through the Vanity Fair of society, to Sodom and Gomorrah, the Cities of the Plain, down to the ninth circle of Hell: have been with him through purgatory (the discovery of oblivion after love and death) to the heaven of the personal discovery: no less than this – *what the whole of a life is for*. We have made this journey (less dreadful than Dante's for it is rich in humour) step by step to the revelation of Beatrice – in this case, the revelation that there is no death. Marcel comes at the end to his Beatrice, not a girl, but a divine assurance.

It was so for Proust, then not so: for his own death-bed was dark, shadowed by the spectre of the mother he believed he had, by his homosexuality, profaned. He saw the black shrouded woman at the door and he cried out in fear. Is it the last trick Time plays, that we should cry out in fear? But that is an antic thought, too horrible to be contemplated. After triumph, what? For after triumph, Time still goes on.

However, fortunately, it will not do. We are made to believe that the triumph was Marcel's: but it was Proust's. He discovered how to make the work, and despite sickness and psychotic seclusion, he completed it. The ripeness was all.

Apart from the device of the recognitions (madeleine, paving-stone, spoon, napkin) there are no tricks of time in this book. It is, with the exception of the flashback, *Un Amour de Swann* (in which almost every major theme of the entire work is stated), a straightforward narrative by chronological progression. From the beginning, it gives the effect of a search, of a young boy setting forth into the great world in quest of – what? At first he hardly knows. This is not the fashionable problem of the search for identity: Marcel is fully cognisant of who he is, and his roots are deep in society. After a while he believes that he has a vocation for writing, but all he manages to produce is an article for *Le Figaro*. (This runs counter to the life of the author who, before achieving *A la Recherche*, wrote, and suppressed, a prentice novel of nine hundred manuscript pages, *Jean Santeuil*, and the wonderful critical essays, a trial of strength for the great work to come, which were later gathered together under the title *Contre Sainte-Beuve*. The old idea of Proust wasting years in dilettantism and social climbing has now been dispelled.) It is not until late in the book that he realizes the object of his search, which is nothing less than that for Time itself.

It is, despite its length and complexity, a wonderfully lucid novel, and the climax, when it comes, is brought about by a display of marvellous intellectual force and clarity.

Not a depressing book. Essentially it is, as has been said, a 'young man's book', full of the excitements, joys, discoveries and despairs of youth, sparkling with humour and irony. If it contains much tragedy, if friendship comes to seem an illusion, love a delusion, if beautiful men and women are degraded by, often made almost ridiculous by, age and the propinquity of death, all this is *used* for the final purpose, as if the writer were carrying back from the well of Time a vessel filled to the brim with dancing water, of which he will not spill a single drop. The work is shaped like Vinteuil's septet, which culminates in a strong-beating shock of pure joy, an analogy made clear by Proust as his novel progresses and the septet grows slowly out of scraps of almost unreadable paper lovingly hoarded and transcribed by the two young women who broke the composer's heart.

A la Recherche comes to an ending entirely affirmative, far more so than Molly Bloom's ecstatic but capricious 'Yes, I will, Yes'. *Le Temps retrouvé* is the title of the final volume. It could have been the title of the entire book.

Of all very great writers, Proust was the most avid in the search for affirmation. Himself a man of considerable moral courage, he took it upon himself to find answers. There is no sign of such searching in the preliminary sketch, *Jean Santeuil* which, even when the circumstances of its discovery and patching together by Bernard de Fallois are taken into consideration, is lacking in direction. This is, however, a most interesting book, shedding light upon what Proust was like before he took the tremendous moral grasp upon himself from which *A la Recherche* resulted. The 'snobbery' of which he has so often been accused was certainly present – ragingly present – in parts of *Jean Santeuil*: but recognizing this, he learned to *use* it for quite determined purposes, to make it work for him through his new-found irony.

I have said elsewhere that what makes the great work so morally tough is that behind Marcel, the Narrator, we sense a 'second Marcel', mocking, critical, undeceived. There is no 'second Jean' in *Jean Santeuil*. Proust learned how to make fine metal out of his own faults, even when he could not entirely overcome them. He turned his writing itself into a tremendous moral exercise: as Marcel grows up from the coxcomberies of adolescence to the wisdom of middle age, so Proust grows with him. *A la Recherche* is by no means a fully autobiographical novel, yet the writer and his book are curiously at one. We never know Marcel's surname, but in our hearts we cannot stop believing that it was Proust.

He was a stern moralist, sometimes almost too stern. Homosexual himself, he still thinks of homosexuality as a vice, and its men and women accursed upon the Plain. The truth was that, unlike Gide, he did not love his own condition and wished that it had been otherwise with him, as once it might have been. Yet the archetype homosexual, the baron de Charlus, is drawn with charity and humour, even when he sinks low enough to become a habitué of Jupien's brothel. It is part of Proust's genius that he can make this incident seem funny and even a little touching: in other hands it might have seemed disgusting, and no more than that.

The only major character in the book from whom he withholds charity is Morel, the violinist whom the Baron loves. There is an odd failure here: there are even times when Morel seems to be set apart from this particular work like a fragment of a painting which has escaped varnishing. We believe in him as an artist, but it is hard to credit that there is really nothing else to be said for him. He remains an ungrateful, deceitful scoundrel in a world where men and women may be sacred monsters steeped in Time, but are never – what shall one call it? – mingy. One cannot believe that Morel will ever grow to the status of splendid monstrosity with the years.

I do not claim that *A la Recherche du temps perdu* is a totally perfect book: but, because of its intellectual force and its use of the intuitions, it is a great one, certainly the greatest of this century. It is also a very strange and original novel, which yields more and more with every re-reading. For me, it is impossible to close it without a sense of exhilaration, and perhaps with a touch of regret that the taste of the madeleine may never come to one's own salvation.

References

INTRODUCTION

1 *Du Côté de chez Swann*.
2 Ibid.
3 Ibid.
4 André Gide: *Journals 1889–1949*, translated by Justin O'Brien, 1947.
5 In his essay 'Sainte-Beuve et Baudelaire', posthumously published in *Contre Sainte-Beuve*, Proust tells us that he had hoped to reconstruct '*le monde de la pensée de Baudelaire,*

ce pays de son génie, dont chaque poème n'est qu'un fragment, et qui dès qu'on le lit se rejoint aux autres fragments . . .'
6 *Fils de Réjane*, 1952
7 *Marcel Proust: the Later Years*, 1965.
8 *Marcel Proust: The Fictions of Life and Art*, 1965.
9 *Le Temps retrouvé*, translated by Andreas Mayor, 1970.

THE MAKING OF A NOVEL

1 Quoted from a holograph manuscript in Proust's hand belonging to the University of Illinois; the manuscript bears the title *Comment le Savant peut-il conclure du fait à la Loi*. The present essay is based on a talk presented on 9 April 1964, in Baton Rouge, for the Louisiana State University series of Lectures in the Humanities.
2 See Germaine Brée's description of the Proust archives in the Bibliothèque Nationale, Paris, in *French Review*, vol. *37* (Dec. 1963), pp. 182–7.
3 Paul Souday, *Marcel Proust*, Paris, Simon Kra (1927), p. 11: '*Français et Latins, nous préférons un procédé plus synthétique. Il nous semble que le gros volume de M. Marcel Proust n'est pas composé, et qu'il est aussi démesuré que chaotique, mais qu'il renferme des éléments précieux*

dont l'auteur aurait pu former un petit livre exquis.' – Souday's review of *Swann* first appeared in *Le Temps*, 10 December 1913; cf. Douglas W. Alden, *Marcel Proust and his French critics*, Los Angeles (1940) p. 173, item 54.
4 Henri Ghéon, *La Nouvelle Revue française*, XI (1 January 1914), pp. 139–43. Cf. my edition of Proust's *Lettres retrouvées*, Paris, Plon (1966), pp. 127 and 129.
5 Joachim Gasquet, in *L'Eclair*, 11 December 1919: '*le plus épais des improvisateurs*'.
6 Jean de Pierrefeu, *Le Journal des Débats*, 12 December 1919: '*M. Marcel Proust était connu pour des pastiches habiles et malicieux lorsqu'il publia, quelques années avant la guerre, un volume compact, sans commencement ni fin, bizarrement intitulé Du Côté de chez Swann*.

REFERENCES

Depuis lors il a joint à ce premier livre un second qui le prolonge et il en prépare deux autres sur le même thème. Rien ne prouve qu'il s'arrêtera en si beau chemin. A mon avis, la fatigue ou la mort seules peuvent l'arrêter dans la tâche qu'il a entreprise de rechercher le temps perdu par lui.'

7 Marcel Proust, *Correspondance générale*, vol. VI, Paris, Plon (1936), p. 116: '. . . *je viens de commencer – et de finir – tout un long livre.'*

8 III, 900. All quotations from *A la Recherche du temps perdu* in this essay refer to the Pléiade edition, by MM. Pierre Clarac and André Ferré, Paris, Editions Gallimard (1954), in three volumes. Translations are my own.

9 *Du Côté de chez Swann*, I, 92.

10 Ibid.

11 *Le Côté de Guermantes*, II, 215.

12 Fernand Gregh, *L'Age d'airain*, Paris, Grasset (1951), pp. 118–19; cf. *L'Age d'or*, Paris, Grasset (1947), pp. 132–3.

13 Jacques de Lacretelle, *Les Clefs de l'œuvre de Proust*, in *Les Cahiers Marcel Proust*, vol. 1, Paris, Gallimard (1927), p. 190.

14 Marcel Proust, *Textes retrouvés*, Urbana, University of Illinois Press (1968), p. 217.

15 In a letter addressed to René Blum, which I date as of 23 February 1913, Proust writes: '. . . *il y a beaucoup de personnages; ils sont "préparés" dès ce premier volume, c'est-à-dire qu'ils feront dans le second exactement le contraire de ce à quoi on s'attendait d'après le premier.'* Léon Pierre-Quint, *Comment parut 'Du Côté de chez Swann'*, Paris, Kra (1930), p. 44.

16 Marcel Proust, *Contre Sainte-Beuve*, Paris, Gallimard (1954), pp. 291–7; cf. *A la Recherche du temps perdu*, I, p. 145.

17 Marcel Proust, *Correspondance générale*, vol. IV, Paris, Plon (1933), p. 260: '*Il me dit: "Vous notez tout!" Mais non, je ne note rien. C'est lui qui note. Pas une seule fois un de mes personnages ne ferme une fenêtre, ne se lave les mains, ne passe un pardessus, ne dit une formule de présentation. S'il y avait même quelque chose de nouveau dans ce livre, ce serait cela, et d'ailleurs nullement voulu; simplement je suis trop paresseux pour écrire des choses qui m'ennuient.'*

18 *Le Côté de Guermantes*, II, p. 427. Cf. Marcel Proust, *Remembrance of Things Past*, vol. 1, New York, Random House, p. 1023. My translation is slightly different.

19 That is the main purpose of the investigation that the narrator carries forth in his search for Truth throughout his novel. He seems almost to be referring to that composition he had written for M. Darlu's class when, in *Albertine disparue*, he states: '*Et puis, un seul petit fait, s'il est bien choisi, ne suffit-il pas à l'expérimentateur pour décider d'une loi générale qui fera connaître la vérité sur des milliers de faits analogues?*' In another version of the same passage, he comes even closer to the wording in the title of the lycée composition: '*Et puis, sur un seul fait, s'il est certain, ne peut-on pas, comme le savant qui expérimente, dégager la vérité pour tous les ordres de faits semblables?*' (Pléiade edition, vol. III, pp. 514 and 1103).

THE FAUBOURG SAINT-GERMAIN

1 *Carnets inédits: Bibliothèque Nationale.*

2 '*A l'âge où les Noms, nous offrant l'image de l'inconnaissable que nous avons versé en eux, dans le même moment où ils désignent pour nous un lieu réel, nous forcent par là à identifier l'un à l'autre, ce n'est pas seulement aux villes et aux fleuves qu'ils donnent une individualité . . . alors chaque château, chaque hôtel ou palais fameux a sa dame ou sa fée.' Le Côté de Guermantes*, I.

3 The beginning of an unpublished letter addressed to the comte de Gaigneron.

4 *Sodome et Gomorrhe.*

5 *La Prisonnière.*

REFERENCES
BERGOTTE

1 *A l'Ombre des jeunes filles en fleurs, I*
2 *Du Côté de chez Swann, I.*
3 Ibid.
4 Ibid.
5 Ibid.
6 Ibid.
7 Ibid.
8 Ibid.
9 Ibid.
10 Ibid.
11 Ibid.
12 *A l'Ombre des jeunes filles en fleurs, I.*
13 Ibid.
14 Ibid.
15 Ibid.
16 Ibid.
17 Ibid.
18 Ibid.
19 *La Prisonnière, I.*
20 *Du Côté de chez Swann, II.*
21 *A l'Ombre des jeunes filles en fleurs, I.*
22 Ibid.
23 Ibid.
24 Ibid.
25 *Le Côté de Guermantes, II.*
26 Ibid.
27 *La Prisonnière, I.*

ISRAEL'S WAY

1 A letter from Proust to Count Robert de Montesquiou, Librairie Plon.
2 *Sodome et Gomorrhe.*
3 *Du Côté de chez Swann.*
4 Ibid.
5 *La Fugitive.*
6 Ibid.
7 *Sentiments filiaux d'un parricide : Pastiches et Mélanges.*
8 *Du Côté de chez Swann.*
9 Ibid.
10 *Sodome et Gomorrhe.*
11 Ibid.
12 *La Prisonnière.*
13 Ibid.
14 *Le Temps retrouvé.*
15 Georges Feydeau, 1862–1921, the highly successful comic dramatist.
16 *Le Temps retrouvé.*
17 Ibid.
18 Ibid.
19 Ibid.
20 Ibid.
21 *Du Côté de chez Swann.*

PROUST AND PAINTING

1 See *Literature Through Art*, Helmut Hatzfield, Oxford University Press, 1952.
2 *The Imagery of Proust*, Victor Graham, Basil Blackwell, Oxford, 1966.
3 *A l'Ombre des jeunes filles en fleurs.* Gallé was one of the leading art nouveau designers, famous for his elaborate work in glass. Montesquiou was a friend and patron, and Proust used to commission items from Gallé's studio to give to friends.
4 *A L'Ombre des jeunes filles en fleurs.*
5 *Du Côté de chez Swann, II.*
6 This and the previous quotation are from *Letters of Marcel Proust*, translated by Mina Curtis, Chatto and Windus, London, 1950.
7 *Degas Letters*, edited by Marcel Guérin, Bruno Cassirer, Oxford, 1947.
8 The three men were probably Degas, Ludovic Halévy and Cavé.
9 Proust was probably wrong. Daniel Halévy recalls Degas making this remark. Forain, who took an anti-Dreyfusist and antisemitic

REFERENCES

line after the Dreyfus trial, was no longer on speaking terms with Proust. Proust was a long-standing admirer of Gustave Moreau. The mythological Elstirs which the Narrator sees on his first visit to the Hotel de Guermantes are based on paintings by Moreau.

10 *My Friend Degas*, Daniel Halévy, Rupert Hart-Davis, London, 1966.

11 After the death of Proust, his brother sent Helleu a pair of small bronze elephants which Proust used to keep in his bedroom. The parcel was addressed to 'Monsieur Elstir-Helleu'. I am grateful for this and other information to the artist's daughter, Madame Howard-Johnston. See *Bonjour M. Elstir*, by Paulette Howard-Johnston, Gazette des Beaux-Arts, April 1967.

12 *Propos de Peintre*, Jacques-Emile Blanche, Emile Paul, Paris, 1919–28.

13 Helleu's great-grandfather had been a member of the Council of Five Hundred.

14 According to the artist's daughter Helleu advised Blanche to buy Manet's *La Femme au Gant* (*Portrait de Madame Brunet*). He did not benefit financially from these artistic deals and he would have been horrified at the thought of accepting a commission. He criticized those who did, in particular Proust's friend, Boni de Castellane.

15 Letter to Madame Straus.

16 Léon Daudet was probably the author of this much repeated remark.

17 Madame Elstir is believed to have been based on Claude Monet's first wife.

18 *Le Temps retrouvé.*

19 *Vuillard*, Claude Roger-Marx. Arts et Métiers Graphiques, Paris 1946.

20 *Proust and Painting*, Maurice E. Chernowitz, International University Press, New York, 1945.

21 See Louis Gautier-Vignal in a lecture given at Nice, 1948, entitled *Dans l'intimité de Marcel Proust.*

22 See *Proust et la Peinture*, Juliette Monnin-Hornung, Librairie E. Droz, Geneva, 1951.

23 *Sodome et Gomorrhe.*

24 *A l'Ombre des jeunes filles en fleurs.*

PROUST AS A SOLDIER

1 *Le Temps retrouvé.*

2 *Le Côté de Guermantes.*

THE WORLD OF FASHION

1 In *Sodome et Gomorrhe*, Monsieur de Charlus praises Albertine's dress. 'A dress', he declares, 'may be brilliant without vulgarity, and quiet, without being dull. Besides you have not the same reason as Mme. de Cadignan for wishing to appear detached from life . . .'

2 *Du Côté de chez Swann.*

3 Odette's passion for cattleyas was probably derived from that of Madame Greffulhe. Proust wrote a gossip column for *Le Gaulois*; and in 1894 he described Madame Greffulhe in an article (*A Literary Fête at Versailles*) wearing a mauve gown the colour of her favourite orchids. See George Painter: *Marcel Proust: A Biography,* 1959.

4 *Du Côté de chez Swann.*

5 *A l'Ombre des jeunes filles en fleurs.*

6 Ibid.

7 Ibid.

8 Odette's white guelder-roses – the snowballs – were taken from Madame Straus's salon.

REFERENCES

See a letter from Proust to Laure Hayman quoted by George Painter, op. cit.

9 *A l'Ombre des jeunes filles en fleurs.*

10 Ibid.

11 Ibid.

12 The name Doucet was already famous at the beginning of the Second Empire, when the future Empress wrote to her sister, the Duchess of Alba: '*Je te fais parvenir pour ton anniversaire un charmant manteau de Mme Doucet*'.

13 *Le Côté de Guermantes.*

14 Ibid.

15 Ibid.

16 When hats were enormous, probably during the 1900's, Madame Greffulhe, we learn, was president of a society to encourage the wearing of small hats in the theatre.

17 *La Prisonnière.*

18 Ibid.

19 *Sodome et Gomorrhe.*

TRIUMPH OVER TIME

1 Trans. Stephen Hudson.

Sources of Illustrations

BN: Bibliothèque Nationale

Section I, between pages 8 and 9

Robert and Marcel Proust; Proust with his mother and brother; Proust, Robert de Flers and Lucien Daudet; Proust's grandmother (Mme Mante Proust). Marie de Bernardaky (BN). Marie Nordlinger (Pauline Green). Dr Adrien Proust; Proust's parents' drawing-room, rue Hamelin; Proust and contemporaries, Lycée Condorcet (Mme Mante Proust, photo A. Bouret). *Sortie du Lycée Condorcet* by J. Béraud (Bulloz).

Proust with Jeanne Pouquet and friends (Mme Maurois). Proust by J.-E. Blanche (Mme Mante Proust). Proust and Agostinelli (BN). Proust in 1896 (Mme Mante Proust). Proust by J.-E. Blanche (BN). Proust in 1922 (Mme Mante Proust, photo A. Bouret). Proust's bedroom, rue Hamelin; Proust on his deathbed (Mme Mante Proust).

SOURCES OF ILLUSTRATIONS

Section II between pages 32 and 33

Moriss Column (E. Atget). Bois de Bologne; Polaire in the Bois; The Bois, c.1900; Moulin Rouge (Sirot). Place St Augustin (BN). Bois de Boulogne (J. H. Lartigue). Universal Exhibition, 1900 (Hachette). *Place de la Bastille*, by Luigi Loir (Schweitzer Gallery). Avenue de l'Opéra (Snark International).

Section III, between pages 48 and 49

Reine de Joie, by Toulouse-Lautrec (Victoria and Albert Museum). *Friday at the salon*, by J. Grün (Hachette). *Maxim's*, caricature by Sem (BN, photo Hachette). *Le Cercle*, by J. Béraud (Bulloz). Evening party, 1880's; Sarah Bernhardt (Sirot). Nijinsky in *La Péri*; Nijinsky in 1909 (Enthoven Collection). *The acrobat*, by J. J. J. Tissot (Boston Museum of Fine Arts). *Master of Ceremonies*, by J. Béraud. *La Loge*, by J.-L. Forain (Courtauld Institute). A meet in the forest (Sirot). *La Promenade au Bois*, by G. Boldini (Snark International).

Section IV, between pages 72 and 73

Illiers, engraving (BN, photo F. Foliot). Illiers, church (Doisneau-Rapho). Mme Amiot's kitchen; The Pré-Catalan (photo A. Bouret); The Amiots' garden (Roger-Viollet). Etretat (J. H. Lartigue). Cabourg advertisement (Victoria and Albert Museum). Grand Hotel, Cabourg (Sirot). Deauville (Snark International). Proust in Venice (Mme Mante Proust). Proust in Venice (René-Jacques).

Section V, between pages 120 and 121

Rouen Cathedral, by Monet (Louvre, photo Giraudon). Portrait of Madame Chéruit, by P. Helleu; Mme Helleu, by Helleu (Lumley Cazalet). Whistler by Helleu; Montesquiou by Helleu (BN). Helleu by Boldini (Hachette). Vase by E. Gallé (Sperryn's Ltd). *Young woman undressing*, by G. Boldini (Lumley Cazalet). *The Client*, by J.-L. Forain (Lefèvre). Mme Helleu and her son, by Helleu (Ferrers). *La Revue Blanche* by P. Bonnard (BN). Interior by E. Vuillard (A. Salomon). *Salome dancing* by G. Moreau (Giraudon).

Section VI, between pages 152 and 153

Proust as a soldier (Mme Mante Proust, photo A. Bouret). Barracks at Orléans (Radio Times Hulton). Comte de Cholet; Reynaldo Hahn (BN, photo A. Bouret). 1914 (J. H. Lartigue). The degradation of Dreyfus (Mary Evans). Major Picquart (Radio Times Hulton). Zola on trial (BN). Dreyfus arriving at Rennes gaol (Radio Times Hulton). Two caricatures by J. L. Forain (BN). Military court, Rennes, 1899 (Radio Times Hulton).

Section VII, between pages 168 and 169

Exposition de Blanc by H. Thiriet. Dress of 1890; Dress of 1898 (Mansell Collection). Dress by Paquin; Dress by Redfern (Victoria and Albert Museum, photo D. Witty). *Girl Reading* by L. Anquetin (Tate Gallery, photo SPADEM). Yvonne de Bray (Sirot). Bicycling in the Bois de

SOURCES OF ILLUSTRATIONS

Boulogne (Radio Times Hulton). Auteuil, 1912 (J. H. Lartigue). Ida Rubinstein, by de la Gandara (Victoria and Albert Museum). Dress by Poiret; Dress by Doucet (Mary Evans).

Lady in a feathered hat, by Drian. Dress by Chéruit (Mary Evans). Walkers in the Bois (J. H. Lartigue).

Section VIII, between pages 200 and 201

Anatole France by K. van Dongen (Giraudon). Montesquiou by Whistler; Boni de Castellane (BN, photo Snark International). Robert de Billy (René-Jacques). Reynaldo Hahn; Bertrand de Salignac-Fénelon (BN, photo A. Bouret). Mme Greffulhe (duc de Gramont). Madame de Chevigné (BN). Princesse Caraman-Chimay; Anna de Noailles (Sirot). Madame Straus with friends (photo A. Bouret); Louisa de Mornand (photo A. Bouret); Réjane (BN). Liane de Pougy (Sirot). Laure Hayman (BN, photo Snark International). Sarah Bernhardt by Clairin (Hachette). Madeleine Lemaire; Reynaldo Hahn and friends, caricature by Sem (BN). Jean Cocteau by F. de Madrazo (Arts Graphiques de la Cité).

Colour Plates

opposite p. 16 *Le Château du Cycle*, by Béraud (Musée de l'Ile de France)

opposite p. 42 *La Soirée* by J. Béraud (Musée de l'Ile de France)

opposite p. 52 *Montesquiou*, by G. Boldini (BN).

opposite p. 64 *Le salon aux trois lampes* by E. Vuillard (A. Salomon).

opposite p. 112 *Le Cercle de la rue Royale*, by J. J. J. Tissot (Galerie Charpentier)

opposite p. 144 *Trouville*, by H. de Bréval (Musée de Trouville)

opposite p. 170 *La Maison Doucet* by Béraud (Schweitzer Gallery)

opposite p. 180 *Théâtre de la Renaissance*, poster by A. Mucha (Lords Gallery, London)

The editor and publishers wish to thank all those mentioned above for their kind permission to reproduce illustrations.

Index

INDEX